For Jim,

with memories of a stimulating seminar

Zenn

11·03·05

LIVING LAWFULLY

Law and Philosophy Library

VOLUME 53

The titles published in this series are listed at the end of this volume.

LIVING LAWFULLY

Love in Law and Law in Love

by

ZENON BAŃKOWSKI

Professor of Legal Theory,
University of Edinburgh

KLUWER ACADEMIC PUBLISHERS
DORDRECHT / BOSTON / LONDON

A C.I.P. Catalogue record for this book is available from the Library of Congress.

ISBN 0-7923-7180-1

Published by Kluwer Academic Publishers,
P.O. Box 17, 3300 AA Dordrecht, The Netherlands.

Sold and distributed in North, Central and South America
by Kluwer Academic Publishers,
101 Philip Drive, Norwell, MA 02061, U.S.A.

In all other countries, sold and distributed
by Kluwer Academic Publishers,
P.O. Box 322, 3300 AH Dordrecht, The Netherlands.

Printed on acid-free paper

Printed in the Netherlands.

Że to Miłości balsam brąz ten zlepił...
(Cyprian Norwid)

TABLE OF CONTENTS

CHAPTER 4 DUTY AND ASPIRATION

CHAPTER 5 THE MARKET AND LAW

CHAPTER 6 THE LAW OF LOVE AND THE LOVE OF LAW

CHAPTER 7 DON'T THINK ABOUT IT

CHAPTER 8 REASONING IN THE MACHINE

CHAPTER 9 REASONING BEYOND THE MACHINE

CHAPTER 10 EUROPE AND THE JOURNEY

CHAPTER 11 LIVING LAWFULLY

PREFACE

Having finally finished the book and in starting to write the Preface, I naturally think of its history and genesis. In so doing one realises that, contrary to some of the *diktats* of our governments, the scientific life cannot be totally planned. We might say that, in planning in the detail that we seem to have to in our scientific lives, we lose a great deal – not least in the time taken to constructing plans instead of actual doing scientific work! In thinking of the origins of my work then, I see no clear plan but an idea and a passion followed by a series of jumps that pull in outside influences and stimuli and try to make them coherent within the general concept of my project. And the grace and luck to make sense of, and pull in, the various contingencies that strike us in our life are as important as any well-planned project. As in science, so also in life in general, and for a book that wants in some way to link the personal and the social, to look at living under rules both as a way of living our lives well and living them in company with our fellows in polities, I have had the luck that my scientific life and career places these sorts of questions to the fore.

My first great luck was to come to Edinburgh to work, especially in the Centre for Law and Society at the Law Faculty of the University of Edinburgh. I cannot imagine a more conducive environment to work and live in. One could not wish for a more intellectual and otherwise supportive environment to deal with the themes set out in this book. I wish to thank all those students, teachers, and other workers associated over the years with the Centre. They have all in their individual ways contributed to the success of the Centre as an Institution and to any merit that my work might have. The list of names is endless but in connection with this present work no list could fail to include Neil MacCormick, my teacher and friend whose generosity with his time and friendship I cannot begin to measure, and Emilios Christodoulidis with whom I have argued and discussed the ideas contained herein since he was a graduate student here and who keeps me at least partly true to my old sympathies.

I wish also to thank Claire and Florence Henderson Davis. My meeting them and Charles, now sadly deceased, profoundly influenced the direction of the book. Claire and I collaborated together on various projects whose input into this work was great, especially influencing the theological engagement. I wish to thank them for their special brand of anarchic order; for their joy, trust and hope; for pushing me into places I would never have dared to enter, from theology to contemporary dance.

The first drafts of what were to become the book were written in Belforte in Tuscany where I went, with my colleague and friend Drew Scott, to work, run and rest, over one summer in the beautiful Tuscan countryside. The mixture of work, sport and food was invigorating and I particularly remember our runs through the sunny woods that smelled strongly of *funghi porcini*. I wish to thank Drew Scott for his generosity and friendship and for the long and stimulating discussions on questions of European identity and integration during our daily runs. These continued in Edinburgh and culminated in an ESRC Research Seminar on the Legal Theory of European Integration that we organised and their development can be seen in the book.

Most of the first part of the book was written at the University of Łódź where I was a guest for a month. I wish to thank my host Marek Zirk-Sadowski for his hospitality and help in providing an environment suitable for a Pole to work and play in.

The last part of the book was written at the Benedictine Monastery of Fort Augustus in Scotland where I spent two months taking part in the Benedictine life and writing. Living that life provided the ideal circumstances to write about creativity and order. Looking down Loch Ness in the evening sun showed me the beauty and particularity of the world. I wish to thank the community, now sadly and untimely closed down, for their welcome.

I finished the final part in Australia while a guest of the Universities of Macquarie, Sydney and New South Wales. I would like to thank Wojciech Sadurski, Martin Krygier and Adam Czarnota for their hospitality and help.

Many people have read and commented on the book or sections of it and I would here like to thank, Neil MacCormick, John Bell, Neil Walker, Tim O'Hagan, Roger Cotterrell, Martin Krygier, Alexander Peczenik, Duncan Forrester, Adam Czarnota, Emilios Christodoulidis, Fernando Atria, Steven Smith, Richard Jones, Claudio Michelon, Leonor Moral Soriano, John Holmwood, Kimberely Hutchings. I would also like to thank Emmanuel Melissaris and Joachim Genge for helping me with technical aspects of the book.

Finally, I would like to thank Christine Lauer:

Alles geben die Götter, die unendlichen,
Ihren Lieblingen ganz,
Alle Freuden, die unendlichen,
Alle Schmerzen, die unendlichen, ganz

The book I dedicate to my maternal grandparents, Ś.P. Teodor and Zofia Domeraccy, whose lives knew pain and joy and love, and whom I loved.

CZEŚĆ ICH PAMIĘCI.

INTRODUCTION

IN AND OUT OF THE LAW

In the opposition between law and love, there has been for too long concentration on the *thanatos* of law; of law as the restraining, civilising force that is necessary to hold in check the *Eros* of love, the love central to our contingent, passionate natures. This book aims to redress the balance - but in so doing it will not cast law aside. For we must not forget that love is dangerous and we can only approach it with caution – embracing it wholeheartedly can kill us. So though 'law' and 'love' feature centrally in this book, they will not be seen as opposed. In going beyond this opposition, I want to see how an ethical life and a society under law might be related. Part of my aim then, is to rethink and reconstruct the anarchism that underlay my earlier work in, for example, *Images of Law*[1]. I do this so that one can see how the moral autonomy that anarchism values so highly can be found not in the rejection of law but rather through the understanding of law, of what legality must really mean.

Legality will here be distinguished from legalism, which is what Judith Shklar called the nomian attitude; that attitude and ideology of rigid rule-following which I describe later on in the book. But it is important to note that the nomian attitude can apply to both law and morality - one cannot just think of law as nomian and rule-bound, and oppose it with an anti-nomian ethical attitude or with morality. Both law and morality can be rigid and rule-bound, constricting the autonomous spirit. So the relationship of law to morality is not to be constructed in an oppositional way thus re-conceptualising the anarchist question into when it would be morally right to break the law. Rather what I am concerned with is the very idea of 'living lawfully' and what that might mean.

In the English language 'living lawfully' has rather positivistic connotations of following the actual law and does not have the same register as, for example, the German *Recht*. *Ein rechtschaffener Mensch* is not merely

---

[1] Bańkowski and Mungham (1976)

someone who just keeps to the law - the phrase has the idea of living in a morally correct way. But that is not meant to mean something moral as opposed to the law - it is about morality but it is also about the *law*. The lawful person can both keep the law and break it, but always within the context of the law. In English the rather old fashioned, 'righteous' captures this - thus the righteous person. We can have the same idea at different ontological levels and we can, for example, apply this way of looking at it to the state as a whole. The *Rechtsstaat* then, is the state living lawfully; the lawful state with the same connotations that we noticed at the individual level in our 'righteous person'. It is not the positivistic sense that the Rule of Law can have, that the state is bound by the laws of the land.

It is in this sense then, that the aim of this book is to explore what it means to live a life under the law. In general social terms, I mean by this questions of the rule of law, constitutionalism and democracy. But these broad questions of social and political theory get broken down into moral and ethical questions. What does it mean to say that a society should be governed by rules? What sort of ethical life does that entail? The way we answer that question is to go into questions of what it means for us to use rules as reasons for actions. What effect does that have on our moral and social life? In particular, does it somehow take over our moral life, give us a way to escape decisions that we should take for ourselves, take away the force of love from our lives?

But can and should we escape the 'net of rules'? Iris Murdoch in her novel, *Under the Net*, amusingly details the comic and sad escapades of her hero who, in existentialist manner, is trying to gain freedom by escaping the ever present net of rules, is trying to find his true autonomy in the face of the heteronomy of rules. Is this something that we are all doomed to; to try and strike out on our own only to be hauled back by the rules - our attempts at contingency always broken by the force of rules? Can we live a life outside the law and what sort of life would that be? Or do we have to settle for the life of the law? Is it impossible to live in and out of the law or must we choose one or the other so as not to subvert the alternative we choose? Does a life of law preclude love and does a life of love preclude law? And so part of the theme of this book is that the social questions also raise individual moral and ethical questions; that to live lawfully implies both a question of how I should live in my relations with my fellows and how society should be organised. The question what is a lawful person and what is a lawful society must be looked at together.

I want then to get away from two images of the moral life by using 'lawfully' in this way. The images are the nomian one of legalism and the anti-nomian one, of love, of the 'religion of the heart' which seem to exclude the one from the other. The best way of seeing that is a particular (and incorrect) Christian view of the relations between itself and Judaism where Christianity was seen as sweeping away the rigid rule following of Judaism. This view gets both that relation and Christianity wrong. Though Christ often ignored the law he did not come to sweep it away[2].

> 'Think not that I have come to abolish the law and the prophets; I have come not to abolish but to fulfil them. For truly, I say to you, till heaven and earth pass away, not an iota, not a dot, will pass from the law until all is accomplished.' (Mt 5: 17-18)

And Gillian Rose[3] documents how in Judaism itself there were similar tensions between the rigid following of the rules and some sort of flexible ways of dealing with love. Law and love in both those systems are actually held in tension. I have thus used many theological images in this book. For the sense of lawful that I have used is something that is found and used in these theological discourses. The implications of this for my argument is that the moral life should be seen as not one or the other of law and love, but as the interlinking and tension between these two. So it is not law or love, rather the precarious intertwining between the two that we are seeking. Law and going beyond it are inseparable and, in a sense in which I will explain, in breaking the law you are fulfilling the law. Truly to follow the law implies being able to break it and recreate it anew - in breaking the law you are following it. But, and this is important, neither does it imply doing away with the law.

This is not just a religious question but an important question for ethics and social and political theory. Theological questions, as Hegel says, are ways of looking at important philosophical questions. And, in the West, the connection between the two discourses has been close and mutually reinforcing. So, just as for Hegel, the Incarnation was the theological way of looking at the central philosophical problem of the relation between the universal and the particular, some of the images I will use, especially of those the parables, will shed light on central philosophical and social questions.

The questions that the book is concerned with then, are deep problems of practical reasoning and social method which run through a wide range of debates. In the book itself I touch upon debates in personal morality, aesthetics, epistemology, social and political organisation, institutional design

---

[2] For this argument see Bańkowski and Davis (1999)

[3] Rose (1993: chapters 1-3)

and the form and substance of law. In one sense, each of these debates is specific and has its own concrete problems and questions, its own register. But at the same time one can see within them a 'deep grammar' of similarity. What they are all concerned with is the articulation of autonomy with heteronomy, freedom with regulation, love with law. They are concerned with how the heteronomy of system articulates with the desire to be free, and the creative impulse, of autonomy. My argument is that this is not to be seen as the never ending oscillation from one to the other, of it being our fate to be pushed from one side to the other with no principle of choice. Instead, I want to argue that the articulations here should be seen, not as contradictories, but rather as tensions. They are worked out in a middle area which is risky and uncertain but one which we must inhabit if we are to live as the beings that are we, at the same time autonomous and heteronomous.

In this book the institution of law has a privileged position and discussion of it runs throughout the entire book. This is because, as a special and authoritative form of practical reasoning, it raises in an acute form the problem of living in the middle and of the articulation of heteronomy with autonomy. The reasoning the law uses here might be called parabolic reasoning, and stresses the importance of allegory and the actual narratives that the law encounters. It is thus appropriate that the book is written in a metaphorical and allegorical style - much of the work is done through the telling and re-telling of stories and examples. The method complements the thesis. But though I concentrate on the institution of law, I have run this articulation through many different concrete debates since it is instructive to compare them with the institution of law. Though my style has been allegorical, I have throughout the book pointed to the connections and family resemblances and the lessons to be learnt from them.

The first chapter introduces the theme of these articulations or tensions by relating the issue of personal morality, should someone obey a law they think wrong, to the question of social organisation, of democratic ordering. The debate focuses on the problems of living in the tensions of commitment to society and freedom of the individual. In the next two chapters I examine, through the optic of the *Antigone* of Sophocles, what legalism can mean in personal practice and in debates in legal theory about the institution of law. Chapter 4 produces some tentative solutions and introduces the notion of legality, which neither transcends the tensions nor takes one side or the other. Rather, it is responsive in accepting the tensions implicit in living in the middle, in the space between them. Chapters 5 and 6 go to the level of society and argues that the tensions are not to be seen as the binary oppositions of a traditional right/left divide. They examine how these problems, and indeed solutions, are instantiated in differing forms of society and the moral forms of life implicit in them. The next three chapters deal with the institution of law and especially legal reasoning. There, I try to show that the middle is a place where what I call 'parabolic' reasoning operates. I make much use of machine and computer analogies which, along with a discussion of creativity, allow me to re-conceptualise anarchism as the creative breaking of the law; as something that can only come about in the context of the law, through knowing and following the law. In this way I try to work out the notion of 'living lawfully'. Finally, I try to work out my themes in a concrete example centred around the debates concerning the governance of the European Union and the debates concerning European Identity.

In conclusion, I argue that a recognition of the centrality of the articulation of heteronomy and autonomy allows us to see how many debates have been trapped in structures which are in thrall to these oppositions. So many positions in all the areas and debates I will look at have, explicitly or implicitly, equated their substantive positions with a more or less autonomous or heteronomous structure of reasoning. One cannot satisfactorily escape this tension, though we might try, and we cannot locate ourselves in a fixed point on the continuum. My claim is that the tension between heteronomy and autonomy is part of the grammar of practical reasoning and an underlying premise of social organisation and institutional design - accepting that is the way forward. That, as I shall explain, is what gives our lives and our institutions integrity and unity. And it is in that spirit and trust that I begin.

CHAPTER 1

NIE POZWALAM

INTRODUCTION

I aim in this chapter to introduce the general themes of the articulation or tensions of autonomy with heteronomy, freedom with regulation, love with law. In particular I look at the tension between the freedom of the individual and the commitment to the collective. The debate seems to require either commitment to society or freedom of the individual. I will show that the debate cannot resolve itself into one or the other because both are important and worthwhile and both have, at the same time, their negative sides. We are not fated to have to choose one or the other. They do not exclude each other as being contradictory – rather they articulate in uneasy tension to make ourselves and our social institutions whole. It is that tension that we must learn to manage and in the understanding of it that I go on to explore what it means to live a life under law.

In beginning of this task, it is perhaps appropriate to look to why living under the law has been seen as a problem; to look at the most comprehensive attack on law, that of anarchism. Anarchists have always distrusted law. Tolstoy (1972) says that the law is based on violence; is in the interests of the ruling class; involves mystifying through the 'science of legislation'. Instead of making things clear, it builds up a huge opaque apparatus of its own, comprehensible only to its acolytes. Direct responsibility is evaded. Anyone can deny responsibility for what they have done as merely carrying out the law. Two different prongs in this attack can be discerned.

The first is that law has been captured by a group of people and used for their own interests. Crudely, law is used by those who have to rob those who have not. More modern studies have indeed shown that lawyers' high sounding phrases often mask naked self interest. (Bańkowski and Mungham,

1976: chapter 3) That 'the interests of justice' often mean my interests. Legal aid means aid for lawyers and not by lawyers. But does this mean that the Rule of Law as an idea (or ideal) is thereby flawed? In part yes. If that is how it is in practice, then that is what the ideal actually means. All else is illusion. In part no. For, for many radicals, the law has been captured by a particular group who use it for themselves and not for the good of others and society. But, it is argued, the law can be re-captured, can be used to do good. Can it? There is a strange coalition between right and left here. Both think that it cannot. Both think that is so because the law is inextricably linked with capitalist, market society[4]. Its instrumental use will, for the former, destroy it as law. For the latter, it will merely reproduce capitalist society.

But it is the second prong of the anarchist attack that I wish to concentrate on here. That goes further. It is not concerned with law's connections to a particular form of society. Rather, it is concerned with what is the moral meaning of legality. What it means to live under the Rule of Law. What it means to live under rules in general. It is this question that I want to take up. MacCormick (1989b) gets at the problem when he morally defends the Rule of Law or what he calls legalism. He gets to the heart of the problem. Legalism suggests some sort of rule-bound way of living, both personally and socially. Here we see the crux of the ethical point that I want to discuss. Is there something wrong with surrendering our lives to rules? We are, as the phrase goes, 'slaves of the law in order that we might be free'. But why should we be slaves? This is not a question of who controls the society and for what reason. It is about the moral implications of placing ourselves 'under the governance of rules' (Fuller 1969) as we try to live our lives among our fellows. What does it mean for the individual and society to organise in this way?

I start, as for me is appropriate, with Poland. The Republic of Poland-Lithuania (1569-1795) was not, as Davies (1981) says 'a resounding success' but political anarchism was one of the principles of the democracy that its aristocratic democracy adopted. Davies goes on:

> 'Its watchword – '*Nierządem Polska Stoi*' ('Its by unrule that Poland stands') contains a paradox that Proudhon himself would have admired, and comes close to Bellarigue's famous slogan of 1848, '*L'anarchie , c'est l'ordre*'. Its laws and practices were inspired by deeply rooted beliefs in individual freedom and civil liberty which, for the period, were exceptional.' (p. 321)

One of the institutions of this form of aristocratic anarchy was the *Liberum Veto*. This was a device to help procure unity and meant that any debate in the

[4] see Sypnowich (1990: chapter 3)

Sejm, the Assembly, could be halted because there was no agreement (*nie ma zgody*) by reason of a single *veto* or *nie pozwalam* (I do not allow). Debate would only go on when that disagreement was resolved and that might take hours, days or indeed could mean the end of a bill, even if the majority were in favour. This of course, led to several problems and many bills, especially tax bills were blocked for some time. Andrzej Fredro, who was Marshall of the *Sejm* in 1652, Davies recounts, wrote supporting this institution and its 'paradoxical philosophy of anarchism'. It was supposed to protect the wise against the stupid majority, kept the King in check by keeping him poor (it was difficult to get taxes through). Gradually it became used to paralyse government completely until hardly any sessions of the *Sejm* were able to pass legislation, law making at that level broke down.

Davies shows how this anarchism which was supposed to protect against tyrannical power ended up supporting Russian autocracy since the form of governance made itself incapable of organising against Russian power. But whatever its outcome, this mode of governance, 'its paradoxical philosophy', and its fierce belief in the autonomy of the individual raises deep questions about democracy and law. It is to these that I now turn.

TAKING PART

Robert Paul Wolff explores the questions raised by the *liberum veto* in his book *In Defence of Anarchism*[5]. Here he takes the story of Stephen, a young American who does not want to fight in Vietnam. He asks under what circumstances would Stephen, even though he thought he should not fight, think it morally necessary to go. When, in other words, would it be right for the state to insist and for him to accept even though he thought it wrong to do so? The best and most acceptable reason for going would be that Stephen is so involved in the society that he is compromised and thus personally barred from refusing to go. This is what the argument that says he has participated in decision making comes to. So in a sense, to continue with the legal analogy, we are looking for what actions would count as personally barring or stopping Stephen from refusing to go. These actions would best take place, Wolff says, in the context of some sort of democracy or democratic ordering of society. Wolff then goes on to take a closer look at various forms of democratic ordering.

He denies representative democracy could satisfactorily solve Stephen's dilemma. Under that system, we take part in the decision-making procedure

[5] Wolff (1976)

by voting for people who then make the laws that govern our lives. In what sense, asks Wolff, do we take part? Is it not the sense that we voted for the person and/or party and the policies that they support? This does not reflect reality at all. In the first place we do not know and cannot know what a particular candidate thinks on all issues. Anyway, one of the points of representative democracy is that we expect candidates to make up their own minds on some issues. In a system of parties we might, however, argue that we are implicated in the decision because we know what party a particular candidate is in. Therefore, since we know what the party stands for, we know in general the candidates' positions. Thus we can have a fair idea of what sort of decisions they are likely to make. We are implicated in the decision-making process because it is the general line of decisions that we approve in voting for a particular candidate. If we vote for a socialist party we cannot complain if we are taxed more to organise better social welfare provision, even if we do not want to give up our 'hard earned' money. If we vote for a conservative party, we cannot be surprised when the return to individuals is given priority over provisions for society in general; when privatisation is more important than providing public service. But the argument from the party system is itself removed from reality. For these days, it is not clear what parties stand for even in a general way. In the British context, the examples I used are not at all clear cut. Parties do not disclose, nor do they know, their entire programme. Nor do they seem to have any shame in departing from it. The argument from representative democracy then does not force Stephen to fight. He is, he could argue, in no sense taking part in any of the actual decision-making. He merely chooses people who then make what decision they like, within, at best, certain constraints.

What other forms of democratic ordering are there then? Wolff next considers direct democracy. He considers this the best argument that can be put forward to make Stephen go against his will to Vietnam. But, for him, it fails also. It fails because it fails to consider another question about what it means to take part in decision-making. Above, we considered what it meant to take part in decision-making in the sense of choosing people who in some sense represent you. But does actually voting for a decision, rather than choosing people to represent me, mean that I take part in the decision-making? Let us first consider the case where everyone agrees but one person, who nevertheless manages to have his view implemented. Here we must say that there has not been participation in the decision making. This would be the case not only if there were some sort of fraud or tyranny involved. It would not be just the possibility of fraud that drives us to say that there would be no taking part in a decision in a system where the wishes of most people can be ignored, even if that is legitimate according to the system.

The first difficulty can be explained by taking the example of the Scottish referendum on self government held in 1979[6]. Those who wished self government to prevail had to win an affirmative vote of a majority of those voting and the proportion of those voting affirmative had to be at least 40% of the whole electorate entitled to vote. The first condition was satisfied but not the second. The question is what to think of those who did not vote? We can say that they took part in the decision making procedure since they had the chance but decided not to do so. But how are we to count them? The referendum conditions meant that we effectively counted them as voting no. But would not counting them - or discounting them - as abstentions be fairer?

Further difficulties can be shown by taking the example of Northern Ireland. Unionists there have argued that the minority of Catholics there has too much influence and that the wishes of the Unionist majority are ignored. On the other side the argument goes that it is the wishes of the Catholic nationalists that are ignored. The mistake made from the Unionist side is taking a part of Ireland (and not the whole) as the base line from which decisions about majority and minority influence and rights can be made. If one accepts that taking all Ireland as the base line is unrealistic, then one runs into an infinite regress. For what is there to prevent this same argument being applied to each area where a particular national grouping is strong. Why should we not have separate referenda, and thus enclaves, in areas like West Belfast and Tyrone or Derry where Catholics are particularly strong. This sort of argument would lead to the cantonisation of the country. We can see the implications of that in what was Yugoslavia[7].

But this is not only an argument about baselines. For the implications of this argument go further. The point at issue here is what is to count as a minority and, more importantly, what is to count as a majority. For we are too ready to think the answer to that question obvious. But is it? Take the Scottish referendum again. It was argued that the conditions effectively imposed a majority of over 50% of those voting and that was unfair. Why? After all some entrenched provisions in constitutions around the world require greater majorities than 50%. We do not think that to be unfair or problematic. The question becomes; what conceptually is a majority? We may say that a majority obtains when there is more on one side than the other. This is a rather

---

[6] See Bradley and Ewing (1997) for the referendum held on 11 September 1997 (in terms of the Referendums (Scotland and Wales) Act 1997) and Himsworth and Munro (1998); Mitchell and Leicester (1999) for the recent referendum.

[7] On the other hand 'all Ireland' is an equally contentious and contested base line, a cultural label of disputed political significance. But the point still holds.

arithmetical way of going about defining a majority. What makes following what 51% want fairer than saying it must be 80%? The (arithmetical) minority seem to lose out both ways. For in the case of the 49% we might think that the voting blocs are so close that it would be wrong completely to ignore the wishes of the 49%. In the case of the 20% we might think that here are a minority that need permanent protection because they will always be in the minority. A figure in between, where the minority is neither too large nor too small, might be appropriate. But how do we find that number? We cannot find it by the laws of arithmetic. We have to produce a procedure for finding that out and that will itself be subject to the problems that I have described. How many people must assent before we can accept that decision as just? What percentage of dissent can we take as acceptable? I mean here that level where the dissenters will still be counted as being bound by the decision and we can justly say that they have participated in the decision making. This will not be solved, as I have argued, by the arithmetical sense of the term of majority. We have here an ethical and political question.

Wolff argues that, looking at it from the point of view of the minority, this problem is insoluble. Even if there is only one person left in the minority, that person can say that they have not participated because their view has not been taken into account. The arguments against this position will be subject to the same problems of what is to count as a majority. A regress will be set up until we come to a minority of 0%. For Wolff, this leads to the conclusion that the only acceptable solution to 'Stephen's problem' is a system of direct democracy with unanimity as the voting rule. This will ensure that everyone participates in the decision making process in both senses. It is only in this case that Stephen will rightly think himself to be obligated. He has not acted here heteronomously, by virtue of a law which someone else has made. For it is only in this case that Stephen will have acted under a law that he has made for himself. That is the only case where we can say that he has acted autonomously. And we arrive back at the *liberum veto*.

THE INDIVIDUAL AND THE COLLECTIVE

We might say then, that part of the argument for unanimity is that no arithmetical majority is natural. One can always ask the question why should the fact that one more person thinks x be reason that *x* prevail and one can go on doing that until we get to unanimity. Where should we stop? To begin to answer this question we must ask ourselves what we want. If we are interested in bringing a society closer together, then we will be more interested in coming closer to the unanimity principle, whereas if we are just concerned with a decision making procedure which will, in a minimal sense, hold, then we will come closer to a simple majority system. Why? In the former, we are interested in the group as an entity whereas in the latter we appear only to be interested in individuals. We only add individuals up - group cohesiveness, except in a minimal sense, is not important. In an earlier paper (Bańkowski 1977a), I tried to answer Wolff's problem in that way. It depends upon which view of society one starts off with. Wolff, I claimed, started off from too individualistic premises. A view, which sees society as constituted by individual atomistic units coming together will see the individual in society in a particular way. For that view means that each atomistic unit must give up some of its autonomy. This will be more the case in modern and complex societies than in more simple ones. The base unit of society being this sort of individual, the loss of autonomy will inevitably be seen as the basic and key sacrifice that is made for society. Any solution to Wolff's problem will always be geared towards the individualistic perspective.

If, on the other hand, we start from a perspective where it is society that comes first and constitutes the individual, then we have a different view of it. Loss of autonomy is not viewed as so important since autonomy is constituted by the society in the first place. The question of the relationship between individual and society obviously comes up. Stephen's problem however has not the same force as it does in Wolff's discussion of it. Why? Because it becomes a question of what is the correct way of acting for Stephen, given that he, as an individual, is constituted by that society. He is not something that came from the outside. Thus one cannot think, as in the first case, of his giving up something that was previously his and his alone, that was nothing to do with the society. It then becomes a question of what sort of ethical ideals you start off with. With the ethical ideals of individualism one looks at the world from the point of view of the individual person and their cares and worries. The individual is sovereign. It is what it wants that matters and nothing else. With a more communal or collective ethical ideal, the individual becomes less important and it is a matter of what solution is best. The individual is viewed not as sovereign but as part of the community and it is that person-in-the-community that must be taken into account when working out a solution. The fact that *I* want (or don't want) something is never perceived as the final determining factor.

This argument does not attempt to deny the problem. Rather it attacks the centrality of the problem. It claims that the grip that it holds on our psyches is something to do with the societies that we live in. In other sorts of societies, this problem might not have the same centrality and grip. In a sense it is a matter of emphasis. The heroes of one sort of society are the individuals. In order to remain true to themselves, they stand out against the chaos and pressures of a world forever constraining and impinging upon them. The heroes of the other sort of society do not have the former's sense of self - that is a negative quality. They work, without thought for themselves, for the good of the community and to build a better world. The former are called by the latter, 'bourgeois individualists/or romantics'. The latter are often seen by the former as falling prey to the herd instinct; losing their sense of integrity and morality.

Koestler's novel *Darkness at Noon* exhibits well some of these points. Rubashov, the old Bolshevik, knows that he is not guilty of the crimes of which he is accused. Nevertheless, he is persuaded to confess to them for the good of the party and the future society. This novel can be see in two different ways, depending upon one's point of view. On the one hand, it can be seen as the story of an individual whose integrity is destroyed by a totalitarian and authoritarian system. On the other hand, it can be seen as the story of someone who sacrifices himself for the good of the society of which he is a part.

But we must be careful not to let this polarise into a clash of 'community' *versus* 'individualism' with no answer in between. This leads to its own political problems. On the 'community' side of the coin, one can see societies where individual rights are totally denied. Where the individual only has meaning for the collective. But the 'collective will of the people' can mask great individual power. This can also be seen clearly in Koestler's novel where, in the end, Rubashov sacrifices himself for party members, who run the powerful apparatus. Socialism of this sort, as practised in the countries of the old Eastern Europe, masked great individual power. Doing something 'in the name of the people' often (if not always) meant doing something for yourself.

But it is not this tendency to fraud that is the root of the problem. For bad faith is not necessary to bring about the effect I have described. The basic point is that here all individuality gets lost in the collective. The sense of self is lost. People do not see each other as individuals but only groups or 'collectives'. Moreover, they do not see themselves as anything other than part of the collective. This can be graphically illustrated by the experience of the '60s. Among many radicals 'the collective' was seen as the answer to everything. Most of these '60s communes failed because they had no sense of the individual. They failed disastrously because people in them could not act as individuals. One person sneezed, everybody caught a cold or formed a support group. The collective life took over in such a way that the individual was lost.

But it is not just a story about the individual collapsing into the totality and collective. The paradox is deeper than that. For at the same time that that happens we might also say that the collective collapses into the individual. Thus in some Christian sects, the community of God *becomes* God and thus the individual in the community is given up for the community become an individual again. We can see the political consequences of this if we look to the experience of fascism and the organic community. There, citizens are lost in the community, the *Volk,* but at the same time that *Volk* becomes an individual. In this way the actions of the leader are justified because *I* am onewith that leader - not in the sense that I participate in the decision making but that I really am he. Thus I cannot complain if something is done to me because I am the individual that does it. We do not have to look to the extremes to see that. The neo-corporatist forms of governance in the 1960's and 1970's and the emphasis on 'community' among radicals served to mask many undemocratic and authoritarian practices which were justified in the name of the community which became identified with the community worker or community leader. (Bańkowski and Mungham 1978) So putting the problem in that dichotomous way means the individual and the collective collapse into each other since there does not seem to be anything to keep them apart.

In looking at what happens when the individual and the collective collapse into each other we realise that the problem that Wolff is addressing and indeed, the *liberum veto*, is more than merely about the individual and society. It does appear that the sort of autonomy that Wolff is talking about would entail that we must be alive to the permanent radical possibility of changing our mind. But this means more than merely some *ceteris paribus* clause. The promise creates a new obligation, it is not shorthand or a summary for the reasons which mean that there is an already existing obligation to do something. It is a separate and independent reason and thus founds its own obligation. But then, in the case of promising, I compromise my freedom and autonomy because I am in thrall to the promise and its authority. I am in a heteronomous relation because I can only be released from it by someone else. This, since we have to think of ourselves as beings that can only make laws for ourselves, as autonomous beings, would be compromising my freedom and dignity. And indeed some anarchists have gone so far as to say that promises are wrong as being a heteronomous form of authority. Thus, as Green (1988) shows, Godwin (1976) a strict utilitarian, thinks them wrong. His grounds are that before the promise there was a reason to do *x,* or not, and the promise at best provides an additional reason for doing something that ought to be done anyway. But we must do the right thing for the right reason, if we are truly to be moral. The promise might give us an 'additional inducement' to act but that

> '[The] last temptation is the greatest treason:
>
> To do the right deed for the wrong reason'. (T S Eliot 1988)

This is the brunt of Wolff's argument against the authority of the State. I promise to obey the state but why should that promise heteronomously bind me? Indeed, as Green says, the paradox goes further for it is difficult to see, on this argument, how any form of association could be binding at all. And this makes the anarchist position paradoxical. For, to the anarchist, the way out of the heteronomy of the state might be through voluntary association and the collective ethic that we talked about above. For this expresses fully the desire to bring people closer together. However these associations will be founded upon some sort of contractual or promissory basis . What is to prevent them from falling foul of Godwin's argument? But it also threatens the basis of Wolff's solution. For why on the argument as it has gone, should unanimity bind? It might bind on the occasion of the deliberation but why later? The only thing that appears to make it binding beyond that time would be some sort of promise but, *ex hypothesi*, that would give me no moral reason for following it later. I would have to see if it were the right thing to do all over again if I did not want to compromise the freedom and dignity of my autonomy. To concentrate on the collective as a way out of the conundrum does not really solve the problem. It merely transfers to another ontological entity which can be treated as though that were an individual even though of different ontological status. For, if as we saw above, there is no space between the individual and the collective, they collapse the one into the other and produce a sort of collective individual[8].

LIVING THE LAW

But here we get to the heart of the idea of living a life under law and rules. For the implication of all this is, as I said above, that we must all be alive to the permanent possibility of changing our minds, that we can never take the rule as a fixed reason for our doing something. But if that is the case, then what is the sense of the rule if we must decide in each case that it does apply? And anyway the point of the rule is to prevent that. Why would we have law otherwise? The point is a mixture of morality and epistemology. I do not

[8] See Green (1988: chapter 2) for this argument

mean to say that law is indeterminate because meaning is always vague. Rather it is to claim that applying the rule is something different from finding its meaning. Whether a rule is correctly applied is a question that has to be determined not only by the meaning but by the particular circumstances of the situation and therefore has to be adjudged each time anew. That is a decision that we have to take and not let the meaning of the rule make that decision for us. If we allowed that to happen we would be, as Wolff says, surrendering our autonomy. And it is precisely the point of the rule to take that decision away from the particular circumstance and locate it in the universality of the rule. We can make this happen by refusing to take these decisions and thus make the rule more and more like a computer system which is programmed merely to apply the rules according to its programme. Consider as an example the cash machines that banks use to dispense cash to their customers. All users have a card. They insert this into the machine. They then key in their private code and the amount of money that they want. The machine checks the status of their account, the amount of withdrawals that they have made. Depending on their status, it then gives them the money or not. There is no argument. You cannot plead with it. You cannot show how here, for pressing and important reasons, it should read the rules differently and give you the money. There would be no bank teller to step out and tell you that in this case the rules need not apply. We would have surrendered all to the heteronomy of the machine.

Why do we want this universality? One answer would be that it is this that brings us rationality. Consider some monkeys on a south sea island[9]. Here, on a beach, the monkeys had found grains of rice mixed in with the sand. They wanted to eat the rice but it was impossible since it was inextricably mixed in with the sand. One day one monkey found that by throwing the mixed ball of grain and sand into a rock pool, the grain and sand separated since the grain floated to the top. Soon all the monkeys learnt this trick. This was seen as a display of a modicum of rationality by the monkeys. But what is it that counts as rationality here? Consider the case of one monkey. How does one monkey learn that throwing the mixed grain and sand into the rock pool will produce food? It is something more than remembering and repeating the chance occurrence (the throwing of the ball of mixed grain and sand into the rock pool) that produced grain the last time. Though that memory might be strong, there is as yet no principle that will connect it with the present time. The first separation of the grain from the sand occurs because the monkey accidentally throws the ball of mixed grain and sand into the rock pool. What happens the next time the monkey wants food and is confronted with rice

[9] This example is taken from one of David Attenborough's nature programmes for the BBC

mingled with sand? We can isolate three instances. First, the monkey might remember what happened last time but not connect it with the present time and so not try the trick again. Second, it might by chance throw the ball of mixed grain and sand into the rock pool again and get rice. But this would not show that the monkey connects this act of throwing with the previous act of throwing, even though they both achieved the same result. It might appear just another chance occurrence and the next time it is confronted with the same problem it would still not know what to do. Why? Because the monkey has not connected each separate incident but has viewed them as disconnected coincidences. Third, it might display a modicum of rationality. The monkey displays rationality when it universalises and transcends the particular experience. When it sees that what happened is not something that stands alone. It sees the event as something that can be connected with past and future experiences and it so connects them. This is what we mean by universalising, for the rule 'if you throw grains of sand and rice that are mixed up together into water, they will separate and enable you to eat the rice' is not merely connecting up particular experiences. It is a refusal to see the world as a chaotic universe of particular instances which have no connection[10]. This comes out well in Weber (1991), where he talks of how the world with the coming of scientific rationality loses its magic. Before, the world was a contingent chaotic place and one could not understand what and why it was happening. With the coming of scientific rationality, the world becomes understandable and predictable and so loses its contingency. We can now know the principles behind the world's operation since we can subsume them under universal laws.

One can see the formal rationality which, produced by bureaucracy, is for Weber essential to capitalism in the same light. It reduces the normative world, as something that is arbitrary and contingent, to something understandable and predictable. People no longer do things for all sorts of reasons which we cannot predict in advance but now act according to rules that have been laid down. This makes their actions both understandable and predictable. So this form of universality in the form of law makes our world a more rational place. Just as in the example of the monkeys the particular is transcended and subsumed under the general rule so here the individual action is understood under the aspect of the general rule that prescribes it. Individual behaviour is understood as behaviour under a rule and is thus made intelligible and rational.

---

[10] There is an excellent account of culture among primates in the Times, 17 July 1999.

We do not have the time here to go into the problems that are involved here but it is sufficient for my argument to posit a close relation between universalisation in morals and law (as a normative phenomenon), and science[11]. Law, as Selznick (1966) puts it, is seen as the rational principle which protects us from the governance of the arbitrary will. Law is thus seen as something that makes our world rational, which gives meaning to our social universe. In the same way, we may say that the laws of nature give meaning to our physical universe. Thus we are able to make some sort of coherent sense of our world both normatively and cognitively. We are able to live in it without being subject to the whims of the crowd or any particular person. Our social organisation has some reason behind it, it is not something that is merely run by the arbitrary desires or wills of people.

Arbitrary here is an ambiguous word. It is not merely something having no reason behind it - an act might be arbitrary and have very good reasons behind it. Take the grading of term papers. When a teacher grades a student's paper what he does is essentially an arbitrary act. That is not to say that it has no rationale but rather that it is subjective. The rationale is the teacher's experience and wisdom in his discipline and the art of teaching. It is that particular quality applied to that particular act that we expect from the teacher. We thus cannot check it as action subsumed under a rule because here we do not transcend the particular - it is precisely the good faith of the particular teacher and the particular qualities applied to the concrete act that we want. We have to trust in the teacher. If we think that the teacher has got it wrong (apart from lack of integrity) we cannot check for there is no criterion that we can use apart from his own experience. Going to a second marker does not control or check the first marker for in the second marking we depend on the skill and experience of the second marker which, as in the first case, is hers and hers alone. There can be no way of transcending the particularities and checking against a rule. Now we can see that as a principle of social organisation this leaves a lot to be desired and it is precisely this that the rule of law stands against. Note that the argument here does not imply that people will act in bad faith (though a certain Hayekian argument (see chapter 5) says that eventually they will). The point is that there will be no independent check to say that what they have done is right. As long as they act with integrity it is *their* reasons that are decisive.

---

[11] See Hare (1961) and (1963)

CONCLUSION

The above is what is meant when we say that law constrains the arbitrary will. Normative chaos is subsumed under law which makes things certain and predictable. One might say that the normative chaos is that of democracy in the sense that it is supposed to represent the contingent and arbitrary expressions of individual wills. But it seeks to do something more than merely constrain or control them. For it claims to maximise the expression of each individual voice precisely by subsuming it into the law and avoid the outcome of a society based on the *liberum veto* where in the end everyone loses (and Russia takes over). In this way, as in the example of the monkeys, all the individual voices are transcended and we make sense of them through the rationality of universal law. But that creates a paradox. For though we avoid the chaos of the *liberum veto*, it means losing the very thing that makes the voices important, their essential contingency and arbitrariness. We no longer listen to, or even hear, Stephen's voice and refusal – he has spoken in the law which now makes sense of his action. And his refusal to fight becomes wrong because it is only seen through the optic of the law and thus illegal. We gain certainty and predictability but we lose the individual and our autonomy. Democracy is important for it represents the desires and wishes of people. But the desire to produce a system to enable people to do what they want without having to fit it into some rational plan of the universe which will be dependent on others in fact fits them into that rational plan. Their autonomy is taken away by the demands of a fixed reason. So the desire to maximise autonomy leads to heteronomy for all. For now *I* do not decide what to do but act heteronomously and let the law do so.

Our journey through the *liberum veto* and anarchism has led us *via* questions of the relation of the individual to society or collective, through rationality and contingence and legality and democracy, to deep questions of political organisation and ethics. But how should Stephen live? How should we organise our lives and our societies? What happens when we try to escape the tensions which I argue are an inevitable part of our lives and societies?

CHAPTER 2

AVOIDING CONTINGENCY

INTRODUCTION

How do we live in a world where things can go wrong, where our values can conflict and lead us into situations where we do not know the answer; where whatever we do seems to have unbearable consequences? It seems that one of the requirements of practical wisdom is that we do not needlessly put ourselves in the way of such situations[12]. But we cannot always do that - the world is not something we can entirely control and make safe. Contingency will always break in. We can at least try to structure our lives so that in the ordinary course of events we live at least something of a stable and structured existence. How should we do that? One way is to try and, in the normative world at least, structure our lives so that we eliminate as far as possible conflict; so that we have a structured system for clearly resolving these conflicts. To do this we need a simplified structure of our value commitments, one that will be able to bypass or not generate conflicting demands. For it is these that appear to us to generate the impossibility of the good life. We seek, in short, to avoid tragedy. And this is seen as not only possible but as something that morally we should do. But what sort of world does that mean we assume and want to live in? How does that affect the structure of our law and life? What does it tell us about living a life under rules? We here will raise once again, and expand, the questions from the first chapter. I will undertake that exploration through considering a Greek tragedy, the *Antigone* of Sophocles. And part of the tragedy, I shall argue is in the way that the main protagonists structured their world so that they could avoid tragedy.

---

[12] Indeed, that is part of the catholic doctrine, in moral theology, of the avoidance of occasions of sin (just placing yourself in positions where you know you will be tempted and you know that there is a high probability of your succumbing is wrong).

ANTIGONE

The story of the *Antigone* is simple. Eteocles and Polynices, the sons of Oedipus, had agreed to rule Thebes in alternate years. Eteocles decides to stay in power and Polynices flees to Argos. There, with the king of Argos, he raises an army which attacks Thebes. The two brothers kill each other and the Argive army flees. Creon, the brothers' uncle, accedes to the throne and decrees that while Eteocles should be afforded funeral rites, Polynices, as an enemy of the city, cannot have them. Death shall be the punishment for those that disobey. Antigone, the sister of the two brothers vows to disregard this decree in recognition of her family obligations. She does this and is sentenced to be buried alive by Creon. Haemon, Creon's son and Antigone's fiancee cannot dissuade Creon. Creon changes his mind, the prophet Tiresias having warned him. But it is too late. Antigone has hanged herself and Haemon kills himself on discovering her dead. Euridyce, Creon's wife, kills herself on hearing of this. Creon is left alive seeing where his singlemindness and misapplication of reason has led him.

Martha Nussbaum (1986:51-82) writes of this play in the context of a book on luck and ethics among the Greeks. Her reading of the play is rather different in emphasis from some of the more traditional readings which see Antigone as the pure heroine and the clash as one between higher and lower laws. When the play is talked of in legal literature, it is presented as the paradigm of the conflict between natural and positive law. The *dike* of the Gods against the *nomos* of the state. In Nussbaum's version as with Hegel, Antigone is also flawed. For Hegel the tragedy is one of the dialectical struggle between the family and the state, Creon representing the state and Antigone the family. The two protagonists are thus bound to each other, right in their own terms but wrong in terms of the other's system. Antigone in following the laws of the gods is wrong in the eyes of human laws and Creon in following the laws of the State is wrong in the eyes of the laws of the gods. Both have too narrow an approach. In this dialectical way of looking at it the transformation occurs in the recognition of their mutual guilt and thus allows the synthesis of *das absolute Recht*.

> The true course of dramatic development consists in the annulment of the contradictions viewed as such, in the reconciliation of the forces of human action, which alternatively strive to negate each other in their conflict. (Hegel apud Nussbaum (1986: 203))

For Nussbaum the play is about practical reason, 'it is unusually full of words about deliberation, knowledge, reasoning and vision' (p.51). It starts with confident claims about what it is correct to do in practical situations and ends with the seeming despairing: 'I have no idea where I should look, which way I should lean'(1353)[13]. And yet it asserts that practical wisdom is the most important constituent of the good life. Both of the main protagonists have an unusually narrow view of the world; one that seems to preclude chance and luck entering in; one that gives them safety and security and confidence in their answers. They both take too partial a view but one that appears to shut out conflict. We see in the play how this narrow view of the world collapses. But we must not, according to Nussbaum, see this in the dialectical way of Hegel where the collapse of the two antitheses leads to the *Aufhebung* of the possibility of a harmonious world free from conflicts.

Creon believes that one who is concerned for civic well being displays practical wisdom, the most important attribute of a man - lack of it is a sign of sickness. Creon has many labels attached to him. He is called, among other things, honourable, pious and just. But these labels name separate and distinct virtues which can cut across each other and conflict. Thus to be a friend might demand being impious, or to be pious might mean being unjust. Honour might curtail friendship. And this, as Nussbaum says, would be something seen as normal to the spectators at the play. So Creon, in the beginning of the play, would be expected to have a deep and intractable conflict. He is relative to Polynices and is thus bound by the deepest religious duties to ensure that he gets a burial. But Polynices is not only an enemy, he is also a traitor to the city. Traitors cannot be buried within the city lest civic values be subverted. Creon, as representative of the state, is bound to honour this.

However, Creon appears to have no conflict at all, no painful tension and deliberation. How is this? If we look at Creon's ethical vocabulary, then we see that he has established a single intrinsic good. Though the traditional words are used, they now no longer stand for different virtues, they are all subordinated to what is good for the welfare of the city. What is honourable and pious and just are now actions that lead towards the welfare of the city. Good men are those who direct their actions for the welfare of the city. So just and good are now attributes not just of a man but of a man *qua* citizen. They do not define independent virtues, rather they describe the civic virtue of someone. A just man is just one who always acts for the welfare of the city. The virtues are united in the good of the city.

But this re-definition of the virtues goes much deeper than that for it also appears to embrace those virtues, those of love and piety, that are seen as belonging to opponents of his policy. He does not see the piety of Antigone to her brother nor does the love of a son move him. Creon, Nussbaum says,

---

[13] The translations of *Antigone* are taken from Nussbaum's chapter.

wants to replace family ties by the ties of the *polis*. In a play about brothers and family ties, his first use of the word brother, Nussbaum points out, is in respect of the close connection of one city ordinance to another: 'And now I will proclaim something that is brother to what preceded' (192). Conflicts in respect of family loyalty cannot arise if the city is the family. On this way of looking at it Polynices is of course no relation to Creon, he is an enemy and outside of the city, and thus no question of value conflict comes in: 'And as for anyone who considers any *philos* to be more important than his own fatherland, I say that he is nowhere' (182).

And this way of looking at it also shapes his view of sexuality. He does not tell his son not to let his passion for Antigone weaken him from the correct path because she is 'bad' as not civic minded. Rather he cannot understand how someone who is healthy in the sense that his practical wisdom is directed at the good of the city can see a woman like that as sexually attractive: 'A man who has not 'thrown out his wits' will find an unpatriotic spouse 'a cold armful in bed' (650-1). Even the gods are bound by this deliberative rationality, it is unbearable and inconceivable that they would want the burial of Polynices:

> 'You say something unbearable when you say that the gods take kindly forethought for this corpse. Could it be that they tried to cover him out of exceeding honour as if he had done something good, this man who came to burn their temples and shrines, their very land, and to scatter their laws to the wind? Or do you see the gods honouring bad people? It cannot be so.' (280-290)

Here we see echoes of Kant and how he thinks of God as bound by rational moral deliberation[14].

Creon has then created a world where there can be no conflict in values and tragedy cannot happen. This is so because, as Nussbaum shows, there is one supreme good. This is simple, it contains no internal oppositions, has a common currency in which all other values can be expressed and is always able to be seen at the bottom of all values. That good is expressed in the city and it is that 'ship of state', to use his imagery, that guards us from the wild sea and the contingencies of everyday life. It is that that keeps us secure and safe. Thus the just man, and also the pious one, will just see everything in terms of the city. There will be no conflict. But Creon fails because the city is more complicated than he wanted it to be - It is not a simple good. This also mirrors one latter day version of Creon' hope, that of utilitarianism whose

---

[14] I examine this notion in the context of Abraham and the sacrifice of Isaac at the conclusion of chapter 4.

single supreme good, happiness, turns out to be far more complicated than its mere reduction to pleasure implies. He fails because finally, in his despair at the death of his son and his love of him, he recognises how complicated the deliberative world really is. Not everything can be subsumed into the city and civic virtue. His practical reasoning was too narrow.

Though it might be said say she makes morally superior choices, Antigone is not the wholly blameless heroine. She is also narrow in her views. According to Nussbaum, this is not only to be seen in the narrowness of her perspective but in her conflict avoiding aims. In this respect she makes the same mistakes as Creon but with different virtues. Antigone too is guilty of attempting to simplify a complicated world. If we only listen to her we would not realise that there has been a war. We would not know that Polynices the brother of Eteocles came with the Argive army to conquer Thebes and was defeated. All we know is that a brother rests unburied. Antigone who subordinates everything to the duty to the family does not see anything else. It is not that the war is seen and discounted for various reasons, it is invisible, it is not relevant and so not there. She sees the brother demanding burial rites and not the enemy and traitor set on defiling the city - but they are both there. This is like Creon who sees it from the other side - he sees the traitor defiling the city and not the family member crying out for burial. Both draw a line, one round the city and one round the family and neither can see out beyond it. That is the narrowness of their vision which makes life easy and conflict free. Like Creon she redefines her central virtue. For her, the act of love of family is more like piety than any feeling. She is cold to her sister Ismene when she acts in, what, for Antigone, are impious ways. Feeling and passion, as we ordinarily see them, are shown by Ismene: 'What life is worth living for me, bereft of you?' (548) and Haemon whom the chorus sees as inspired by *eros* and to whom Antigone addresses not a single word in the play. The love she feels is a form of duty, it is not some contingent beautiful event. It is something that we are born to, a function of our family relations. In perhaps one of the most famous lines in the play, 'it is my nature to join in loving, not to join in hating', she expresses not a devotion to love in general but to the *philia* of the family. Her simplification of this leads her to produce a rank ordering among the family dead and she thinks of her life as one solely and utterly devoted to them: 'You are alive' she says to Ismene, 'but I am long since dead to the end of serving the dead'. The safe life of duty requires the death of life. Her ambition is to be in the world below where there is no possibility of error or wrong doing.

Both Creon and Antigone have so simplified their deliberative lives in the cause of safety that they have altered the structure of their emotional lives.

For Creon someone is loved because of his or her civic qualities. Antigone does not love anyone as themselves but as servants of the dead or themselves dead. They both appear inhuman. It is Ismene and Haemon who show the human emotions. Antigone and Creon both want to produce a simple world to avoid the complexities that abound. They both turn themselves inhuman in the attempt and fail.

THE FEAR OF FAILURE

They appear inhuman because they want to do that all too human thing, they want not to fail. They want to create for themselves a world where that will be impossible. The play details the tragedy (ironically) of their failure. One of the most important things here is the search for certainty . We can see how in doing this both Creon and Antigone lay claim to the law. They both try to protect themselves in the armour of the law but in doing so they lose the humanness that they are supposed to preserve. The problem here is not the search for an answer; practical reason demands that we have answers to practical problems, we do not just leave them and ignore them. Nor is it just the search for a correct answer *per se*. It is rather the idea that, notwithstanding the possibility of various solutions, our way of getting at the answer fixes the problem and we do not have to go any further. The search for certainty means that the answer will be treated as right. Though we may know that we can, in theory, go further that soon is pushed out of sight. And so we get the heteronomy that we saw in the last chapter. For the deliberative reasoning of Creon is bad because it precisely does not use all the relevant material. By enclosing himself in the law of civic virtue what happens is that the decisions are made for him. Once the system is set up, then the answers are there and one does not have to think about what they may be .

The phrase 'Don't think about it' is a good metaphor for what I have in mind. It sounds innocuous and non problematic. But it is often used in contexts where it shows some of the tensions and problems that I want to address. One might, to comfort or help someone in the grip of some crisis which seems to paralyse them, say something like, ' Be philosophical, don't think about it'. The incongruity of this comes from the fact that 'philosophical' is used ambiguously. It can mean either something like 'stoical' (you must bear 'the slings and arrows of outrageous fortune') or it can have the more standard sense of having a propensity to critical reflection. There is also a moral ambiguity here. For there is a sense in which we think that we should be able stoically to bear our troubles, pushing them from our minds and getting on with our daily lives. Yet at the same time, the moral life consists precisely in reflecting on our troubles and not just bearing them except in the sense that we critically think about our afflictions and bear them knowing that this is what we have done and accepting the consequences. And these things frighten Antigone as much as Creon. Creon sets the laws of the state and acts in thrall to them. Antigone though rejecting the system of state law, does not reject law, she applies, as rigidly, the law of the gods.

They both act heteronomously in respect of these laws. But in a further twist of irony they also appear to act as tyrants. One might see Creon as at first the enlightened civic humanist knowing that through the state we are able to live in virtue, and thus the safety of the ship of state is important. But when this becomes of overweening importance to him, we see a change and he turns into a tyrant who claims that his laws must be obeyed, that he alone knows what is for the good of the city. Antigone likewise: at first she seems to be upholding the laws of the gods against the impious demands of Creon. Soon however, the chorus see her as *autonomos;* not the sense of the previous chapter but as someone, like Creon, 'maker of her own laws' improvising her own piety, the sole interpreter of the laws. They are both so obsessed with the idea of not making a mistake that nothing must be allowed to come in the way; no uncomfortable ideas and reasons must be allowed. So their autonomy is merely the heteronomous thrall to their obsession. They make the same moral mistake. Antigone, though she appears to be acting selflessly is in fact exhibiting a form of selfishness. If we take the model of good deliberative action to be taking all selves into account and not unreasonably privileging any one them, then the selfish person unreasonably privileges their own self and the 'selfless' wrongly privileges all selves against themselves[15]. Deliberative action in this respect is dangerous because one could go wrong by over-favouring yourself but you cannot escape from that by totally ignoring oneself.

OPPOSITIONS AND TENSIONS

What I have been suggesting is that we can see the *Antigone* as what happens when you seriously and rigidly try to live a life of rules. But what is the solution then? I have presented the play, following Nussbaum, in such a way that it gets away from the binary opposites of the two protagonists. But the play has of course been read as a clash of opposites. Thus Hirvonen (1997: 245) puts the oppositions in this way:

ANTIGONE	CREON

[15] See Finnis (1982)

divine law	human law
Natural law	statutory law
law based on tradition	law based on enactment
Justice of caring	justice of coercion
principles	Rules
family	State
private	Public
interior	Exterior
Individuality	Social
emotions	Reason
irrationality	Rationality
eros	Logos
duty	Order

Now of course it is true that these oppositions exist but the problem is how to deal with them. We can look at this in two ways, both of which I think are incorrect. In the first place we can think of them as opposing principles which in their clash come together to a transformation and resolution/reconciliation. And this is the Hegelian view of it which Nussbaum rejects. We might also see the principles as being contradictory and the choice always oscillating between them. The way I have put this appears to posit a sort of dichotomous thinking with pairs of contradictory or countervailing principles as CLS would have it; the choice oscillating from one side or the other, depending upon what political and social framework the society has[16]. This is not a good way of looking at it either. Rather those principles are held in tension in societies. It is not a matter of choosing one against the other but rather what weight to give to them in any particular circumstance, as Dworkin (1986) argues. Principles are not binary. They are not like rules in the sense that following the rule automatically means denying the contrary. We may take, for the sake of argument, the principles of community and individuality as contrary[17]. This does not mean that using the one in a particular case will deny the other for all other cases or in a coherent scheme[18]. One would say that in the particular case the one principle has more importance than the other. In the general scheme of things they are both correct principles which can live happily together. Thus in certain cases individuality will be stressed whereas in others it will be community. But it is not to be seen as a zero sum game. These principles are to be viewed as being held in tension rather than as something we have to choose between. My point is not only that we are not forced to choose one or the other. I want to claim that both are necessary. Not only

[16] See Kelman (1987); Jabbari (1992); Ward (1997)

[17] See Unger's (1986) discussion of this.

[18] See Moral's (2000) working out of this in the context of European Environmental Law

instrumentally for the better working of society, but also morally for an ethically more aware individual and society.

LAW LEFT RIGHT BEHIND

But though there are these many opposing principles in *Antigone*, the central one, at least in the way that we have looked at the play seems to be between law, that way of circumscribing the world and the opposing principle which might be seen as contingency, love or passion. I do not want to claim that one can subsume all of Hirvonen's dichotomies in this all encompassing dichotomy, that they, and other oppositions that we discuss map easily on to that one. Rather they will run across it and each other, there will be a criss-crossing and family resemblance of oppositions. That is what I mean by living with the tensions. In what follows, I show examples of this.

a) The rule of rule and utility

Here the political debate is important as well. For in some way the central debate is between nomianism and anti-nomianism. Some Marxists, and to some extent, supporters of CLS see law in bourgeois societies as something rigid and inflexible; beyond the control of the citizen. It is something that is controlled by a ruling class. What we have here is something of an irony. For this view stems, in part, from seeing the law and the market linked and thus connected to capitalist societies. And with this view the right would agree. For the right the market and law are a heteronomous system but our autonomy is preserved because through it we are enabled to do what we like. We will that we have that sort of system and thus preserve our autonomy. For the left there is a heteronomous system but through it we are not enabled to do what we like. The social world becomes something that is rigid and inflexible. The differences in description are not very dissimilar . Thus one might too easily identify the opposition of nomianism and anti-nomianism with a left /right political divide, for law stands firm and is the sole guarantee of our doing no wrong. It is the instrument of that inflexibility. I am not responsible for anything as long as I do not, in the narrowly defined circumstances of my personal interaction, commit a wrong. Thus a Kantian argument about lying. To Kant's view that the categorical imperative knows of no exceptions, is often put the point that lying, for example to save a life, would be justified. To this one can reply in the following manner. When you are faced with a situation where it appears that you must lie in order to save a life, your doing so might, at the cost of doing a wrong, save that person's life. However consider the following story: in order to protect someone from a murderer you tell that murderer that the person is in a place where you believe he isn't. The murderer goes to the place where you lyingly directed him and finds his victim there, the victim having gone to what he thought was a secure place to hide. You are then responsible for the death of that person since, albeit from the best of motives, you did wrong and the consequences of that were murder. If, on the other hand, you merely tell the truth the empirical consequences are irrelevant to your responsibility because you followed the rule of right. Here in a sense you are hiding behind the law afraid to face the possibility that your intervention does not work. Once you intervene in the causal world then you are responsible for the results of your intervention. Following the law of right is not in this way intervening in the world because you are acting in the realm of the *ought* and are thus protected. You thus do not have to think about what might happen. This is also used as an argument for not intervening in the law and in the market which we deal with in chapter 5. We cannot know what it is right to do morally but we can at least know what is wrong - so it is better to circumscribe our lives with general rules which at least keep us from doing wrong. Again it is best to follow the rules which define the market because if we intervene contrary to them we do not know what will happen; an argument, as we shall see, against welfare and thus against the opposite of law, as shown in the play, that is love. This view surfaces politically on the right and reached its apogee in Britain under Thatcher[19].

The left want the system of love or welfare and intervention to ensure that people get the best life possible, the rules must not get in the way of that. We must not hide behind bourgeois law in order to achieve social justice. Universalist reason, as we saw in chapter 1 is flawed because it prevents us from arriving at this goal. It demands that we follow and create a coherent and consistent order and that is impossible. Nothing is determinate, there is just the never ending dance and oscillation of countervailing principles. We must then act in favour of the working class or as, now, the 'community'[20]. We saw in the previous chapter how for both left and right this 'community' can become highly individualistic and so individualism always seems present, even in supposedly collective societies. But it can become highly collectivistic in that collectivism becomes present even in individualist market societies. Thus we saw how to make moral life simple Creon (and Antigone) had to reduce every problem to a single currency to which all value expressions could be reduced. The drive for this simplification made Creon a tyrant wanting to use everyone for his own ends. He no longer saw them as particular people, as men *qua* men; but rather as units of the civic welfare and so no longer distinct but a collective mass. Ironically one might say that in having this, as we saw below, quasi utilitarian outlook in order to make his world safe, Creon opens the way to the opposing view. For though putting everything in a single

---

[19] See Raban (1989)

[20] See Etzioni (1995); Christodoulidis (1998b)

uniform good was supposed to make everything easy it opens up the way for dispute. For who knows what actions will result in the welfare of the city or not. The Kantian argument about lying which I discussed above is there precisely to protect against that unknown. So though utilitarianism seems to favour substantive justice and deal with the particular it also has a collective taint. So utilitarianism cuts across both law and love. On the one hand it appears individualistic, attached to the concrete person seeking to provide substantive justice rather than follow the rigours of the law. On the other hand it is the agent of the circumscribing and safety that the law provides. It is the way a single currency of good is produced and in this way makes other things and people invisible. Remember how radically invisible the single good of both Creon and Antigone made things for them, even their erotic responses.

In respect of hedonistic utilitarianism then, the implication of this is that things become seen merely as instantiations of utility. Thus playing football or reading a book are not really different activities but merely different aspects of pleasure. They then become lost as particular activities; they are lost in the universalistic principle of pleasure. This mirrors the way, for Marx, that the market operates. Everything becomes the same through money and lost in that 'universal commodity'. So much so, that in the end, as Marx says, it is not I that go to the theatre or the dance hall or to eat, but my money (Marx 1974). Law also exhibits this. The individual gets lost in the universal rule. I follow the law but do not give alms to the beggar who is in the street yet beneath my line of vision.

Utilitarianism has, in that sense, the totalitarian tendencies that some ascribe to community. For the individual gets lost in the mass of undifferentiated happiness. The irony is that parts of both the left and right agree with the analysis insofar as it speaks to the totalitarian tendencies of utilitarianism. The former thinks it comes from its abstracting and universalising tendencies whereas the latter thinks that this is precisely what it does not do properly. For the left utilitarianism is to be equated with capitalism - Marx reserved his greatest scorn for Jeremy Bentham, that 'genius in the way of bourgeois stupidity'. For the right utilitarianism epitomises the totalitarian tendencies found in socialistic societies where everything is done for some nebulous good.

b) the market, democracy and law

If we take the idea of the 'market' and the rule of law which is associated with it, we see similar crossovers. For the left the market and the law that goes with it is seen as the acme of individualism. Where all that is important is what the individual wants. The group is unimportant and irrelevant. There is 'no such thing as society' and it is only individuals that we deal with. In the end all we have is selfishness and greed. This is expressed in rights in the law. They are treated as things that enable the individual will to stand supreme no matter what damage it does to society[21]. And again we get another tension. For law and democracy seem to stand in tension. We saw in the first chapter how democracy could be seen as the individual arbitrary wills of people and thus set against the rational universality of law. For the right, here we have the paradigm of universalistic reason. Universal laws are followed and everyone is treated fairly because they are treated equally under these laws. At the same time this does not derogate from the free expression of the individual will. Thus here as well, there are both particularistic and universalistic connotations.

But there is a paradox here, summed up in the phrase, 'we are slaves of the law in order that we might be free'. Democracy could also stand for that passion which confronts the narrow and circumscribed worlds of Antigone and Creon. But our states are founded on a notion of democracy whose fundamental principle is the Rule of Law and these, at key times, hold in check our democratic expressions. The law seems to require that we act at times ignoring what people want because that is what, for example, the constitution says. Thus legality protects us from the 'tyranny of the majority'; that is a situation where, because there is a permanent majority and a permanent minority, the former can impose its will on the latter. Constitutions and Bills of Rights tend to make that more difficult. Without them the majority can, in the name of democracy, ride roughshod over the minority. We only have to look at the situation in Northern Ireland to see what can happen to minority groups without the protection of written norms like Bills of Rights etc. And yet there is a paradox here. Postema put it well.

> '....the attempt to take certain foundational matters permanently off the political agenda, rests on the assumption that the basic terms of political association in a democratic polity can be settled once and for all by some extra-political act. This is a mistake, I believe. But it is understandable because to reject this assumption is to embrace something of a paradox. If enduring legitimacy of a democratic constitutional regime depends on the willing allegiance of its citizens to the fundamental terms of association it defines, then not only our commitment to these terms, but the nature and scope of these terms, must be constantly open to reformulation. Precisely *because* of the overriding political importance and pervasive political influence of these terms of association, their precise determination and contemporary significance cannot be entrusted to others, either our political ancestors or some contemporary élite...The paradox in this idea lies in the fact that according to it the very terms (pre- conditions) of democratic association and so of democratic politics are to be settled *by* democratic politics. Yet, there is no alternative, consistent with our

---

[21] See Campbell (1983) and Dworkin (1977)

> commitment to democratic self government in a pluralistic community.' (1989: 126-7)

Though Postema is talking of constitutional settlements where the problem is more obvious, it is my contention that this paradox applies to law and legality generally. In some sense we think of the rule of law as instantiating democratic liberty. At the same time, if we look at legality as part of the pre-conditions, then we see that utility and justification come precisely from its ability to be 'at arms length' from democratic politics. The point of law seems to be to foreclose discussion and reflective thinking. Yet at the same time we think that this is an important part of the just organisation of society; something that demands, as Habermas argues, critical reflection and discourse (Habermas 1986b). It becomes all the more problematic when we insist that a free society depends upon the Rule of Law. Here again we cannot simply produce a right/left divide. For some of the left this tension was not a problem[22]. They denied that a free society did depend on this. The law was something to be dispensed with because it prevented autonomy. For some of the right this was also true[23]. They insisted on virtually no rules, the market mechanism could take care of all. Thus the right wing anarchists who also held that law in general prevented freedom. For the less extreme on both sides it was seen as something that was necessary as a framework within which people could be free and therefore people could be held to have willed it. But it was something that was a regrettable necessity. Wolff's argument, which I presented in chapter 1, attacks the latter. For it can be seen as holding that the 'framework' cannot hold. In the end, it always has to collapse into a form of anarchism - either of the left or right.

CONCLUSION

What we have been studying in these two chapters is how to live a life under law. And for us here this is not meant to be taken as merely a social thing, concerned with the social and political ordering of society. Thus just as justice does not merely, in Greek ethics at least, refer to the just ordering of society but also to the just man, so law and to live lawfully refers not merely to living in a 'law abiding' manner in society but refers in some way to individual in the same sense as the just person above. To live lawfully is not something about how you live in your public life in the state but about how you live rightfully. So the lawful man is the good man not because he obeys, when appropriate, the laws of the state but because he is good and virtuous. The word *Recht*, as we saw in the introduction, captures this in that one can apply it both to the state, as in *Rechtsstaat* and humans. In applying to the latter it

[22] See Fine (1979)

[23] See Rand (1966) and Rothbard (1982)

means not just one who follows the rules of the former. In English, the rather old-fashioned 'righteous man' captures this and though it does not really sound very well when one talks of the state. But, because *Recht* means a quality of living then, we can say of the state that it lives righteously in the same way as the individual does. Thus to think of it as living under the law (for both states and humans) is perhaps not the best way of describing it since that appears to think of it as following the law and nothing more. Though we might have problems of when to break the law, and we would be breaking them in the name of superior laws, it could not be defined as lawful acting. Now this might appear to be the law and morals debate again; when is it right to break an immoral law? Is that really a law? The *Antigone* showed us that this was not the case. It showed how lawful living entails a risk and tension between various different principles that are always present in our lives.

We looked at the *Antigone* as a story of what it is to be frightened of unrestricted deliberative reasoning and inevitable tensions that arise therefrom. We construct a clear world where laws, of the gods or the state, give us certain answers. What this does is put us in thrall to the rules. What happens? The world becomes simple and clear for us. We know the rules give us the answers since being universal, they are all encompassing with no situation being outwith their scope. This makes everything else invisible; we only see the situation as defined by the rules and are blind to everything else. Thus Creon does not see a nephew, but rather an enemy of the state. Antigone does not see her fiancé Haemon at all, she speaks not a word to him. In wanting this clarity and certainty; in eschewing the danger of value conflicts with their attendant risky choices, we act heteronomously as machine-like objects set in motion by the rules of law. Our autonomy vanishes.

The above is a description of the individual moral actor in their personal relations, but it is a question of social ordering as well. We saw that in Stephen's story. Here the problem, though it appears to be one of whether Stephen should break the law is, in reality, about how he can take part in the society without losing his autonomy. How he can be creative and take his decisions on the reasons which apply to him at the particular time without being lost; in other words, how can he apply substantive justice without it being lost in the mass of rules. For welfare, as a form of love, seems to demand particularity and that is something that we saw, in the Antigone story, is lost by the rules. We cannot be creative and rule-bound.

And we can widen this to the political ordering of societies and broader political currents. Here we can see how democracy becomes opposed to law. Law prevents the people deciding. The ruling class hide behind the law, as did

Creon. At the same time market and law are linked and the market, as with law, gives us certainty - this time in our economic transactions. So love or welfare is thrown out because it destroys the certainty of the rules of the market. They take away the risk that our interventions might go wrong and at least guarantee us security.

But in looking at it as an aspect of the distinction between right and left, we see that it is not as simple as it seems. For then we see that there is a reason for rules, that living under rules has historically protected people and given them at least some of the autonomy that, on they way we have looked at it, the left seem to support. Indeed of the things that we have talked about, as coming from the leftist camp, freedom, individuality, risk etc. are part of the right's programme as well. We talk of market socialism and welfare capitalism - the greed, because of its individualism, of capitalism, and yet the freedom of the individual under socialism. The point seems to be, as I said above, that we cannot map the dichotomies and distinctions that we have talked of above easily on to a left/right divide. Nor can we easily map them on to a distinction that seems to embrace all we have talked of, that of law and love. Why? Not because it is not, as I shall argue, an important distinction. Rather if we see law and love as a distinction in the sense of a dichotomous contradiction, we map all the other distinctions on to it, lining up one set with love and good and the other with law and bad. So we create a neat divide and simple choice rather than seeing a difficult and messy choice. The choice is messy because the distinctions run across each other and we have to hold them in a necessary and inevitable tension both in our individual and social moral lives.

If we see them as separate, and therefore as there being a continuous oscillation of the zero-sum game, we can produce a simple left/right divide. Both agree as to how to describe capitalist societies. Both sides think of them as being entities where the market is inextricably linked with the rule of law. Both then have different moral opinions about life in such societies and its effects. But since they both see it on the oscillation that I described above then both see the one as irredeemably good and the other as irredeemably bad. Law crowding out love on the one hand and love crowding out law on the other. One can either live under the law or out of it. Living in the creative tension of being in and out of the law is impossible. And this is a moral and cognitive failure. For in, living in the law, for example, we become like Creon and Antigone because we see no way out. Letting in even a bit of contingency will threaten to destroy the edifice that we have built up and so we protect it even more. We are frightened of our contingency. Living in love, we are afraid to let in law because we are frightened of the way the law will make us legalist, machine-like automatons. So in protecting our contingency even more we either descend into nihilist chaos or paradoxically become as authoritarian as we claim the law-based societies are. Societies based on love turn into bureaucratic machine like societies such as those of Eastern Europe or nihilistic chaotic ones such as those of Maoist China. And likewise societies based on the security of law turn into authoritarian dictatorships, where the law becomes the property of a small group. If we truly want to live lawfully, in the sense that I have talked of above, we must see neither side as having moral right; that Antigone and Creon just went too far in the circumstances in opting for safety and security. In the next chapter we turn to see how that world view of Antigone and Creon, and thus the mistakes that it incorporated might be seen in actual practice.

CHAPTER 3

LEGALISM AND LEGALITY[24]

INTRODUCTION

How does the world view expressed in the *Antigone* show itself in practice? Some have argued that such a stance and ideology is very common among members of the legal profession and thus in the practice of law and law itself. I deal in this chapter with rationality in law and in our response to law. Autonomy in morality seems to us to be fundamental to moral agency, and from that point of view it seems that we confront positive law as something extraneous to the individual will. Is the fate of the law-abiding citizen then that of a heteronomous being, bound by an extraneous will? What does that mean for the society under law? This chapter attempts to show what it means for society to live that sort of world view. What is that world that we here describe? It is best characterised as that of legalism, seeing the law merely as a heteronomous system of rules. This world demands the complete opposition of law and love (see chapter 2). But since my aim is to deny these binary oppositions, I will end the chapter by suggesting that living the life of law does not necessarily demand the world view of legalism as we have described it; that there is a moral stance contained therein that one could autonomously adopt, freely taking the positive law as one's guide to conduct so far as it goes.

But first I turn to legalism. I will isolate and describe legalism as a moral world view that is not just peculiar to law. It is something that runs across moral and social political life. It can and does operate as the ideology or governing principle of organisation of law and lawyers in a particular sort of society. But that does not imply that law and legalism are *eo ipso* systems of organisation that we must do without as politically and morally unacceptable. I

[24] A version of this chapter appeared as 'Legality without Legalism' which I wrote jointly with Neil MacCormick for a *Festschrift* for Aulis Aarnio, *'The Reasonable as Rational'* , edited by W Krawietz, R Summers, O Weinberger, G von Wright 2000. I wish to thank Duncker and Humblot, the publishers and Neil MacCormick for allowing me to use it.

argue that rule systems do not necessarily need to be legalistic; that legalism is taking reliance on rules too far. And, though this is difficult precisely to measure, the difference can be shown. The answer which I want to put forward in the following chapters which is what I have called living lawfully might also be called legality. And that differs from legalism by just two letters.

SHKLAR AND THE MEANING OF LEGALISM

Judith Shklar (1986) describes the legalistic attitude well. For her it is an ethical attitude. It represents correct social and personal conduct as a matter of rule following, and the rules as fixing the rights and obligations that we have. It is thus both a personal ethic and a social ideal. It reaches its high point, Shklar claims, in the legal systems of the modern Western World. It thus also serves as an ideology for those who value these institutions; for those, like lawyers, who are professionally involved in staffing and running them.

It is a moral attitude that wants to insulate law from politics, preferences and the like. Though it is something that specifically originates in lawyers' thoughts about the world, it seeps through a wide spectrum of opinion and people. Legalism, as an ideology, can run across the institutions of morals and law. Thus some moralities can be highly legalistic while others are the exact opposite.

As Shklar points out, the great philosophers of the western tradition have insisted on morality as something that can be deduced from prior rules. This is so even if these rules are, as in Hobbes and Hume, based on the passions. For Hobbes and Hume the reason that we have the particular rules that we do is something do with the way we are as animal beings. Thus for Hume (1962) we have desires for comfort and procreation which drive us to construct societies on the basis of 'artificial virtues'. These virtues, justice being an example, do not directly relate to some drive that we have. Rather we construct them in order that we achieve certain ends that are based on drives we have - 'Reason is only the slave of the passions'. We then follow the rules that constitute this virtue even when it might not seem to be in our immediate interest. This emphasis on instrumental reasoning is used by Hume to debunk those who see these virtues as part of some objective morality or natural law. For him the strict rules that surround the rituals of primitive societies are little different in principle from the rituals that surround, for example, the way that we buy and sell property, or the regard that we have for the sacredness of ownership. In both cases the rules are artificial, a product of human artifice, but their very point is that we must observe them meticulously. They serve a useful end, but only provided we follow them without direct regard for the end they serve.

The Humean approach applied to developed legal systems yields what H. L. A. Hart (1961)[25] calls the 'minimum content of natural law'. Given certain facts about human nature and the fact that we want to survive, we can know that we have to have certain sorts of rules in society. Thus the fact that we are not immortal but are both highly vulnerable and approximately equal in strength means that we have to have rules that regulate the use of force in society, and enshrine a right to life and to personal security against violence. Likewise, the need to use the products of nature to secure individual and group survival points to the need for some form of property law regulating people's rights to use of and access to material things. Rules are not in fact of value in themselves; but the values they serve are effectively served only where a reasonably strict attitude to the rules is maintained

Kant[26], by contrast, might be seen as the high priest of a rule based morality. We can see this in the categorical imperative, ordaining that we shall act only under a maxim that can be universalised as a rule for all. We see it in the insistence that our emotions and inclinations, even our needs, in the phenomenal world cannot determine what morally one ought to do. What is important is following the rule of right. Acting in the form of law is good in itself.

What contrasts with such legalistic moralities? It is the abundance of irrationalist moralities, based on the heart and on feeling or 'the will to power'. Existentialism, and the 'flower power moralities' of the sixties also come into consideration. But we must be careful not to dismiss these alternatives out of hand. 'All you need is love', even when seen in the context of the heady days of dope smoking might not seem a satisfactory alternative to Kant. But what it does point to is that social values can be legalistic or non legalistic; that saints and heroes are as important as rights and duties and that morality always aims towards supererogation. Here the question of what is 'owed' does not have pride of place. What we might distinguish here is moral systems that depend on ideas like 'authenticity' or being 'true to oneself'. These can easily collapse into irrationality or worse. Thus the ethics of the heart, moral action must be out of the compassion or feeling that you have for someone, can easily collapse into mindlessness. What is right to do is what you feel. It can also collapse into the more totalitarian tendencies of doing what is in the 'blood'; of the importance of the 'superman'. Here also we can see a 'situational'

---

25 See chapter 9

26 See Murphy (1970)

ethic. What is important is an appreciation of the particular situation and what it is right to do in the unique circumstances of that particular situation. This can depend upon the careful weighing of reasons or, as in act utilitarianism, the careful calculation of what the consequences will be. It can, however, collapse into an excuse to do anything at all. Thus the alternative to Creon might indeed be worse.

Religion also provides us with an example. Christianity has been seen as a legalistic religion, especially in the Pauline tradition[27]. But there has always been a strong sector in the church which has stressed the opposite. Christianity was a religion of love and that what mattered was not so much following the law as being pure at heart. Jesus came to destroy the old law. It is well illustrated by the Pharisee as he stands in the temple proud that he obeys the laws and is not like the sinners. Jesus damns that Pharisee. One can also see here the emphasis on mysticism and the rejection of ritual that goes with some of the expressions of Christianity and indeed other forms of religion. What matters is oneness with God rather than ritual and rules. Shklar quotes Petrażycki (1955) who sees the important distinction as not being between law, morals and religion. Rather we must look to the distinction between legalistic and non-legalistic values. We may then place forms of social ordering on a continuum, running from the legalistic to the non-legalistic.

Petrażycki thinks that the term 'morality' ought to be limited to autonomous 'other worldly', self-imposed duties, a view he ascribes to Kant. Here we see an ambiguity in looking at Kant. He can be considered as reaching the acme of a rule based morality and thus of a form of legalism. Yet he is also taken as the epitome of autonomous morality. Indeed Wolff (1976) considers him to be just that. The categorical imperative is something that you set for yourself. It is thus a case of acting autonomously. But it is a rule. Though you make it, it applies in all instances in which its conditions are fulfilled. This point can be made clearer if we look to the difference between generality and universalizability. I can intelligibly make a rule that only applies to a single person. That does not negate its status as a rule for it applies universally each time the conditions for its application are fulfilled. It is a law because, though it might apply only to me, I know that each time the conditions that the law specifies are fulfilled, it will apply and therefore I have to follow it. The rule now commands me in the sense that I do not have to look beyond the conditions of its application. I might have set it but it now has a life of its own. That is because I do not command myself each time. The

---

[27] Another view of the Pauline tradition, to the contrary, engages directly with the themes of this book, law and love. See Sanders (1991)

command now passes out of the contingency of my particular situation and commands because the conditions of application are fulfilled and that is enough. To adapt the example of the monkeys used in the first chapter. When the rational monkey throws the ball of mixed grain and sand into the rock pool in order to get food, it does so not because it did this at some previous time and got food, because it chose (commanded itself) so to do. What happened previously is irrelevant because now it has a rule that says throwing balls of mixed grain and sand into the rock pool brings food. The rule, as we showed in chapter 1, takes over what I did. I am lost because the fact that I (or the monkey) told ourselves what to do is irrelevant.

In the law, legality is expressed, for Shklar, in what she calls formalism. It is in that way that the law gets the requisite degree of impartiality. It is viewed as a system of perfectly clear and consistent rules. These contain precise and 'scientifically' analysed terms, elaborated out of perfectly analysed and synthesised concepts, the concepts being unvaryingly used in the same sense throughout the whole body of law. Law is treated as a self contained and autogenerative system which needs to be kept distinct from politics in order to organise our lives. Politics is a dirty business and it is only through the pristine objectivity of pure law that we can have clean systems. This can also be seen in the 'World Peace through World Law' movements. Law, which is right, will replace politics, which is power even if hidden power. Thus law is cut off from being contaminated by politics and has a history of its own. International law is a 'primitive stage in the history of law'. Though law in general has 'clouds of history trailing behind it', the content of this is seldom spelt out. It is as if law is its own history, prompted by its own internal mechanisms[28].

Legalism is uncompromising because rules are, according to Shklar, binary. They either exist and apply or they do not. So legalism has nothing to say about relations between incompatible systems of rules except that one set must be binding. Shklar says:

> 'The urge to draw a clear line between law and non-law has led to the construction of ever more refined and rigid systems of formal definitions. This procedure has served to isolate law completely from the social context within which it exists. Law is endowed with its own discrete integral history, its own 'science' and its own values, which are all treated as a single 'block' sealed off from general social theory, from politics, and from morality. The habits of mind appropriate, within narrow limits, to the procedures of law courts in the most stable legal systems have been expanded to provide a legal theory and ideology with an entire system of thought and values. This procedure has served its own ends very well: it aims at preserving law from irrelevant considerations, but it has

[28] Bańkowski and Mungham (1976: 32-38)

> ended by fencing legal thinking off from all contact with the rest of historical thought and experience.' (pp.2-3)

Though legalism's ideal of objectivity through formalism depends upon some sort of consensus, it is not the only thing involved. Legalism prescribes agreement through rule-following. Though the theory uses rules to create agreement, rules also presuppose that agreement. Thus we can see that natural law theory is not exempt from the ambit or ambitions of legalism. It is the rules that are important, not how they are arrived at. For legalism the power of natural law would lie in the rules that it generates and not in the nature, God or practical reason that might be said to produce them. The particular moral view that natural law has, becomes infected with the neutral ideology of legalism. Rules save the day and evade personal responsibility - see Antigone.

This is not to say that laws do not encompass the values of the particular culture that they find themselves in. Legalists and lawyers admit that. The claim here is rather that no matter where the rules come from, the effect of legalism is to make them appear objective and unchangeable. Legalism doesn't so much deny the connection between law and values as hide it and tuck it away from view. Since it concentrates on the rules to the exclusion of everything else, the rules lose their sense of contingency. They dominate the entire moral universe. They are the islands of stability in a chaotic universe. This kind of view is something of the sort that was set up as a target of criticism in *Images of Law*, and it plays a similar part for many proponents of Critical Legal Studies[29]. This concentration on law and the rules can tend to make us forget that it is we who make the rules and we that can change them. We see ourselves instead as the technicians of rules that we do not and cannot challenge. The morality of law (or of legality) becomes one of legalism; of the purely technical manipulation of rules. The rules appear as though they have a life of their own which cannot be challenged. They control us rather than we control them. What we concentrate on is the rules themselves; rather than to look at their instantiation in the social context. *Fiat iustitia ruat caelum* or as Kant would argue, one should act on one's universalizable maxim no matter what the consequences; never tell a lie, not even to save a life.

LEGALISM AND LEGAL THEORY

Shklar connects systems of legal theory which do not, at first sight, seem at all closely connected. Thus analytic positivism, natural law and the American realist movement are seen as connected by their link with legalism. She does

---

[29] *op. cit.*

this by making a connection between, legalism, formalism, and the felt need for certainty. Let us examine her view of these theories in turn.

a) Positivism

For Shklar, analytic positivism, and positivism in general, have an easy connection to legalism. Positivism in all its forms is concerned with looking at law as a system of rules, divorced from other branches of human affairs. It is this that makes it necessary for positivism to separate law from morals. This can be seen as an aspect of the search for certainty. Since morals are seen as subjective and unclear as with all aspects of value, then the only certainty that can be got is from rules. They are clearly and objectively out there. They do not depend upon the subjective preferences of the people. This certainty, for positivism, is achieved through formalism. A formalism which, as we have seen, means the ability to make clear and objective deductions from rules. The certainty stems from the agreement but it is agreement directly through the rules. Not as in the case of natural law which takes an agreement, and in some cases at least, transforms it into rules. Shklar claims that positivism ignores the social conditions necessary for the creation of agreement in any particular society as irrelevant to that certainty produced by the rules. Thus it is important to show how values, especially in the shape of morality, do not impinge and indeed are separate from law.

The claim that morals were internal whereas law was external was one historically important way in which the claim that values did not impinge upon law was argued for. Shklar examines this argument. To understand it, she claims one has to see how this distinction stemmed from a Christian context. For Christians it was the difference between sin and immorality and not that between law and morals that was important. Sin has to do with the personal relationship to God that everyone has. It is something between you and God. The state of sin is the breaking of that relationship with God. When we are in sin we are in Hell because we can no longer stand to be within the burning love of God. It is that state that is internal. Immorality is what we externally do. Every act of immorality is necessarily sinful but the immoral actions can be private or public and there is a debate as to whether only public (as opposed to private) violations of common morality can be subjected to criminal sanctions. But this is about public and private behaviour and not internality in the sense of sin. Sin cannot be touched by law for in the end only you can mend your relationship with God. The church can help you. It tries by enforcing certain precepts in order that you might not fall into the state of sin. But it cannot, in theory, touch the actual relationship. The law can never get at the internality that is the essence of sin.

Shklar emphasises that this did not mean that governments stopped trying to punish sin. But it was only when sin stopped being generally believed in that punishing morals came to be seen as such an outrage. It is only, then that punishing morals becomes an issue. For before the practical question, by and large, of both theologians and governments was whether acts (of immorality) that were private, but not in that internal sense of sin, should be punished. Now, when sin was taken out of the picture, there was only morals left and that started to become internal in the sense of sin - sin was subsumed by morals. However it was not only religious moralities that stressed this internality. Consider the morality of motives that lays emphasis on the motive of the act. This extends the scope of individual autonomy. By making the internal the distinguishing feature of the moral it stands against external pressure on the individual. For how can one be made to think right? Thus external demands for compliance are not only wrong but they do not have any real effect on the internal and thus the morals of the individual. The individual may do what he is forced to but that will not make them moral. 'Iron bars do not a prison make'

Law then, might be reserved for dealing with human beings in gross while morals deals with the personal and particular. But all of this takes us back to that autonomy that Petrażycki wanted to be reserved for morals. Let us see how this might come out in the way law and morals might be treated by some positivists. How do you separate moral rules from legal rules? For Hart (1961) and those that follow him that is a grave difficulty. For the theory rests on the definition of what makes practices in the world rules of obligation. This is done first of all by showing how the idea of habits, used by Austin (1954) and Bentham (1823), relating as they do to observed regularities of external behaviour, are inadequate to explaining the notion of rules. To understand the normativity of rules we need to reflect upon the human attitude to the things they do as a rule as distinct to what they do from habit.

> '[I]f a social rule is to exist some at least must look on the behaviour in question as a general standard to be followed by the group as a whole. A social rule has an "internal" aspect in addition to the external aspect which it shares with a social habit and which consists in the regular uniform behaviour which an observer could record.' (Hart 1961: 55)

There are two other aspects to this distinction. Deviation is regarded as behaviour which is open to criticism and that criticism is regarded as justified or legitimate. These are aspects of what Hart calls the 'internal point of view'. But there is, as MacCormick (1981) points out, danger of circularity here. For the internal point of view is supposed to depend upon a critical reflective attitude while that is itself explained in terms of justification and criticism. We should therefore best see this in two aspects. First a cognitive attitude, seeing patterns of behaviour in seeming random human actions. Second in a volition which comprehends some wish or preference that the act or abstention from the act be done in the envisaged circumstances. So rules of obligation depend upon patterns and attitudes. But how, on the basis of this, can one distinguish morality?

For Hart, in primitive society there is no distinction between morality and law. But there may develop dispute-settling procedures. Out of them might come institutionalised systems with enforcement procedures and institutions for authoritatively making decisions. From this a specialised system of rules could grow up. We can see here that the problem is solved by situating the law as such into institutions of this kind. In the process of the institutionalisation of certain rules as legal rules, it is of course possible that they will diverge from the morality of various groups in society. So we get the question why or whether people should morally obey the rules laid down by the institutions of law. Institutions then are the key. The only thing that differentiates legal from other rules is their special institutionalisation. But as we have seen legalism has precisely nothing to say as to the relationship between different systems of rules. All it can say, as a matter of binary logic, is that one must be valid and the other invalid.

This last is the point reached by MacCormick (1994). The argument that follows from the point can at least to some extent be mapped on to the internal/external distinction discussed above. This represents law as being distinguished from morals not only by its institutionality but also by its heteronomy. Morals are the realm of personal responsibility for a subjectively binding, hence in principle controversial, judgement of right and wrong. Positive law can secure objectivity and a degree of interpersonal certainty, but at the cost of being heteronomous, externally imposed. We may indeed need this objectivity and relative certainty in order to be able to live our lives in society without endless conflict and dissent over every morally significant issue that arises. We need it precisely because of its crucial difference from morality. So law and morals are conceptually quite distinct, but they complement each other[30].

One can see how this contradicts Shklar's argument. For what she is arguing is that both law and morality can be on a continuum of legalistic or

[30] See also Campbell (1996)

non-legalistic. Here MacCormick is reserving the legalistic for law and the non-legalistic for morals. His is a version of Petrażycki's argument. But it is not one that denies the relevance of law to morals. The position here lies beyond Hart's in the way it makes the conceptual and institutional distinction, but also in its claim that the two main forms of normative order complement each other. At the bottom line, however, this remains a position within the camp of positivism. The work of the legal scientist is concerned with the legal side of this complementarity.

But properly understood, both law and morals have inbuilt tensions between autonomy and heteronomy. The question is how are they to be articulated. In that sense then law and morals are not conceptually distinct and the way that we normatively organise our lives is not a mixture of law and morals. Living lawfully might take in many different institutional systems and they will be a mixture of heteronomy and autonomy, law and love, of certainty and uncertainty, of nomianism and anti nomianism. When dealing with law then, we must view the relation between autonomy and heteronomy as something internal to law. It cannot be solved by expelling autonomy into another, though complementary, normative and conceptual framework. That way may lead to an unacceptable form of legalism.

b) Natural Law

For the natural lawyers it is quite clear that the attempted purification of law does not work by bracketing law off from morals. But for Shklar it is seeing the fragility of consensus that leads natural lawyers to seek something that will produce the conditions of certainty. This does not imply that legalism is thereby eschewed. In fact from that certainty springs a strong rule system which overrides all other systems. '*Lex iniusta non est lex*'.

Finnis (1982) has attacked this view. In a sophisticated analysis, he shows how this is not in fact true of natural law systems. In them, the legal and the moral do not either match up or cancel each other out in that binary way. His emphasis on practical reason does much to make his view of natural law non-legalistic in Shklar's sense. But one can see the germ of truth in what Shklar has to say. For in his treatment of authority, Finnis adopts a conventionalist view with elaboration. For him authority has no necessary or unitary origin. Society by society, we confront it as it has there turned out to exist. What matters is not how the persons or institutions that enforce societal co-ordination have come to be in a position to do this, but the fact that, somehow or other, they are in fact to some extent able to do this and to have their directives treated as authoritative by others. The mode of achieving authority does not so much matter as the fact that the authority is effective in its role. For what practical reason demands is some sort of co-ordination. Authority is legitimate in so far as it can achieve co-ordination, even where it falls short of setting terms for co-ordination that match up to what is morally ideal or even entirely satisfactory.

It is here that we can see the force of Shklar's point. For it is at this intersection that the slide begins. Certainty is only guaranteed by the rules which, in the end, are made by the person in authority. Shklar is making the point that historically natural law has used a particular form of certainty to produce, in some cases, legalistic systems. This is not a necessary truth about theories of natural law. Her point is that they are not in themselves immune from a legalistic morality. The converse is also true. For legalism as a practice does need agreement. The classical liberal view is that the agreement comes from the rules. But legalism does not, as we have seen, look beyond the rules to the social conditions that make up that agreement. This agreement is in fact extremely fragile - a fact which extreme market liberals such as Hayek (1982) recognise. For them the 'great society' is extremely fragile. But guarding this fragile good is the price we have to pay for living any sort of civilised life. The agreement brought about by rules does in fact need a whole complex of agreements and consensus among those who are part of the legal order. Without this it would be very difficult to keep the system going. That is why, according to Shklar, judges find natural law theorising so congenial. It gives them the solidity of agreement that is a necessary pre-condition of the certainty that the rules produce. It is a way of guaranteeing that possibility. For Shklar then, natural law theory's greatest ideological function has been to produce a pre-fabricated set of rules that people want.

c) American Legal Realism

But this does not only apply to natural law theorising. Shklar also tries to show how this quest for certainty can be found in American Legal Realism. She thus dubs it the 'first cousin' of legalism. At first sight the Realists were far removed from legalism. They were interested in social reform and wanted to effect the New Deal legislation. They were thus committed to arguing that the law was not a pre-ordained 'brooding omnipresence in the sky'; precisely the sort of arguments that the Supreme Court was using in order to block the New Deal policies. They were influenced by psycho-analysis. Frank (1985) attacked law as being the outmoded expression of the father figure which we all still hanker after. He argued for a law administered by judges who, through analysis, could administer socially sane policies without being hamstrung by legalism in the shape of the father figure. In fact the entire Realist attack was an attack on the formalism dominant in the law schools of the time.

They claimed that the law in action was more important than the rules in the book. Thus one had to look to what actually happened rather than looking for legal rules in text books. This is the beginning of sociological theorising in the law. The implication was that the rules were something that did not just 'exist' but were socially produced. To know them one had to look to that social process. They went further than that. They also claimed that, however the rules were produced, they did not have to be followed as a matter of logic. There was no tight logical connection between rule and decision. A rule could be made to justify almost any decision. So the judges who claimed that they were only following the rules when they struck down New Deal legislation were hiding behind an ideological smoke screen. They struck down the legislation, not because they had to, but because they did not like it.

Now this is obviously the sort of particularising, non rule-bound way of looking at it that is profoundly non-legalistic. But the problem then arises: if you reject all father figures and see the law as something creative, how do you know that what you decide is right? The opposite of legalism cannot be chaos, there must be some sort of order. Frank (1942) in fact, came to look to certainty after all. What drove him to this was the complaint that the Securities and Exchange Commission, which he came to be in charge of, was operating in a ruleless and arbitrary way. His argument against these charges was that the courts could not provide the certainty that was craved. For they had no means of producing the accurate facts without which sound decisions could not be made. His Commission, which was staffed by experts and investigators, could. Ironically, the 'fact scepticism' of Frank was not an epistemological scepticism about the possibility of finding objective facts in the world. Rather it was an attack on the trial process, which he claimed was not able to produce them at all[31]. He thus proposed an inquisitorial form of process which would be staffed by experts, trained in getting at the truth of the matter. He thus, Shklar says, produced a way of getting at certainty while attacking the traditional court system. The experts were there in the same way as the law was 'there'. And this expertise took on a neutral, clean aspect in the same way that the law did. Thus chaos was reduced because the law's certainty was founded in the agreement of experts who could make the law predictable and safe. Producing certainty through the law of the expert.

---

[31] See Frank (1973); Twining (1984)

LEGALISM, FORMALISM AND CERTAINTY

There are echoes here of the way that in the perversions of a communitarian political ethic, 'community' can come to be a mere cloak that covers the wielding of arbitrary power by the few. But we have to be careful here. Shklar's strategies for presenting Natural Lawyers and the Realists as 'first cousins' to legalism are rather ambiguous. For it certainly does not seem like the legalism that we first described. The certainty that is generated does not stem from rules. It comes rather from vague and shadowy bodies of knowledge, that cover the power of the few who claim the expertise to know this. It is precisely the sort of 'rule in the name of the people' or 'rule by experts' which those in favour of rules fear will happen if law is jettisoned. For the position under scrutiny does not appear to be formal or formalist. We saw that a mark of legalism was its certainty. But it is also its formality; it does not matter what the result is as long as it comes through the rules, the due process of the law.

But for the realists and the natural lawyers substantive justice matters; the correctness of the particular decision in the particular circumstances is also important. Legality works with formal justice which ignores the material circumstances of the case as long as the rules are followed. Everything is treated equally under the laws. Whereas in substantive justice, the rules are not so important as getting the right decision. But, one might reply, this sort of formalism also occurs in the rule of experts. In the end what matters is whether the result was generated by the expert. This is also a form of formalism. The only test of the correctness of a decision can be whether an expert in good faith made it, for the experts are the only ones that can know. Therefore the criterion of validity is, as in positivism, a formalistic one. One of pedigree, though the pedigree might be different. And one can see how Creon, and Antigone talk over the laws of the state and the gods until only they are allowed to know and certainty is guaranteed.

But there is also, for Shklar, a sort of ideological relation. For lawyers and judges are trained and attuned to the need for certainty and objectivity in the law. They will automatically, if law seems to fail, look for the certainty that these other forms engender. If they begin to fail then they will go back to the old ideas. Thus Shklar says, when the New Deal, the ideological driving force of the Realists was won, Realism was driven more and more to legalism. In their later work, some of the leading Realists came to seem to be nothing more than enlightened legalists. At the same time, the zeal for creativity etc. in legal education led to a counter trend which started to reinforce legalism again[32].

[32] see Duxbury (1995)

We can see, in some respects, how this story is once again being repeated in the CLS movement in America.

What we have discussed are all ways of putting certainty into our lives by some sort of formalism. This might be achieved either through formally established and rather strictly interpreted rules, or through formal recognition of the conclusions of experts, or through reliance on an objectively cognisable natural law. This formalism can in many contexts seem, or be made to appear, highly attractive. Yet it is open to abuse and can in various ways, Shklar claims, lead to tyranny and stultification in social life. But what of legality? Is that linked to legalism and the negative ideology that flows from over-reliance on rules? Legalism and legality seem to be closely linked and legality turns out to be rather negative because contaminated with legalism. Shklar seems to me to be confused. At first she makes the distinction. Narrow legalism is not to be conflated with the noble theory of legality. We can see this when she discusses the Nuremberg trials. Her attack on them was not on the ground of what they brought about, but on the use of the trial-form to bring that about. The error or even crime was to represent the Nuremberg process as a legal process. The justification of the trials could only be, according to Shklar, political necessity. They could teach the German political elite what the loss of legality meant by conducting a trial which, though it could not be justified by legality, was fair in stating reasonably exact charges and then proving them by recourse to incontrovertible evidence. The solution under its guise of ostensible legalism worked because it brought back respect for legality among the German elite who then fashioned Germany into a Rechtsstaat. This could not work in Japan because the Japanese did not have a legalistic culture to appeal to. Most saw the war crimes trials as the work of conquerors acting as conquerors will always do.

These arguments seem to suggest approval of legalism as a policy which can, in certain cases, provide a way of showing respect for legality. The implication of this is however, that the two do have close connections. Yet Shklar nowhere explains clearly how or on what points the two do differ. She does, as we have seen, argue that legalism is not only to be connected with law but spreads across all forms of ordering as well, notably morality and politics. But her view of what it in fact is, is rather more difficult to detect. Is legalism to be defined by the need for certainty and formalism, described in the way we have talked of it above, or through rules? In the beginning it is rules that she singles out for attack. Her examples contrast nomian and anti-nomian systems in law and morality. Later, it appears that she sees the defining feature of legalism as formality and certainty. In this light, she comes to portray nomian systems as being the ones that are necessarily legalistic because they necessarily aim to produce that certainty and formalism. Hence her book is ambiguous. It is no wonder that lawyers, as she says in the second edition of *Legalism*, looked at her work askance. For they saw her attack on rule-based solutions as approval of a more radical anti-nomian posture in law than that which she actually favoured when she came to explaining her own liberal and tolerant ideology.

We can see this problem much more clearly in the mistakes of *Images of Law*[33]. Here a radical anti-nomian position was put forward based on utopian marxist political premises. The idea was that the law fixed things in such a way that it produced solutions that were clear and certain but did so at the cost of neglecting things outside of this world. The law was captured by groups of lawyers who arranged these things in their own interest while claiming it was in everyone's. Much of this can be seen as a way of looking at the safe world that the protagonists in the Antigone wanted to create for themselves. Law acted as a way of pretending to depoliticise the world. It neutralised people's power both by 'overt repression' and by the 'ideological' legitimation of authority. An example of this was the inquiry into the British Army's methods of interrogation in Northern Ireland (the so called 'disorientation techniques').

Little space was devoted to questioning the morality of what were virtually disorientation techniques. If it could be shown that it was legal then it was beyond question. In this way political questions are not only deflected but are made to seem entirely inappropriate. As long as the given social order is said to be legal then the world is all right. It is good because it is 'legal' and 'legal' stands outside the social structure and guarantees it (Bańkowski and Mungham 1976: 13).

What was being claimed here was that the law translated questions of morals and politics into questions of legal validity. In doing so, it deflated important questions because all that came to matter was whether the law was followed or not. This had the effect of channelling political action into legal pathways and thereby defusing it. In a sense this was part of an argument against legal activism. At that particular period this was seen as an important channel of social change. Bańkowski and Mungham's argument was that this did not work because in the end it merely transformed that activism into law. Everything seemed all right as long as the legal battles were won. But this ignored reality or the world outside law where nothing much necessarily changed. So their argument was that this form of legal activism aided only lawyers and those others who had an interest in the expansion of the law. Part of what they wanted to argue was that though, at that period, one could show

[33] Bańkowski and Mungham (1976)

that law and lawyers had an interest in 'bringing the law to poor people', the converse had not been shown. Lawyers had this interest because of their material interests. This played an ideological function in legitimating society and thus defusing conflict. They argued that 'bringing law to the people' quite often had the effect of taking away people's problems. They were replaced in a legal form. This form they could not understand or do anything about. They showed how the law would translate a social problem into a series of legal problems which did not necessarily get at the actual problem. Thus problems of poverty and bad housing conditions were translated into questions of the rights of tenants. This did not address the question of lack of housing stock and the means to buy or rent it. Problems of crime and vandalism are seen as something to do with lack of enforcement of the law. This disregards the various social conditions that might be said to be important contributing factors. They used the example of the trial to show how often the discourse of the trial changed and deflected the message that the protagonists wanted to get over. The person charged with some crime cannot recognise what he has done in the language and process of the trial. The political activist finds his political message taken away in the trial. One can see this latter view echoed in the work of Christodoulidis (1998) where he argues how law, as a self-referential discourse makes it impossible to express a 'reflexive politics'. Law made the world safe.

Now much of what they said about the practice of the law was and is true. One can still see great fights about legal aid, one can still see the law defusing political battles and social problems are still treated as legal problems and nothing more. In part, as we shall see later, their arguments as to the relationship of law, or at least a legalistic form of law to capitalist societies were true and Hayek and others agreed. But it was in their practical prescriptions that we can see the mistakes. The solution for them was, as O'Hagan (1984:10) says, to 'devalue structures, relations and rules relative to 'direct actions'. One might call this the political message of complete autonomy; a sort of anarchist prescription for social action. It is clearly a moral argument about how humans should act in the world; an anarchist message for complete autonomy.

CONCLUSION

How does it fit in with our story? Let us turn to Antigone again. The protagonists want a secure, clear, and narrow world, thus safety and certainty and the desire to create a conflict free world. In this sense then, the play is about the fear of risking oneself and the machinations that one does to avoid that. Now rules are one of the clearest ways of doing that and so the play and we in this book deal with all the various dichotomies and tensions as endemic in rule-based societies. But we can also see how the rules can themselves get subverted in the desire for certainty. How people claim to be experts and know them, be sole interpreters as Creon and Antigone tried to be, and all in the cause of certainty. Shklar's view is that lawyers will always go back to rules for their certainty and so it is nomianism that she attacks. But of course her moderate political view makes her not totally opposed to law, hence her ambiguity. In *Antigone* love was opposed to this safety and certainty. But that was not, as we shall see, anti-law. Rather it was the acceptance and the embracing of the necessity of risk in one's moral life which could involve rules and certainty as well. In *Images of Law,* because love was seen as the opposite and contradictory of that, it was seen as the anarchist autonomy of a sort of spontaneous creativity - a celebration of the plasticity and infinite change in human life, that sort of life that Iris Murdoch in *Under the Net* debunks. One might say that notwithstanding all the Freudian theorising of Frank, the American Legal Realists, did as Hart says, behave like disappointed absolutists - if law cannot be certain then we should not have it. Law must be certain or it cannot be anything. In a way much argumentation in CLS behaves the same way - if law cannot be absolutely determinate, then it is indeterminate and we must celebrate its plasticity. But the fact that law cannot be seen on a 'model of rules' does not mean rules are not very important in it.

My aim here is to show how legality or living lawfully can be insulated from the attack on legalism in its negative connotations, and to show how a reliance on rules does not necessarily lead to that admittedly negative ideology of legalism. Here it is important to note that formalism and certainty, which for Shklar are the defining features of legalism, are something which she sees people as always turning to. Of course, they must. States and other durable social organisations must order themselves in ways that are intelligible to those whom they govern, even when in their democratic forms the people governed also participate in governance. To this extent, the legalism that insists on rules and on their being followed especially by those who hold power in government is no more than insistence on legality, and legality is a real virtue in forms of government.

It remains true, however, that rules without the underlay and aspiration of principle and ideal with which they creatively mesh can be the implements of tyranny. Approaches to interpretation that ignore or undervalue the need for attention to principles, and to the consequences of decision judged against implicit ideals and principles of law are thus undesirable. Legalism is indeed the vice of this narrow governance of rules, unleavened by aspiration or ideal. It is to the manner of this leavening that we turn in chapter 4.

CHAPTER 4

DUTY AND ASPIRATION

INTRODUCTION

In the last chapter we saw how the world of Creon and Antigone was realised in practice for law and lawyers and the connections to rules and certainty that it had. We saw how in this legalistic world view there was both a psychological and a cognitive problem. How the desire for certainty led to the fixing of modes of ordering both of oneself and society by heteronomous rules; how the strength of this desire was so great that even when rules were seen as wrong the only way to deal with them was by dispensing with them. For rules were seen as something that must be obeyed; either you obey them or you do not have them. That is why some of those keenest in their proclamation of the plasticity of life are really legalists who cannot cope with the burden of rules.

There is also a cognitive mistake which runs as follows: if life is not completely certain then it must be uncertain; positions where there is this flexibility in that there is tension between certainty and uncertainty are unstable and collapse, the one into the other. We must therefore, because the principles are counterposed in this way, stand for one side or the other. Thus having attacked one side, proposing a solution which implies that there is some good in that side appears contradictory. Shklar then, whose views on legalism and the world view of lawyers was in many ways similar to Bańkowski's and Mungham's, appears somewhat contradictory in her positive proposals. On the other hand, Bańkowski and Mungham made the mistake of thinking there is no alternative. In denying this earlier view through my claim that one can hold the principles together in some sort of tension, I do not want to propound that liberal view which claims that the solution lies in a compromise which can be found and established, that there is 'one right answer' to the problem. Rather, I want, as we shall see, to argue for a continual tension with there being no possibility of fixing the one right compromise. But it is important to remember that living lawfully will not totally eschew legalism; that legality, as I called it in the previous chapter, does not throw out the need for certainty entirely.

NONET AND SELZNICK

I now turn to another sociological view which looks at this ideology in practice. From there we will be able to go to the beginnings of a solution. The view is that of Nonet and Selznick (1978). They have a typology to deal with some of these problems. Legality and legalism are seen as different things. The question of the link between political power and the idea of a 'model of rules' is dealt with. They distinguished three modalities or models of how law operates in society. This was for them a developmental model. But the 'inner dynamics' of development, is not concerned with the 'iron laws of history'. Nor does it make normative judgements that the latest stage in the development is best. The three modalities can be summarised as; i) repressive law, where law is a servant of repressive power; ii) autonomous law, where law is a differentiated institution capable of taming repression and protecting its own integrity (or autonomy); iii) responsive law, where law facilitates the response to social needs and purposes(p. 14).

Writing in the 70s and in the context of developments in the USA, they saw a crisis in law. For some law was used to create the just society, for others it was naked repression. In dealing with the crisis, there was, for them, a low risk and a high risk strategy. The former implies seeing law as giving the vital ingredient to social order. This implies the strict obedience and fidelity to law, without changing it, of officials. The high risk strategy sees order as part of the problem. What sort of order being an important moral question dependent upon one's views of the needs of society. For them law is a historical phenomenon whose forms depend upon contingent circumstances and events. However, in order to be able to look at the phenomenon over different times and places we need some sort of broad definition to fix our enquiry. For them, law emerges when questions arise as to who has the 'right' to define and interpret obligations. Law then is connected to questions of authority. It is this question of authority that is, as we shall see later, vital for the relationship between heteronomy and autonomy. They look to variations in legal ordering, the role of coercion in law, the interplay of law and politics, the relation of law and state to moral order, the place of rules, discretion and purpose in legal decisions, civic participation, legitimacy and obedience. My aim is to use their seminal early work to enrich and refine my arguments, conclusions and solutions.

a) Repressive Law

Repressive law is characterised by a close integration of law and politics. Law is subordinated directly to the governing elite. It is a pliable tool and thus official discretion prevails. The separation of spheres is unknown. This official discretion makes law very uncertain as a means of certifying rules and official decisions since nothing is fixed. Repression however, must not be identified *per se* with coercion. It is the uses of coercion and the quality of consent to it that counts. It occurs in situations where society and political order are weak and the powerful have to fall back on repression. This is not, they claim, limited to the nascent embattled state. In fact, its supreme example comes from modern totalitarian superstates. They quote a fragment of the Laws of the RFSR:

> In the interests of economizing forces and harmonizing and centralizing diverse acts, the proletariat ought to work out rules of repressing its class enemies, ought to create a method of struggle with its enemies and learn to dominate them. And first of all, this ought to relate to criminal law, which has as its task the struggle against the breakers of the new conditions of common life in the transitional period of the dictatorship of the proletariat. (p. 36)

It is important to note that this subordination of the law to political power and to *raison d'état* is not necessarily mal-intentioned. It is the weakness of the order and the inability to count on the allegiance of the citizenry, that makes politicians and others with their backs to the wall see this as the only way. Though this mainly occurs in nascent and totalitarian states, repressive law can occur in seemingly liberal societies. It can occur there in two ways. Governments cannot satisfy the demands of the public for justice or welfare and have to resort to thrusting some aside either by neglect or ultimately by repression. Governments also overreach themselves in that they take on tasks that they cannot cope with except by neglect and repression.

We can see this in the various fiscal crises of modern western states. As government creates institutions to service the ever expanding ends of society, these become subordinated to the needs and interests of the bureaucracy and they coerce as well. There is a dual system of justice. For those who need to be kept in order, law is repressive. It is public and concerned with punishment. For those that 'have' and do not need to be kept in order, it is private and facilitates.

Law also engenders a moralism. Morality is legalised, that is to say it is institutionalised and fixed in conformity to a particular idea of value and order. This also grows into 'legal moralism' which loses sight of the larger ideals of value. This is repressive in the way Freud talks of superego repression, that is to say that the person is subordinated to the needs of the social order. For Nonet and Selznick there are two main features of repressive law; first, the close integration of law and politics which takes place in the direct subordination of legal institutions to the governing elites: secondly, rampant official discretion which allows the law flexibility in fulfilling its objects.

b) Autonomous Law

Autonomous law grows out of the failure of repressive law to deliver any sort of viable legitimation of authority. For it rests ultimately on contingent power. They summarise the chief attributes of autonomous law as follows:

> 1. Law is separated from politics. Characteristically, the system proclaims the independence of the judiciary and draws a sharp line between legislative and judicial functions.
>
> 2. The legal order espouses the "model of rules". A focus on rules helps to enforce a measure of official accountability; at the same time, it limits both the creativity of legal institutions and the risk of their intrusion into the political domain.
>
> 3. "Procedure is at the heart of law". Regularity and fairness, not substantive justice, are the first ends and main competence of the legal order.
>
> 4. "Fidelity to Law" is understood as strict obedience to the rules of positive law. Criticism of existing laws must be channelled through the political process. (p. 54)

Autonomous law is separated from politics. Its aim is the legitimation of power. It does this by standing outside that power and casting some restraint on it. The law as an institution becomes autonomous, celebrating its specialised institutions and concerned only with them. But the price of this is a detachment from substantive values. In repressive law, legitimation consisted in the blanket certification of the source of power. Now the concern is with a justification of its use. But the price of this is political subordination. In the end autonomous law, like repressive law, is tied closely to the political order. In effect, say Nonet and Selznick, a historic bargain is struck. Procedural autonomy is purchased at the price of substantive subordination. The courts defer on policy issues. In return, they have the power to control access and the conditions of participation in the legal process. The government is one actor among many and subject to these conditions. Due process and procedure become all.

> The outcome is that a morality of means comes to encompass the whole of legality and justice. Substantive justice is derivative, a hoped-for by-product of impeccable method. But formal justice is consistent with serving existing patterns of privilege and power. (p. 67)

The 'model of the rules' becomes the central feature of this mode of law. This is so because rules give clear limits. They are able both to restrain political power and make legal institutions (the judiciary etc.) acceptable to the state. This is so because close adherence to the rules limits their power as well. Legality is the good side of this system, legalism the bad. They use Weber to show how the system can be seen as being like modern bureaucracy. For Weber (1954), it was both the harbinger and standard bearer of the rule of law.

This also points to the close connection with this sort of rule based way of ordering activity and capitalism. Weber, for example, saw a close connection between the development of a highly rationalised form of legal administration and the development of large industrialised capitalist economies. Here, the predictability and order of the law helped the capitalists in their decision making. At the same time, according to Weber, there occurred increasing use of bureaucracies as institutions for administering work. Here abstract rules are very important since it is they that enable there to be accountability and adequate supervision of the staff at the lower end of the pyramid. 'The red tape' of bureaucracy was there, in the first instance anyway, to protect and guard rather than obfuscate. For Weber, this was all part of a movement which he called 'rationalisation'. Most attention is paid to maximising efficiency since the most pervasive value is control over the environment and prediction of the future. To further this, there is an increasing separation between means and ends and law is concerned with means questions. Bureaucracies and legal institutions are not committed to any particular set of values and can serve any political system. Thus these three factors, abstract formal rules, bureaucracies, and the division of means and ends promote both efficiency and the values required for capitalism. We can thus see why legalism has such a strong hold in the sort of societies that Weber describes; why people can think that the rules ought to be obeyed, right or wrong, because they are the rules. The tendency of capitalist systems according to Weber was towards ever increasing formal rationality. This description of the late 19th century bureaucracies showed how they provided a social and administrative guarantee of social justice and the rule of law. The uniform and regular application of rules is an effect of that institutional structure. Conversely however, this guarantee may turn into a threat since the connection between efficiency and due process is only contingent. Precisely because the rule of law is dependent upon maximising administrative efficiency, it is thereby at the mercy of changing perceptions of efficiency and expediency and changing demands on legal and para-legal institutions. If the situation of the administration changes through, for example, increased volume of work, then formal rationality may cease to be the most efficient method of administration and autonomous law is at the mercy of the bureaucracy.

In a functioning system of autonomous law however, formalism, attention to procedure and 'the artificial reason of the law' become its hallmarks. Answers come from procedure and the substantive is forgotten. Obedience to the law becomes the mode of good political conduct. It constrains rulers because it holds them accountable to rules. It demands of the rulers fidelity to the law. But the other side of this coin, and part of the historic bargain that they talk about, is that autonomous law demands unconditional obedience by the citizens to lawful command. The lawfulness of which is determined by the specialised institutions of autonomous law, mainly the courts. This modality does not understand Stephen's dilemma - he has to go and fight since it is his side of the bargain.

c) Responsive Law

For Nonet and Selznick autonomous law leads to what they call responsive law. As we saw, for them formal justice is consistent with existing patterns of privilege and power. But

> The sense of fairness is affronted when a system that prides itself on the full and impartial hearing is unable to vindicate important claims of substantive injustice. The justice of autonomous law is experienced as sham and arbitrary when it frustrates the very fairness of expectations it has encouraged. In time, the tension between procedural and substantive justice generates forces that push the legal order beyond the limits of autonomous law. (p. 67)

The result of autonomous law can thus be the erosion of the Rule of Law since a caste grows up who are used always, in their legal reasoning, to criticising authority. This and the advocacy associated with arguing a client's case inevitably leads to a rights' based jurisprudence. Responsive law is the third way of dealing the crises of integrity. Here, there is a strong commitment to a distinctive mission. People can be held accountable to that mission by external controls. Responsive law tries to get a kind of openness in institutions with its integrity by looking to social interests. But this is not mere pragmatism -it can be called the 'Sovereignty of purpose'.

There are problems however. In the first place the progression, notwithstanding the disclaimers, seems to go in a linear historical line. From repressive to responsive, they each generate the dynamic to go to the next. But, as we shall see, autonomous law is at least as likely to generate repressive law. There are tensions in all of the modalities that can generate each other. My concern is not to produce a scheme of how this has happened but to ask how some of the tensions that arise can be accommodated in a fair and just system of organisation.

RESPONSIVE AUTONOMY?

To this extent one can also say that it is clear that the normative sympathies of Nonet and Selznick lie, in that book, with responsive law. Law is seen by them, following Fuller (1969), not as something coming from the central state but rather as something stemming from peoples' interactions. In a way this makes the law political because it diffuses legal authority. It encourages participation in law as part of the political process. Law then relaxes central control and institutions take on their own power at the 'grass roots' etc. But this democratising and participatory nature is fraught with the problems of some interests being overlooked. Responsive law's central concern is competence, as legitimacy was that of autonomous law. Judicial activism and social advocacy strained autonomous law to the limits. Responsive law is not concerned with individual rights but rather with institutional design to achieve ends. It is interested in new ways of increasing visibility of decisions, new organisation units etc. Legality here means the progressive reduction of arbitrariness in positive law and its administration. Regulation is its paradigm function. This is not just legal in the narrow sense but describes new ways of going about things. It is not just administrative law in the sense of judicial review but concerned with positive design. These two tasks blur the distinction between politics and law and attempt a new polity. Autonomous law in a sense dies because law is no longer a separate entity backed by its own 'artificial reason'. Responsive law is, in this sense, like repressive law. But there is a wide moral gulf between them. Here it is a way of expanding legal values into positive responsibilities in government by the reintegration of law and politics.

But the problem remains that this appears to have thrown out autonomous law altogether. Repressive law and responsive law seem only to differ in intent. O'Hagan (1984) sees them as trying to achieve a kind of synthesis of the two previous forms and wonders whether this would not in fact lose that society the protection of formal law. The problem is similar to that that we noticed with Shklar. For in putting forward their solution, which was bracketed by O'Hagan with Bańkowski and Mungham (1976), and Unger (1975; 1976) as utopian and anomian, it is not clear whether or not they have lost sight of the good of autonomous law. In his later work Selznick (1992) makes clear that he does not want to get rid of the good that autonomous law has brought and he subtly looks at this new legal mode of arguing. I would agree with much of what he says and much of my later discussion will be in that spirit. However it is still ambiguous as to whether what he is trying to do is a synthesis and move beyond (the Hegelian *Aufhebung*) that we rejected earlier.

When he thinks of principles as being the key point in this form of law in that they mediate between law and justice he quotes MacCormick (1994: 439) with approval as saying that legal principles are 'the meeting point between rules and values'. Here there is a recognition of the good of rules. He then goes on to say that the critique of positivism by those such as Fuller and Dworkin puts the emphasis in law back on to principles, upon the indeterminate as opposed to the determinate. But the trouble with Dworkin is that his emphasis on principles gradually takes over and one begins to lose sight of rules entirely. In his earlier work, he says that law consists not only of rules but of principles and policies. Gradually policies become things that stand outwith the law and are contrasted with rights which, it appears, are what principles have become. Rules disappear from the picture and one gets the impression that the enemy of law is policy (though how that is connected to rules one does not know). Furthermore, his obsession (at least up to and including Law's Empire) with 'the one right answer' puts us in mind, ironically, of how Shklar characterised the Legal Realists. In Dworkin too, we see the search for certainty with everything finally subsumed in the coherence of integrity. There is safety and there is certainty - risk has gone. He plays the Antigone to the positivists' Creon. The rigidity of the law is reproduced under the guise of community[34].

Fuller, on whom Selznick has relied in earlier work, also presents problems. Selznick sees Fuller as anti-positivist in his reliance on principles in the law. He is here referring to the 'inner morality of the law' and the famous eight principles. Now this is very like Selznick's concept of institutional morality. It clearly works in arguing the law is not a normatively free project; that it has at least some value built in the kind of institution that it is. But it is not clear that this helps. For what are the inbuilt values? In many ways they might be

---

[34] It might be argued that Dworkin's concern with the 'one right answer' is not about certainty. Dworkin, according to John Bell, to whom I am grateful for this comment, draws upon Fuller (1978) for his discussion of principles and policies. Fuller is there concerned with justiciability and rules and principles help to delineate issues capable of rational debate and solution through adjudication. Thus Dworkin, as Fuller, is concerned with issues of rational debate rather than the actual right answer. In some respects this might be true but the problem then is that what he says is not particularly distinctive and he becomes a sophisticated and nuanced positivist as, for example, MacCormick (1994a: chapters 8-9).

taken to be those of autonomous law if we take that, as we shall see later both right and left do, to be representative of capitalist societies. Fuller (1969) contrasts 'managerial ordering' with the regime of governance by rules. In very general terms this could be seen as the contrast between bureaucratic/administrative systems such as found in the old eastern Europe, welfare and economic systems (or, in Dworkinian terms policy oriented systems), and systems of rule governance, the institutional morality of which consist of the famous eight principles of the 'inner morality of law'.

The point here is, that for him much of this legal ordering reaches its apogee under capitalist societies and he quotes Pashukanis with approval to this effect. And it is here, as Weber notes (see chapter 1) that we find the emphasis on predictability and certainty, the drive to take away the magic from the world. Fuller is not against managerial regulation and in fact thinks that in the appropriate places it is necessary - but for society as a whole the governance of rules is appropriate. Thus Fuller appears to be saying that governance of rules is important but we can allow within this ordered spaces of chaos. This is precisely the liberal view of the market society, where we have rigid frameworks to allow people to become autonomous within them. The problem with this is, as we shall see later, that the framework takes over, what Marx called commodification, and what now might be called juridification[35]. The principles then become internal to the law and important in making the law less rigid, but they are still within.

The paradox with Fuller is that though he talks of the system of 'governance of rules' and appears to link it with autonomous law, he also seems to approve of and see it as what we called legality. He thinks of law as being interactive and communicative between citizens and between law receivers and law givers. It is in that that we find legality. Indeed he contrasts it with the directive nature of managerialism. However all this is allusive and suggestive. We also get an idea of the way forward in an area which Fuller would not recognise, in his discussion of the relations of managerialism and legality. There he is not only talking of regime boundaries. In his subtle discussion of managerialism one can see how in part it also embraces forms of the governance of rules. This could be taken as the basis of a way of living with the tensions that we have talked about.

DUTY AND ASPIRATION

We still have to get clear what legalism is. We cannot examine Nonet and Selznick's claim before we do that. Both they and Shklar see it as the bad side

[35] see Teubner (1987); Habermas (1986)

of legality and equate it with formalism, with the 'model of rules'. In Shklar's case also, with the quest for certainty. But it is still not clear what it is. The implication of the sometimes too close equation with autonomous law is that you cannot have it and any other form of law. Some would say that this is not only cognitively but normatively correct; that any other way leads to arbitrary power. Others would deny this and say that that sort of system leads to stultification and affirms existing power; that its fixedness is ideological, hiding the political preferences of those in power. Law, they say, is flexible and can never be fixed, and that is something good. But this is mistaken. Legality consists in the articulation of autonomous and heteronomous systems. We need heteronomy as well as autonomy. We cannot collapse the one into the other

The problem is then how to marry these two incompatibles. If law is flexible and plastic, then how can it be hard and determining? How can it be so in a way that is not ideological and a mask for the power of some? If it is hard and determining, then how can it be flexible and plastic? What I want to suggest is that it is not formalism, rules, and certainty that are the problem. The problem rather, is excessive reliance on them. Legalism is a form of nomianism taken to excess. One might therefore argue that legality need not be cured of legalism. It merely should not have too excessive a reliance on it. Legality is nomianism understood correctly or as Nonet and Selznick say, 'the ideal of legality needs to be conceived more generally and to be cured of formalism'[36].

What is 'too much' here? Here Fuller can help us, especially in the distinction that he draws between the morality of aspiration and the morality of duty. For Fuller, the morality of aspiration is most plainly exemplified in Greek philosophy. For the Greeks morality was not about right and wrong but rather what was fitting conduct and what was not. If one failed to realise one's capacities one was condemned, not for not fulfilling one's duty, but rather for failure to live up to what one was. The morality of duty, as opposed to aspiration, starts from the bottom rung of the ladder. It says what you should not do rather than ask that you live up to something. We may, as did Adam Smith, use the analogy of grammar to make this point clearer. The rules of grammar are the essential rules without which one cannot write and make oneself understood. We need them to be able to make human communication possible. The rules of good writing or style, on the other hand,

---

[36] *op. cit.*, p. 108

> 'are loose, vague and indeterminate, and present us rather with a general idea of the perfection we ought to aim at, than afford us any certain and infallible directions of acquiring it'(quoted by Fuller 1969: 6)

Let us take another two examples. Wróblewski (1992) deals in a careful and painstaking manner with the concepts of validity and justification and examines their use in the various ideologies of the judicial application of law. The detailed examination of these concepts is an important starting point for anyone interested in developing any normative theory of law. It is the point from which one can be creative but without which one's theories risk degeneration into shallowness. One can draw an analogy with art. Here it has been argued by some that non-figurative painting can best be done by those who have been classically trained. True creativity then, it might be said, is derived from discipline. It is only then that your creativity allows you to start changing the rules of the discipline. Non-figurative art is not a matter of just slapping paint on to a canvas. The analogy of grammar and writing reinforces this point. It is only those who have mastered the rules of grammar who can then go on to write well and with style. It is only those who have got to this point that are able to play with the rules of grammar. Neither is writing merely slapping words on to paper.

The best way to explain the distinction is to tell a story. Suppose someone asks how he can be a good husband and love his wife. My reply might be something to the effect that he has to be gentle and kind. But this might not satisfy my legalistic interlocutor. He thinks this is too vague and wants some more specific rules that he can follow. I reply that he should give his wife flowers every week; go to a good restaurant once a fortnight; and agree to at least 75% of her requests. This satisfies him and he goes off and duly follows these rules. When he comes to me some time later, aggrieved because his wife has left him, what do I say? He thinks he has done what is necessary - he followed the rules that I gave him. But his mistake would have been to think that was enough. More was necessary and he would only have learned what that was if he had not ignored my fine but vague phrases. But you cannot specify them.

One might say that following my rules was the morality of duty - a *sine qua non* of being a good husband. But being a good husband demanded something more than that - he had to look to the morality of aspiration in which the rules were embedded. The story is not meant to say that one has no duties to one's partner. I did not tell my friend to do those things out of a malicious sense of humour. Rather, I thought that if, as seemed clear, he was incapable of knowing what it was to be good and kind, then perhaps these rules would teach him. They failed because he did not see that that was not all there was to it. If you understood the aspirations behind the rule you would see that the letter of the rule did not have to be followed no matter what the cost. Rules are there to help you understand and they can be re-formulated in the light of that learning.

Another example might make this clearer. Suppose I am a vegetarian and thus refuse to eat meat. I must remember that the point of my practice is not exhausted by the rule, 'do not eat meat'. There might be occasions when I have to re-formulate my rule. If the aspiration behind the rule, the moral practice that I hold to is not to cause unnecessary suffering to sentient beings then obvious there will be occasions when I think it right and proper to eat meat. Suppose that in a strange and poor country I am invited by poor people and meat is offered. What am I to do? Am I to turn this down because I do not eat meat, being a vegetarian. Or, am I to weigh up the hurt and suffering caused to my poor hosts by my so doing against the suffering to the animal which, by the standards of Western factory farming, was not treated particularly cruelly? The decision might be difficult. However I would not necessarily be betraying my ideals if I did eat the meat.

Turn to the parable of the Good Samaritan. The lesson of that parable is that one should love one's neighbour - a category which, as Jesus implies, is rather wide. But look what happens in the law. In the case of Donoghue v Stevenson 1932 AC 599 Ld Atkin said:

> 'The rule that you are to love your neighbour becomes in law: You must not injure your neighbour, and the lawyer's question: Who is my neighbour? receives a restricted reply. You must take reasonable care to avoid acts or omissions which you can reasonably foresee would be likely to injure your neighbour. Who then, in law, is my neighbour? The answer seems to me to be persons who are so closely and directly affected by my act that I ought reasonably to have them in contemplation as being so affected when I am directing my mind to the acts or omissions which are called in question. This appears to me to be the doctrine in Heaven v Pender as laid down by Lord Esher.'

What the law lays down as one's duty is the sine qua non without which loving thy neighbour would be impossible. But this clearly does not exhaust the possibility of love nor does it mean that the person who merely does not injure his neighbour, so defined, is really loving his neighbour. For that, you need a morality of aspiration, which is given in the parable Jesus told. Loving your neighbour means more than following the duty of the law and you will not even understand what that duty is unless you look to the aspiration guided by the story. At the same time it does not mean that you should include everyone you meet in the moral community, rather that we should, as Fuller says, aspire to enlarge that community at every opportunity and aspire to include, if we are able, all men of good will.

Legalism is to mistake the minimum duties of law for legality and the whole of law. To say that all laws can be seen as merely the morality of duty without looking to the aspirational parts of it. An example from legal theory might also help. The practice theory of rules founds moral rules on social practices. It has been put forward, among others, by H L A Hart (1961). A problem with such a view is whether it can account for a critical morality. How can a lone vegetarian in a society of meat eaters criticise the social practice of meat eating? One answer would be that the social practices about meat-eating have been misdescribed and that we should restate them. On closer examination, we might see that this imaginary society had no social practice treating meat-eating as obligatory. Rather, it had a practice of condemning cruelty to animals, or indeed to all living creatures. The difference between the vegetarian and the meat-eater could then be seen as a difference within a single moral practice. The meat-eater's cut-off point for drawing the line between unacceptable cruelty and acceptable treatment of animals would simply be lower than that of the vegetarian. The practice would be the same, that of avoiding cruelty to animals. They would both be participating in it. We thus circumvent the problem of making the lone moral critic's position intelligible. For we can look at the practice to be criticised in a way which enables us to see the criticised and the criticisers' points of view as aspects of the same normative practice. The difference being that along the continuum of that practice the one places the point of obligation somewhat lower than the other. That point is what we might call the morality of duty - beyond that is aspiration[37].

What legalism does is to mistake the rule that expresses the duty as all there is to it. It forgets that it is merely a point on an aspirational scale. We mistake the actual rule as being all there is to it. We have to look at the rule of duty within the context of the practice of aspiration of which it is a part. Though we have duties for which one might say that legalism is appropriate, this does not mean that they are written in stone. For aspiration will sometimes mean that the *sine qua non* of duty might have to be changed. At other times, duties that seem set in stone can be seen as an imprecise way of helping us to get to the aspiration which will also change those duties. An example of the former case can be seen when the duty is seen as more aspirational. It imposes too heavy a charge and breaking it would not be hypocritical as long as one held to

[37] MacCormick (1981)

the aspiration of which it is part. The latter case would be when the detailed rules enable one to come to an understanding of the aspiration for which they stand. This would enable one to break the rules, the better to follow the aspiration. Thus when the enlightened Christian moralist tells his perplexed student who finds it almost impossible to follow the church's complex and detailed moral teaching, 'All you need is love', he could mean both of these. He does not mean the love of the flower power days, rather that the rules are to some extent aspirational and should not be read as imposing impossible demands. That is why failing to follow the rules need not be hypocritical. To call it so would be to mistake aspiration for duty. And this is how legality differs from legalism in that sometimes the rules have to be changed for the higher aspiration. Aspiration and duty feed off each other.

The question remains. We have a continuum which makes up the rule. It moves from duty to aspiration. But where is the pointer that marks the dividing line to go? That, of course is a matter of judgement and balance. Once it is made however, that part that is the morality of duty becomes inflexible and determined, for that is its nature. The aspirational part acts in the way that I have described. The duty part can still be changed for aspiration is always in play. But once done it is something determined and not flexible. We might use the idea of defeasible rules to express something of the idea here.

The duty /aspiration distinction is very important and it performs a number of tasks. In the first place it has the connotation of going beyond, of reaching out as against something that is firm and certain. At the same time a relation between the certain and the uncertain is expressed. This is where it gets problematic. It can imply that the duties, though important, are not as important as long as you stick to the aspiration. Though duties have a language of failure and success, aspiration does not and we can never fail as long as we try to reach beyond. Secondly it implies a minimum standard, something without which a practice cannot be undertaken. Thus the rules of grammar or drawing. But it also means that you will not get very far if you think that that is all there is to it. You will not be a great writer if you know thoroughly the rules of grammar, though you will be able to communicate. The Pharisee, standing in the temple, makes this sort of mistake. However there is more also. Thirdly then, it can imply that the duties are ways of getting at the aspiration. For example in teaching my child about social relationships, I will not necessarily say that all you have to remember is to act in such a way that will not involve your hurting someone; that everything you do will have the respect of the other in view. I might indeed say that but also give my child a set of defined duties in acting with people. My hope is that in following these, the child will learn what it is to respect someone else. And when it has some idea of that aspiration, when it is on the road, then it will be able to throw away some of the duties. It will know, for example, when it ought to lie. Here the duties are ways of getting you on the road and are then dispensable. It is important here to note that this does not mean that you can discard all duties. Otherwise we can get a sort of gnosticism, once you know the secret teachings you have no need of rules or duties anymore because you are safe in the aspiration.[38] The person on the road of aspiration will always need duties, but though, as opposed to aspiration they will be rigid, they can be changed.

I do not therefore use the word 'achieve' in respect of aspiration because that would be to imply that the aspiration can be known clearly. For Fuller, it is important to show that you do not have to have an idea of the excellent in order to know what your duties are. For what is appropriate as the *sine qua non* of a particular institution does not have to be known by reference to the best example. Thus, to take grammar again, one can have that without having a notion of the finest style. In this I agree. We do not have to have the notion of a particular end in view in order to seek excellence or work out what our basic duties are to be. However, we must recognise that we do have an end and that it does reciprocally interact with our duties. We should not think of our duties being all we can hold on to because we cannot know the excellent. In fact what we can see above is a constant movement between these different versions of the duty/aspiration distinction.

The problem here is about the internal and the external; about going out from the security of the law and coming back in again; about law being both standing in and out of it. Selznick (1992) tries to get at this by seeing principles as a way of changing the law internally, but at the same time as being launching pads for going outside of the law. I will look at this more closely when we look at legal reasoning in respect of our main themes about how in some ways we can see mechanisms that propel us out and into the law. And that is what law is. The duty/aspiration distinction also gives us a way of seeing this. What is important to see is how law should be seen as the articulation of these two spheres, that of duty and aspiration - that good legal decision-making is, paradoxically both in and out of the law. And this is the ambiguity in Fuller. He identifies law with the morality of duty but legality seems to be something which, as an interactive concept, is something more than that; something which also has the flexibility of aspiration.

---

[38] We can see the example of some Christian sects where this meant a complete abrogation of any rules of sexual morality for instance, in the name of the freedom of love. Recent examples include Waco and the Jonestown massacre.

He makes a telling analogy[39]. This both illustrates some of the problems and leads us into the next chapter. He distinguishes two views of economics. My point is not to see if these views of economics are correct but to use the analogy. There are those who see it as exchange relations and those who see it as how to deal with scarce resources (marginal utility). That latter can be seen as something like the morality of aspiration - we have no duties but we aspire to balance the resources that we have in order to live well. We do not need to have a particular view of that end in order to do this - it will be a matter of balance and judgement. Utility is just a word for the good and welfare and when we try and produce a single criterion for it, as Bentham did in the principle of pleasure, we destroy its point. Exchange on the other hand, is for Fuller the *sine qua non* of social life - a way of manufacturing the social product. The question of the articulation between the two economics is one of judgement. Exchange is part of the morality of duty. We are only interested, in the economic judgements there, if there was agreement in exchange. He likens this, through the notion of reciprocity, to law. Thus law is not only part of the morality of duty but reaches its highest point under capitalism. The question there is, where is the equivalent of marginal utility economics in law? This he does not really answer. What this means is that law gets stuck in duty and legalism again. Legalism and legality are again identified. What is more, it becomes identified, as we shall see in the next chapter, with a particular social form, namely capitalism.

CONCLUSION

We conclude again with the *Antigone*. What does the *Antigone* tell us about situations where there are many principles in tension, where in very broad terms, the safety and certainty of law, and the contingency and risk of love collide? As we saw, we do not look in the first instance to Antigone herself for the answer. She, in our terms, was on the side of the law. We must first of all, says Nussbaum, look to the Chorus. What do they have to say about deliberative reasoning? The Chorus first shows how any response will not only be intellectual but will also have recourse to emotion where it is fitting. They allow themselves not only 'to think on both sides' but to feel deeply. They speak of the power of • 'seated besides the laws of right' (781-801), and they side with Haemon; 'And now myself, as well, am borne outside of the laws of right, seeing this; and can no longer contain the streams of tears, when I see this Antigone here going to her bridal chamber of eternal sleep' (802-6).

But they do not see any harmonious vision and their vision is well expressed in the ode to that awesome thing man (332-75). At first that seems

[39] Fuller (1969: 17-30)

to be a history of triumphant progress of that creature who has created so many devices for controlling the contingent. He builds ships and ploughs the earth, captures animals for food. He invents speech and, though he cannot overcome death, he even conquers disease. But all the images of power and success, Nussbaum notes, are undercut by the possibility of problems; 'Clever beyond hope is the inventive craft he possesses. It brings him now to ill now to good'. The whole ode makes us think, says Nussbaum, of the choices human beings are often forced to make between values which sometimes will forever be in conflict. It will not always be possible to make a correct and harmonious choice; the good legislator will sometimes, for example, have to be impious. Again Nussbaum recalls Creon's de-eroticising of civic sexuality. The good civic husband cannot respond to the 'passion that sleeps on a young girls soft cheeks' to 'the madness that turns men from duty.' They must have, according to Creon, civic marriage and sexuality. This then determinedly pushes *eros* away - Demeter holds sway. As Nussbaum says, the Hegelian city, when forced to choose between marriage and *eros* must choose the former. It cannot honour all the gods for then it will have to deal with sometimes irresolvable conflicts. Nussbaum shows how the Chorus goes on to portray this bleak view for the possibility of human life. And this does sound like the world of the early CLS, with its continuous oscillation between two components and no principle of choice.

But the play does not leave it like that. At the end of the play Tiresias talks of what must be done to show correct deliberative reasoning as against the simplistic way of Creon. It is, as one might expect, a question of balance. He, and Haemon earlier, speak of flexibility, of accepting the world as it is; bending with it and taking on board its complexities. They use an image that today appears clichéd, that of the flexible tree being stronger than the proud oak. But flexibility does not mean that one goes with every current that is available. He accepts, as at least in part correct, Creon's image of the ship of state as a haven against the contingencies of the world. What is important is to pay due regard to everything. In this way though we can have no complete transcendental resolution we see the beauty of our existence and the world. It is in this way that we get the beauty and mystery of the world. Such a life has time for both love and co-operation in civic law. But what is to be the criterion of our balancing. In some way, according to Tiresias, we stick to the conventions of the city which lead to a rich plurality of values which teach us both the richness of a diverse existence and some of the ways of balancing.

And this appears to mirror Gillian Rose (1992) when she speaks of the relation of law to love, which in the way we have talked of it one can see as the central moral conflict of the play. We have to learn to inhabit the tension between particular and universal, autonomous and heteronomous, law and love. This place is what Gillian Rose calls the 'middle'. That place lies in the negotiation between law and love, particular and universal, autonomy and heteronomy. That area is an anxious place because it refuses to abandon either side of the equation. We cannot call it a contradiction because that implies that it can be transcended whereas we are dealing with and trying to hold together things that pull us in both ways. It is anxious because here there is neither an easy answer or guarantee that our solution has turned out right. We cannot try and find an ideal ending to aim for or try and theorise a new beginning, we must start with what we have and what we are. We need reason and rationality but that itself cannot be justified by reason. We have to have the faith to apply it and bring things within the purview of reason and at the same time to know when our love requires us to discount rationality in order to recreate it again. How do we know when to do this and listen to the voice of love that will recreate the law anew? Let us look at this through the story of the sacrifice of Isaac[40]. God tells Abraham that he must sacrifice his beloved son Isaac. Abraham goes to do this and is only stopped by God at the last moment. What do we make of this dark and terrible story? For Kant it is quite simple. He says:

> 'Abraham should have replied to this putative divine voice: 'That I may not kill my good son is absolutely certain. But that you who appear to me are God is not certain and cannot become certain, even though the voice were to sound from the very heavens'... [For] that a voice which one seems to hear cannot be divine one can be certain of... in case what is commanded is contrary to moral law. However majestic or supernatural it may appear to be, one must regard it as a deception.' (Apud Rose 1992: 12)

So Kant is saying is there is no problem here, do not listen to this voice that is telling you to sacrifice your son. This is not God speaking to you, because God is not going to ask you to do something outside the law, against the categorical imperative. So for Kant there is certainty. But this was precisely not the case here. The answer might have been clear in respect of the law but for Abraham it was not clear because of the voice, because it appeared that God was telling him to do this terrible thing. So he had to take the risk of stepping outside the certainty of the law in order to fulfil the commands of, you might say, the love of God. And in doing that he becomes the father of the law - so in breaking the law, he recreates it differently and anew. But the act of breaking the law is something that is necessary to making the law. He becomes the father of the Jewish law precisely because he was able to break it in the first instance. Why and how does he know that it is right now to change and

[40] See Bańkowski and Davis (2000). I am indebted to Claire Davis for her fruitful collaboration in these ideas which came from a joint research project.

break that law? One of the reasons is paradoxical - it is precisely because he led a life of faith according to the law. Precisely because he was someone who followed the laws, who knew and applied them, was he able to recognise when there was an exceptional pattern and be able to change them. So his act of creation, his act of creativity, in breaking the law and recreating it, stems in the end from the structured life he led under the law. In that sense, his act of love makes the law, but that is only possible because he follows the rules and the laws.

Only by obeying the lawwill one know when the law is to be disobeyed or suspended, and it is only in this suspension that the law itself is continually renewed. This creative breaking of the law can only be effective if it stems from a mastery of the law, in the sense of following and understanding it. But it is not the law that will guarantee the break. However, creativity cannot start *ex nihilo* for that would indeed be chaos. One cannot be a James Joyce and rework the conventions of English grammar without a mastery of those rules but those rules will not guarantee the good of your new style. This again takes us back to Fuller's way of going at the problem and it also allows us to look at some of these problems in more concrete political terms. And it is these we turn to in the next chapter.

CHAPTER 5

THE MARKET AND LAW

INTRODUCTION

As we saw in the last chapter, it was difficult, in their various ways, for our authors completely to distinguish legalism and legality. What is more, the intertwined concepts also become, in Fuller, identified with capitalism and market society and, as we shall see, this is true for writers of the left and of the right. What that means is that society gets identified to some extent at least with legalism and it seems, as we saw, contradictory to say that something good like legality can co-exist with it. It is either law or not. Thus the left think of market societies in a negative way as embodying a full blown legalism which cannot allow for the particularity of welfare. The right agree, they see the form of life in a positive way as legalistic. Neither of them think of these principles standing in tension, 'in the middle'.

We now turn to look more concretely, at how these problems get expressed in concrete political societies. We do this in relation to the problems of the relation of market to non-market societies, and the relationship of social justice and equality. Fuller identified lawand the morality of duty with capitalist societies. How does that then articulate with aspiration or non-market principles. The questions to be asked in this chapter concern, very broadly, social justice and equality. Should the state distribute welfare and resources to achieve some notion of social justice? Is the implication of this distribution some form of welfare state? What are the political consequences of that? Or, is the market the most efficient way of achieving fair distribution? Is the implication of that an uncaring, unloving society? Are market and welfare two inimical principles which will always be in opposition to each other? What sort of ethic do the notions of welfare and market imply? How can we evaluate these rival ethics? On the one hand, the market is presented as the saviour of society. The re-marketisation of society is supposed to bring both efficiency and morality back to peoples' lives. It gives them freedom. On the other hand, the market is represented as destroying any sense of social solidarity. The market's opponents claim that its concentration on the individual and his/her desires gets rid of any caring society that there could be. Crudely, the anti-market side can put the antithesis as one of a selfish society against a caring one. The pro-market side replies in the same vein by saying that 'the road to hell is paved with good intentions'; that all the talk about caring masks a massive and usually progressive disregard of individual rights, coupled with a progressive diminution of economic efficiency.

HAYEK AND THE CASE FOR MARKETS

The parable of the Labourers in the Vineyard is a classic examination of some of these themes[41]. Here, God's love comes up against the labourers' demands to be treated justly. The themes of welfare, desert, equality, justice, contractual rights all come up in varying mixes. However this should be understood in its biblical setting. We can use it here to explicate different visions of society; different moral principles of social organisation. One way of looking at the parable is to say that love is its own reason; that the love of God knows no bounds and He gives to all what they need. But we can turn this into a contractarian argument against the more 'caring society', by pointing out that God is a special case, being all-knowing as well as all-good. Since God knows all, he knows what is best for everyone; being all-good, he can be trusted to will it for everyone; by being all-powerful, he can achieve it for everyone. However, we cannot be God and so cannot know the best thing to do. F A Hayek (1944; 1973; 1976; 1982) has taken this as the nub of an argument for the market and against welfare and state intervention. God might know what every individual human being is doing and what is best for him or her in the context of what everyone else is doing, but this is beyond the capacity of human beings. Caring only works if you know what you are doing.

---

[41] For the kingdom of heaven is like a householder who went out early in the morning to hire laborers for his vineyard. After agreeing with the laborers for a denarius a day, he sent them into his vineyard. And going out about the third hour he saw others standing idle in the market place; and to them he said, 'You go into the vineyard too, and whatever is right I will give you.' So they went. Going out again about the sixth hour and the ninth hour, he did the same. And about the eleventh hour he went out and found others standing; and he said to them, 'Why do you stand here idle all day?' They said to him, 'Because no one has hired us.' He said to them, 'You go into the vineyard too.' And when evening came, the owner of the vineyard said to his steward, 'Call the laborers and pay them their wages, beginning with the last, up to the first.' And when those hired about the eleventh hour came, each of them received a denarius. Now when the first came, they thought they would receive more; but each of them also received a denarius. And on receiving it they grumbled at the householder, saying, 'These last worked only one hour, and you have made them equal to us who have borne the burden of the day and the scorching heat.' But he replied to one of them, 'Friend, I am doing you no wrong; did you not agree with me for a denarius? Take what belongs to you, and go; I choose to give to this last as I give to you. Am I not allowed to do what I choose with what belongs to me? Or do you begrudge my generosity?' (Matt 20 1-15)

From the point of view of society as a whole, humans cannot know what everyone wants. Each can only know what each wants and they need to do.

How does Hayek argue for this thesis? We start off with the idea of order. For Hayek there are two models of social organisation. First, there is the 'spontaneous order'. We can never know everything about social life. In non-command societies, order grows up spontaneously and is self-generating. It requires general rules that have to be obeyed. These can emerge through, and are best left to, natural selection. Secondly, there is a 'constructed order'. This kind of order assumes that there must be some purpose and end to the order as a whole and that intervention can help it better to achieve its function.

For Hayek (1973), societies and social institutions arise by evolution. The criterion of success is the survival of one social form in competition with another. Societies are the product of unwitting actions on the part of countless individuals. No one intends to produce any specific distribution of goods or services; it is merely the product of their countless actions. Hayek calls this spontaneous order a cosmos. Human society as cosmos is the product of human action, but not of human design. This sort of order functions through abstract rules.

> '[I]n a social order the particular circumstances to which each individual will react will be those known to him. But the individual response to particular circumstances will result in an overall order only if the individuals obey such rules as will produce an order. Even a very limited similarity in their behaviour may be sufficient if the rules which they obey are such as to produce an order. Such an order will always be considered an adaptation to the multitude of circumstances which are known to all members of that society together but which are not known as a whole to any one person.' (p. 45)

We have to distinguish this spontaneous order from a deliberately constructed order or *taxis*. A *taxis* functions through rules which are specific for the particular function or effect that people want to achieve with it. They are regulations that are not general in the way that the rules of the *cosmos* are. Rather they are instrumental devices for gaining particular ends. They have a specific purpose in mind and, indeed, they have been made with that purpose in view. The *cosmos*, in contrast, cannot be said to have a particular purpose since it has not been constructed deliberately. It is the outcome of countless intentional actings but not of an overall plan. A *cosmos* merely enables people to harmonise their various competing desires and to pursue them in some sort of co-ordinated and orderly way. It does not pursue any particular goal. The *cosmos* is far more hospitable to complexity than a *taxis* therefore. It does not have to deal directly with each individual and his or her particular needs and desires and try and match them with the needs and desires of everyone else. Instead, it is concerned with the procedure of just co-ordination. It deals with the general and abstract and thus ignores, to an extent, the particular.

Liberal legal order and the market economy can be seen as examples of such an order. Here also Hayek's notion of the 'Great Society' makes its appearance. One of the defining characteristics of such a society is the equal respect and treatment of all human beings under the liberal form of law; this to consist of general and abstract rules. This overarching system of rules, implying a philosophy of right and duty and equal treatment under equal abstract rules is the only rational way that people can live in community. It is a move from the morality of the tribe and the solidarity of the small group to the great society where everyone is equal, united by abstract rules. We do not have the same depth of feeling in such a society but that is the price one has to pay for civilisation. It is no wonder that such a society is very fragile. For Hayek, this is the essential characteristic of Western civilisation. And it is this which makes that fragile entity, the 'Great Society', superior to all others.

This conflict between what men still feel to be natural emotions and the discipline of rules required for the preservation of the open society is indeed one of the chief causes of what has been called the 'the fragility of liberty': all attempts to model the Great Society on the image of the familiar small group, or to turn it into a community by directing the individuals towards common visible purposes, must produce a totalitarian society.

This is what we might call the way of living under rules that we have seen is seen by many as the safe option, as legalism.

A market economy is another component of the Great Society. Here again we see the opposition between cosmos and taxis.

> 'Much of the opposition to a system of freedom under general laws arises from their inability to conceive of an effective co-ordination of human activities without deliberate organization by a commanding intelligence. One of the achievements of economic theory has been to explain how such a mutual adjustment of the spontaneous activity of individuals is brought about by the market, provided that there is a known delimitation of the sphere of control of each individual' (Hayek, 1976: 147).

How does that happen? Adam Smith was one of the first to provide an explanation. He showed how individual actings are co-ordinated through markets not because this is what markets were designed for but because markets turn out to have this property. They do so because in an open market there is a tendency for activities to be co-ordinated. Those are rewarded who produce a commodity that is desired at the lowest price. The market is the most efficient system of communicating the information, in the form of prices etc., that people need to achieve that goal. In the pursuit of their own interest, they are led to favour the general interest. Hayek called this system a catallaxy. This is a system which has no particular end but can be said to have as many ends as there are people who make it up, 'serving the multiplicity of separate and incommensurable aims of its members' (Hayek 1976: 159). Hayek asks us to think of it as a wealth producing game which depends upon both skill and luck. This game allows different ends to become compatible with each other. What is important to note here is that prices are the means of giving information. They show what ought to be bought, made or sold. They are not a reward or punishment for desert or good judgement. They give the information that is necessary for the system to work and resources to be distributed. The chances that everyone can have their expectations fulfilled are thus maximised. It is important also to note that there is no deliberate distribution; momentary outcomes are the result of all the individual transactions made under the rules. If this is the case, then no one momentary holding can be said to be just or unjust since no one chooses that any given individual should have any particular holding.

The metaphor that best describes this process of distributing resources is that of the 'invisible hand'. Invisible should be read here as 'not existing' rather than some superhuman hidden force. There is no God behind the system who co-ordinates everything with some pre-ordained plan of which He alone has the knowledge. Rather, what we have is a system where the intentional actions of many particular people can be co-ordinated and made coherent[42]. This can be effected without these people having to desire the particular outcomes that the system as a whole brings about. However we can also see this as a product of the theology of Smith's time, stemming from Newton's theology and from his idea of the universe as a machine with all pieces fitting together. The function of God, being not to keep it in motion but rather to oil it occasionally. So the market system is designed as a self-contained rational system of co-ordination. In Thomas Chalmers this also played an important part in his theodicy in that God had so arranged the world that the selfish impulses of people were functional in providing rational social order[43]. So the God of the oil-can also becomes the God of the night watchman state. In a world designed like this one does not need intervention, except the occasional oiling. Indeed active intervention would be positively harmful.

---

[42] See MacCormick (1989) for a full version of this argument

[43] See Nicholls (1995)

The parable challenges that sort of story for it shows an interventionist God. There is both an epistemological point and a moral point involved here. Epistemologically, the point is that we cannot know everything. We cannot know all the facts and particulars that exist in the world. We would need to know all these in order to make an absolutely correct decision in the context of the society as a whole and our particular plan for it. Science will not advance in such a way that it will become the equivalent of God. It will be unable to become as God because it has to deal with the world at a general level. This will not lessen the multiplicity of particular facts in the world and will not help us to know them. For (Hayek 1973: 16), it will always be the case that a single human will not be able to know all the 'particular facts which are known to some men but not as a whole to any particular person'. This makes Hayek attack what he calls constructivist rationalism; that is, the idea, stemming from the Enlightenment, that one can design social orders from scratch. Order for Hayek is not like this. Social orders do not have designers in the sense of being the product of deliberate human design. Any attempt to design order would anyway end in failure since we cannot know everything. It is hubris that makes us think we can do so. We can make grand designs which aim at a particular end but what actually transpires will never correspond to the designed aims. We cannot design societies from scratch, we can only go along with the flow of a spontaneous order. This is not, however, to say that reason has no part to play. We can, first of all, learn to interact with the institutions that we find ourselves in and not stand against them, seeking to construct them anew. Secondly we can get round our ignorance of the particulars that might exist by dealing with abstractions and generalities. In practical terms, we have to confine ourselves to making sure that the market runs properly; that everyone plays the game fairly; and that the rules that define the market are followed.

Morally, the argument stems from the epistemological point discussed above. We cannot direct the market order because we cannot know all the particular facts that exist. Trying to do so would in fact distort our ability to do anything at all. Our activity would distort the role of the market as a system for providing information for action. It would, as it were, hold back the hidden hand of the market. Moreover, the attempt to inject some sort of design into the system in the form of planning has consequences for liberty. Hayek (1994) explicates these in the Road to Serfdom. As planners tried to push the society in certain ways, society would gradually become more directive and managerial. There would not be an order where there was no purpose as a whole. Instead of individuals following their own desires aided by information from the market, they would be forced in directions that the planners wanted. This would lead to a lack of liberty; to a lack of negative freedom.

It is important to note that this is not a situation where evil-intentioned planners would force things on unsuspecting citizens. The argument is that even those with good intentions would be at fault. Though they would be trying to act for the good of society, they could not know what this good might be. Neither could they know all the consequences of their interventions. All that they would succeed in doing is distorting the very information mechanisms people use when deciding how best to act. People would not be able to do what they thought was best for them but would have to follow the orders of those who claimed (misguidedly) that they knew better. This would inevitably lead to a totalitarian state. The road to hell is, for Hayek, truly paved with good intentions. Intervention implies a system of legal ordering which Fuller (1969) calls managerialism. In this schema, law is a system of regulation that directs us toward particular ends, paying scant regard to rules or legality. Fuller contrasts this 'rule by managers run amok' with legality. In the latter we place ourselves under 'the governance of rules'. We can see then that our epistemological hubris, in thinking we know what is right, has severe moral consequences.

How do we get round that hubris? Hayek argues that though we cannot clearly tell what is right, we can more easily tell what is wrong. We ought, therefore, to try to refrain from doing wrong. If we follow the rules that we have laid down beforehand, this will at least ensure that we do no wrong. Here we can see the argument for legality; by following the rules we minimise our chances of doing wrong and this is all we have in our cognitive power to do. If we positively try to do good, then since we do not have that cognitive capacity, we will inevitably make mistakes and commit greater acts of immorality.

PASHUKANIS THE CASE AGAINST MARKETS: AND CAPITALIST SOCIETY

What we have seen so far is a view of society based on a market model. Not only is it claimed that this would be the most efficient way of organising society but also that it is the only moral way of going about it. Only in this way, it is argued, can we ensure that people can pursue their own individual interests freely. That the labourers in the vineyard freely contracted to work for a denarius is, on this view, the key point of the parable. Whoever gets what he or she bargained for has no complaint, especially not about others getting what they bargained for. To re-shape market outcomes for some state-favoured purpose, even 'social justice', in fact upsets these bargains. The purposive state is intrinsically illegitimate. For Hayek the 'Rule of Law' provides a framework for freedom and is inextricably linked with market society; it is ideally suited for the market society and does not fit well into a policy of welfare state intervention.

I now turn to consider the view of the Soviet Marxist scholar E B Pashukanis (1951; 1980). Pashukanis, though agreeing with this description of capitalist society, draws different cognitive and normative conclusions. Pashukanis agrees with Hayek that lawand economy are intimately connected. But it is in Pashukanis's way of formulating that connection that we get an idea of his objections to capitalist society. For Pashukanis, the connection is not best described in causal terms; such as that the forces of production cause the superstructure, that epiphenomenal edifice consisting of law, morality, religion art etc. For him, the connection is best expressed by concepts such as 'constitute', 'reflect', 'mirror'. Thus the juridical and the economic are intertwined. One does not cause the other because the market is an 'institutional fact'. Here we might draw on the theory of "institutional facts", as put forward by Anscombe (1958) and Searle (1969). They observe that there are some entities which seem to exist in the world wholly independently of human institutions, and they call these "brute facts". Their existence is, or seems to be, in no way contingent on our will, nor do they result from our conventions and contrivances. Other entities, by contrast, seem not to exist in this way. An example of this would be a goal in a football match for example. If someone asks me what that is, there is no material object which I can specify as a goal. I cannot point to a ball crossing the line and say, "that is what I mean by a goal". And yet I can intelligibly talk of there being a goal. These facts may be called, following Searle, institutional facts,

> '[They] are indeed facts; but their existence, unlike the existence of brute facts, presupposes the existence of certain human institutions. It is only given the institution of marriage that certain forms of behaviour constitute Mr. Smith's marrying Miss Jones. Similarly, it is only given the institution of baseball that certain movements by certain men constitute the Dodgers beating the Giants 3 to 2 innings. Even at a simpler level, it is only given the institution of money that I now have a $5 dollar bill in my hand. Take away the institution and all I have is a piece of paper with various green and grey markings.' (p. 51)

These facts exist then by virtue of their being institutions constituted by rules. Thus a contract in law exists by virtue of the institution of contract which is instituted by the rules of contract. And yet the contract that I make when I get on a bus is not the rules of contract or my act of getting on the bus and paying the driver - it exists in an institutional way.

We can consider the market and economic activity analogously. What we call the 'market' is basically constituted by legal rules, the correct use of which brings about legal-institutional facts, among others the market[44]. In this way law and economy are intertwined and we cannot say the one causes the other. Thus Pashukanis sees the juridical relation as the one which makes commodity producing society possible. For it enables us to have the institutional facts of commodity and exchange. In this sense one can say that free market society exists as something constituted by law. This institutional view of the market says something about the form of social organisation in a society. It led Pashukanis away from the old marxist views which saw law as an instrument of the capitalist class, enforcing its ideology and interests. The implication of that view was that law was a weapon which, though in the hands of the bourgeois, could be taken over by the proletariat and used by them. By contrast, for Pashukanis the part that law played in capitalist society was a uniquely constitutive one. The whole society was constituted as capitalist through its central institution the market. The market was, in turn, constituted through the jural relation. Law then, was a central feature in the form of organisation of a society. We saw, when we looked at Hayek, that this view is also mirrored on the right.

What does this mean? Marx said

> 'It is plain that commodities cannot go to market and make exchange of their own account. We must therefore have recourse to their guardians who are also their owners. Commodities are things and therefore without the power of resistance against men. If they are wanting in docility he can use force. In other words he can take possession of them. In order that these objects can enter into relationship with each other as commodities, their guardians must place themselves into relation with each other as persons whose wills reside in these objects and must behave in such a way that each does not appropriate the commodity of the other, and part with his own except by means of an act done by mutual consent. They must therefore recognise in each other the rights of personal proprietors. This juridical relation, which expresses itself in contract, whether such a contract be part of a developed legal system or not, is a relation between two wills, and is but a reflex of the real economic relation between the two.' (Marx 1970: 1,88)

Pashukanis interprets this analysis of market exchange as follows. Capitalist society is where generalised commodity production obtains. Here goods are, in a generalised way, produced for their exchange rather than their use value. In other words, goods are not produced for their intrinsic worth but in order to exchange for other goods that persons might want. Bread, for

[44] See Rottleuthner (1989); MacCormick and Weinberger (1986)

example, is not produced because it is 'the staff of life' (its use value) but because people want to buy it (its exchange value). What they want it for is irrelevant, as is the commodity's social value. I might just as well produce pet rocks if people want to buy them[45]. This being the case, mechanisms are needed which enable commodities to be transferred and to be owned by those doing the transferring. Exchange cannot operate unless someone owns a commodity and can transfer his or her rights in it. It is clear that I could not sell you the Tower of London unless I owned it. Similarly, I could not do so if society as a whole owned it. If all property is held in common, as in a monastic community, I cannot transfer goods in the same way as in capitalist society - though I may have things for my own personal use. The relation between commodities exchanged in this way is only expressed through the wills of those claiming ownership. This relation of wills is expressed through law, through the juridical relation. It is not the pet rock and the money that are related, but the pet rock that I own and want to transfer and the money that you own and want to transfer. The personal pronouns are the most important descriptors, thus goods become as persons. But this does not, as one might think, make people most important. For you and I become abstract legal persons. The fact that it is the rights we claim in commodities that are most significant means that we are looked on, not as concrete persons, but as bearers of right. This abstract bearer of right, the legal person, only has existence in the commodity that it lays claim to. The irony is that though the commodity becomes as a person, that person is an abstract legal subject which only has concrete existence in the commodity. Marx calls this the 'fetishisation of commodities'. This fetishisation makes commodities, rather than the people who made them, appear to be the movers in social life. We live our life through them. It is not what I put into them that becomes important but rather what they exchange for on the market. We lose control over our own actions. We do not think we can interfere in the process of distribution for exchange follows a logic of its own. We cannot go against the 'invisible hand'. This postulates an individualism where individual interest is all that matters and where 'society' does not exist except as the sum of individual human actions. Things always have to belong to someone, there can be no conception that they belong to society as a whole and be used to benefit that society and the individuals in it as they need.

Pashukanis sees the juridical relation as the one which makes commodity-producing society possible. For it enables us to have the institutional facts of commodity and exchange. The whole society is constituted as capitalist through its central institution the market. The market is, in turn, constituted

---

[45] According to Hayek, as we saw, this shows the virtues of the market as a means of distribution of the social product. It is not dependent upon what planners decide but what people want.

through the juridical relation. Law then, is a central feature in the form of organisation of a society. We saw, when we looked at Hayek, that this view is also mirrored on the right. The rule of law and the political liberties of the west are seen as being inextricably linked with market society. Hayek sees market society as one where distribution is based on a formal principle of equality and a negative conception of liberty and applies universal laws equally to all. Who gets what is determined by the operations of the market. That is fair because the market works on the principle that when people freely buy and sell they exchange goods that have equivalent value. Thus everyone gets what they want. This freedom from coercion, from being told what to do, is guaranteed by universal rules, equally applied.

But for Pashukanis this is precisely what is wrong with capitalist society. Capitalism appears acceptable because of the equivalence of the market. Since everything is equal and free in the market - I freely exchange my goods for those of equivalent value - there seems to be no exploitation. But this is mere formal equality and ignores the realities of the situation. The reality is the exploitative nature of the capitalist production process. There is differential ownership of the means of production, and the surplus value produced by the proletarian is appropriated by the capitalist. Capitalist society may offer freedom and equality but money is unevenly distributed and freedom is the offer 'you can't refuse', the stacked deck, the three card trick. For Hayek, both rich and poor are equally free to stay at the Ritz even though only the former can avail themselves of this opportunity.

Pashukanis wants to replace this formal equality with a system of distribution based on a substantive principle of equality and a positive conception of liberty that treats people as individuals according to their respective needs. Freedom is not just freedom 'from', but the freedom positively to fulfill oneself. This means we cannot just apply a measure to people and treat them equally in respect of it. The rule that everyone is free to go to the Ritz is no use. We have to treat each person individually and see whether they need to go to the Ritz and what they will gain from it. The implication of this is that society is a co-operative venture, where people confront each other in all their facets and not as buyers and sellers or bearers of rights and owners. The freedom of each becomes the condition of the freedom for all and distribution occurs naturally: from each according to his abilities, to each according to his needs.

THE FORM OF LIFE OF MARKET SOCIETY

For both Hayek and Pashukanis then, law has a centrally important role because it constitutes a particular sort of society. Both sides argue that one cannot have a socialist law, in the sense of legality and the rule of law. Since that form is so bound up in the society, to do so would mean accepting a capitalist society. The rule of law and the political liberties of the west are seen as being inextricably linked with market society. Fuller (1969) sets this out. For him our duties stem from some notion of reciprocity. There are three conditions for this. Firstly, duties must result from a voluntary agreement. Secondly, the reciprocity of duty must have some equal value - what I do for you must, in some way, be the equal of what you offer to do for me. Thirdly, the duty must be reversible[46] - the duty A owes to B must, in theory and in practice, go from B to A as well. The rule of law depends on this fact. When people come together to decide the rules under which they will live, they must remember that those who are the beneficiaries now might, at some time in the future, become the obligated. Fuller thinks that the kind of society that best expresses the above is a market society. There, one has free and voluntary exchange. A measure of equality is provided since the system works because the commodities exchanged are seen as having equal value to the participants. I consider a £100 bill and the pet rock I get from you in exchange to have equal value - as do you. The duties are reversible both in theory and in practice - we can be buyers and sellers. For these reasons, he argues, notions of moral and legal responsibility reach their full height under capitalism. For the market society is determined by exchange. This is expressed throughout that society even unto its moral and legal views, those latter helping to constitute it. In this light, we can view the Labourers in the parable as expressing a sort of capitalist morality. What they are saying is that some sense of reciprocity, here defined as equality, must obtain. The exchanges they make for their labour must be equal as against all the other labourers. The rule is not equality of the persons as concrete individuals but as personified in their labour - the commodity they have to exchange. It is only when the commodities exchanged are equal, that the labourers are treated equally. Thus 'equal pay for equal work' - what they deserve is to be paid according to the amounts of work done and to be treated equally. They think this to be the only fair way. Otherwise one gets the despotism of someone who knows what is good for you. That path leads to slavery.

---

[46] Fuller could have expressed reversible a little more clearly since for some, Hohfeld (1966) for example, rights and duties are correlatives, precisely not reversible. But the point here is one that applies to the fundamental structure of the *Rechtsstaat* as a whole, within which all citizens are related to one another as equal bearers of rights and duties (so rights and duties will be reversible at that level). I owe this point to Tim O'Hagan.

Let us take a more concrete example. Examiners do not take into account the welfare needs of students when marking their degrees. We might say that the maxim, 'equal pay for equal work' obtains. For the same quality of work students get the same marks. We do not consider it relevant that one student might have greater need of the degree than another - he is poor and this is his only means of supporting his family. If we did, it would be unfair for many reasons. One of those would be that equality could not prevail since each student would have to be judged differently. Let us look at the case where the moral choices are not so obvious. If social security benefits are to be given on the criterion of need, this gives great discretionary power to those who hand them out. Because each person's welfare will be different, one cannot make a general rule which defines in what cases a particular benefit is to be given. This will depend on the individual judgement of need. One cannot 'care' for an abstract proposition but only for a concrete person. Rules will be more akin to rules of thumb. They will be broken when necessary for the good of the individual or institution. This negates legality and can be, as we have seen, the beginning of the slide into a dictatorial regime. And anyway, it seems unfair to look to need at the expense of equality. This is what the labourers in the vineyard recognised.

Law then, not the 'rules of thumb' that we saw above but the general abstract rules of the 'eight ways' of Fuller are bound up in and constitute the form of life of, capitalist society. We can see this exemplified in the work of and Kamenka and Tay (1975). Using Tönnies (1955) and Pashukanis, they pick out three ideal types of legal-social order. Capitalist society is characterised by *Gesellschaft* law. This arises out of, and constitutes, atomic individualism. The community is not seen as an organic whole, rather it is the sum of individual bearers of rights, all standing equal before the law and all pursuing their own interests. Contract is the paradigm form of such a law. There is a distinction between the public and the private, between the moral and the legal. This type of law is best expressed in individualistic, laissez-faire societies; each individual's interest being just one competing and sometimes overriding interest among many. One can see how equality becomes a key feature of this sort of society. Everyone is equal under the law and everyone is equal in the market. Everyone can do what they want under the abstract and universal rules which apply equally to everyone. 'Equality under the Law' is the slogan of these societies. And it is a powerful one. This is what make it an improvement on and an advance from feudal society which can be characterised as a *Gemeinschaft* society in terms of its ideal type. Here justice is substantial and expressive of the organic community. There is no distinction between public and private, between political, moral and legal issues. All are one in the community but differentiated by status. Capitalist society, with its emphasis on freedom and equality, cuts a swath through the old feudal society where everything depends on status. The individual is set free of the old status hierarchies which no longer bar his advancement. It is no wonder that Marx and the socialists saw capitalism as a progressive force in this era. But they also thought that a new form would replace this. Pashukanis and others, thought that this would be replaced by the 'socio-technical' norm and that this form of ordering would be based on considerations of substantive justice and the consideration of the actual person. Now this form of ordering was seen by Kamenka and Tay (1975) as 'bureaucratic administrative' which

> 'Seeks to regulate an activity and not to adjudicate in collisions between individuals; its fundamental concern is with consequences rather than with fault or *mens rea,* with public need or public interest, or the interest of the public activity itself, rather than private rights or individual duties.' (p. 139)

It is clear how this is a form that would be characteristic of welfare states and those where some overarching purpose (such as the construction of socialism) is given to the organisation of national life. When Pashukanis says law will wither away under communism, he means that *Gesellschaft* type law ought to be replaced by something like the bureaucratic administrative mode.

In some ways this is akin to the managerialism of Fuller and we can see how it would be inimical to the 'governance of rules'. We saw how Fuller thought of legality, in his notion of 'interactive law', as more than merely what (in Tay and Kamenka's terms) could be called law. However this is, as we saw, very allusive, and we can still see 'the governance of rules' as, to all intents and purposes, the law of the market, *Gesellschaft* law. On his view, mangerialism must have its own strictly demarcated spheres otherwise it could contaminate and take over the Rule of Law with disastrous consequences - so the moral case for the market.

But the contamination is not one way. Marx, through his notion of commodification, thought of the *Gesellschaft* form doing the same for welfare and disastrously transforming all our social relations. How ? We can see this if we look at some of the moral criticisms of capitalism and the case for Pashukanis. In *Past and Present*, Thomas Carlyle says,

> 'True, it must be owned, we for the present with our Mammon-Gospel, have come to strange conclusions. We call it a Society; and go about professing the totalest separation, isolation. Our life is not a mutual helpfulness; but rather, cloaked under due laws-of-war, named 'fair competition' and so forth, it is a mutual hostility. We have profoundly forgotten everywhere that Cash-payment

> is not the sole relation of human beings; we think nothing doubting, that it absolves and liquidates all engagements of man. 'My starving workers?' answers the rich Mill-owner: 'Did I not hire them fairly in the market? Did I not pay them, to the last sixpence the sum covenanted for? What have I to do with them more?' - Verily Mammon worship is a melancholy creed. When Cain for his own behoof had killed Abel, and was questioned, 'where is thy brother? He too made answer, 'Am I my brother's keeper?' Did I not pay my brother his wages, the thing he had merited from me?' (Apud Acton 1971: 11)

The claim here is that markets encourage greed instead of selflessness. Indifference to one's neighbour rather than concern. Selfishness and avarice is promoted to the level of a virtue.

Carlyle makes three claims about the way the market economy structures human relations. Firstly, there is the claim that I do not do things for others. I always do things for myself and say, without any justification, that this is the best for others. There is thus no community and no co-operation - everyone pursues their own self-interest. Moreover they have to. If they do not, the market mechanism will be upset and things will get worse. 'You can't buck the market'. It appears that a morally acceptable society can come out of something that, by most moral criteria, is considered a vice.

Acton (1971) attempts to answer this point. He claims that the market does not imply that one uses the economic necessity of the other to help oneself. It is merely the way the economic system works. One does not have to see market activity as 'using others to help oneself'. It could just as easily be conceptualised as 'doing something for someone else in order to satisfy myself'. Here we have something much more like the 'cool self love' of Bishop Butler (1950). The bottom line however, is satisfying yourself. In a sense everything depends on motivation. There obviously is a sense in which this sort of market ethos is morally acceptable. If it were not, we could not make sense of the Christian imagery of 'losing your life in order to gain it'. How far, however, someone can act selflessly for the sake of someone, while knowing it will be for their gain, is a fine question. And this is especially so in a system where the organisation of social life is based specifically and generally upon self interest. A self-interested society makes for a self-interested individual. The rise of the 'Yuppy' in the '80s is instructive. Again this appears to be a version of the theodicy of Chalmers.

Secondly, Carlyle claims that a market society is a competitive one, where 'the law of the jungle' replaces co-operation. This is a strong theme in the moral criticism of capitalism. Competitiveness generally is attacked as unworthy. For a while[47], this extended to discouraging competitive games as inculcating the wrong sort of values. Do they? One must, as Acton says, distinguish competition from rivalry. In rivalry people want to defeat each other as well as gain the prize. In competition this is not the case. Defeat of others is not wanted for its own sake. They are indifferent to the other competitors except as a means to the end of winning. 'The law of the jungle' with its connotations of Hobbes and anomia is a misnomer when talking about competition. There are rules in competition. It is not the case that 'anything goes' but rather that everything must be done according to the rules. Again, we are dealing with a question of motivation here. It is a fine point as to whether a society based on competition will not slide over into what Acton calls rivalry. In the real world there is a fine distinction between wanting to win; wanting to win and wanting the other person not to win; and finally just wanting the other person not to win[48]. Some of the activities of our more famous entrepreneurs fall into the latter category.

But it is in Carlyle's third point, which is about what a market structure does to human relations in general that we can see what Marx meant about commodification and the spread of the market. Accepting Acton's point about competition creates a problem of its own. For in competition one is indifferent to the other person - what is important is following the rules of the game. The other's success or failure is not a matter of your concern. Your only relation to your fellow competitors is as someone else following the rules. You only care that they follow them. It is, as Acton says approvingly, a rather impersonal relationship. But this is precisely what some see as the morally questionable. For we are completely indifferent to one another. Except in so far as we have obligations and duties to each other under the rules, we do not have to care. This is the attitude exemplified by Carlyle's mill owner.

We can see the equality and indifference that the market needs and promotes operating in the *Gesellschaft* order. It cuts through the old feudal society, attacking status and substituting the equality of all under the law. But how does this equality work? How can we consider people to be the same when they are so obviously profoundly different? What happens is that we strip away from them all the things in respect of which they are different. Finally we come to something in respect of which we can say they are the same and can be treated equally. But this is not something concrete. Rather it is the abstract concept of the legal person. It is as legal persons, the abstract bearers of rights and duties under the law, that we treat concrete people equally. Thus the real human person becomes an abstraction - a point at which

[47] Among the so called 'loony left'

[48] Many football supporters might recognise themselves in this.

is located a bundle of rights and duties. Other concrete facts about them are irrelevant for the law. What this amounts to is that the law ignores as irrelevant the circumstances and material conditions of the particular concrete individual. We are equally able to go to the Ritz in theory but only those with money actually can. We are all equally able to sleep under the bridges of the Seine. Treating unequals equally merely compounds inequality.

What is more, treating people as abstract makes them abstract (the way in which the commodity and the person merged in Pashukanis). They become things and not real living persons, who feel and care. You do not help a person but give them their rights. It becomes worthier to visit your dying mother in hospital because you have an obligation so to do rather than because you love her[49]. The person's attitude to self would also be affected. Self also disappears into this abstract point. The concrete person would not do anything only his abstract self would. He would not experience except in so far as the buyer and seller in the market, and thus the commodity, would. What is meant by this can be seen in the way art becomes corporate entertainment, sport is experienced on the TV etc. And here it is not the motivation of the person but the way that the nature of the market structures human relations that gives this effect. The things that bind us, the one to the other are no longer anything else than the prior web of rules that has defined our relations and our duties and rights to each other. Contract, what we owe and are owed to each other, becomes the paradigm of relationships here. We no longer ask, 'what do you need?, but 'what are you owed?' Marriage, on this view of it, becomes for Kant

> 'an agreement between two persons by which they grant each other equal reciprocal rights, each of them undertaking to surrender the whole of their person to the other with a complete right of disposal other it.' (1979: 167)

and thus for Hegel a contract for sexual use. This might now be expressed in the way in which, in the drive for justice in the marriage relation, there is a tendency, feared by feminist communitarians[50], of contractualizing that relationship. Cohabitation contracts try to pre-determine all the intimate

---

[49] See Anscombe (1958b)

[50] Mendus (1989) makes this argument. She sees contract as the pervading legitimatory form of liberal society. She suggests that feminists too readily accept this as appropriate for marriage.

See also Pateman (1984) who says:

'The conception of marriage as something contractual is part of the theoretical stock of liberalism...the keystone of the contractarian view of marriage is the doctrine that individuals have a right in one another's bodies. The right follows from a conception of individuals as owning the property they possess in their persons and bodies; one individual can thus have a rightful access to, or sexual use of, the body of another only with the consent or agreement of, or through a contract with the property owner. The marriage contract establishes legitimate access to the body of a spouse' (pp. 80-81)

details of ones life together and so define what love is. Marriage or a stable relationship becomes a form of flat sharing.

This structuring spreads for many reasons and just takes over all other forms mainly because of the force of the market and that form of ordering in our lives. But of course we can also see how this is also the case because it has moral merits - co-habitation contracts are not bad, their excess is[51]. This structuring scythed through the status relations of feudal life and *Gemeinschaft* forms of social ordering. And it will help us in dealing with more managerial forms of social ordering.

CONCLUSION

This phenomenon, also called juridification by Habermas (1986) and others[52], starts producing the legalistic morality that we talked of and structures its forms of life. So there is a distinct way of acting which is in that sense rule-like or legalistic. Recall the cash-line machine example we gave. You put your card in the machine and key in your PIN number. If you are in credit and various conditions have been fulfilled, then you get your money. But if you have no money or have already taken out your quota for the day, no cash is issued and there is no arguing. The machine does not see you, the person who might need the money there and then for all sorts of pressing and important reasons. The machine is not interested in you it only 'sees' the card. It sees (reads) that and it says that no money is to be given to you. What you think or what you can say is unimportant. You have now become the card. You no longer exist for the bank and it is only your card that exists. We have used the example of the machine to make the example more graphic. The machine could be the social security clerk as he or she applies the regulations, you as you follow the law.

It is in this way that love is negated by rules. For love and fellow feeling cannot get in the way of the operation of the rules. But of course, there is a plus side to all of this which we see if we take the perspective of the labourers in the parable of the Labourers in the Vineyard. Here the rationality of rules is all important. Think of the cash machine analogy again. Say these machines become tellers who care. They do not see you as the cash card. Rather they see you as someone in need. Their love goes out to you and they give you money. But if they keep doing this, listening to their feeling, then where will all the money come from? Will the bank have any left? What about the depositors? For the sake of helping a few they might have harmed the many.

---

[51] See Biggs (2000)

[52] See also Teubner (1986; 1987)

It is the rules and the machine-like activity of the law that keeps that in check. What one needs is a way of knowing when to stop acting like the machine and not follow the set patterns. When to let the person in the card break out. Or, to put it more prosaically, when creatively to break or re-think the law. Or to put it in market terms, when do we need non-market principles? The relation between these is what we turn to in the next chapter.

CHAPTER 6

THE LAW OF LOVE AND THE LOVE OF LAW[53]

INTRODUCTION

We saw in the last chapter what happened in this dichotomous way of thinking; that one way of life pushed out the other. Both sides have a problem with allowing in any of the other side. If we leave it to the cash-line machine of the last chapter, it will take over and we will never be able to break out of that cycle. The story recalls those science fiction dystopias where law application and enforcement is given over to the hands of a computer/robot. That machine takes over in such a way that humans cannot break in. It just applies its programmes in a relentless way with no regard to concrete reality. If this is too fantastic then think of what happened when world stock markets crashed. One of the causes was automated systems of selling - sell orders being automatically triggered at certain prices. This had a reinforcing effect and created a sort of amplification spiral which drove the price further down, which generated more sell orders and so on. This had its own inexorable logic and nothing could be done short of destroying the whole system by pulling the plugs out.

On the other side it is as though concrete individuals take over and nothing is able to control them. Once you say that sometimes the rules have to be ignored, you can never just follow them because in each case of applying them you have to decide whether to apply or ignore them. Hiding behind the rules means that you do not have to decide the raw moral questions each time - not a bad thing as we shall see. But if you say that in certain cases you do not have to hide behind the rules, what is going to tell you that this is such a case unless you look at each case? And then, why do you need the rules?

---

[53] I am grateful to my colleagues in the 'After Socialism Project' of the Centre for Theology and Public Issues' where this material was originally discussed. This is a reworked version of some material that appeared in the outcome of that project as 'Beyond Fear' (Morton 1998). I wish to thank Andrew Morton, Steve Barron, Graham Blount and John Hughes for making that two year project so stimulating and friendly.

Put in this way the view on both sides is that market and welfare, law and love, cannot be conjoined. It is a zero sum game, having one implies the absence of the other. Thus the market is said to drive out welfare and love in our society and a welfarist society is said to drive out law and legality. But it is not as simple as that. It is not one or the other and furthermore, it is not a transcending synthesis either. In this chapter we explain how one cannot separate love from law; how they are not mutually opposed but that the latter is implicated in the former; how the arbitrary explosion of love carries within it the seeds and bonds of rationality. This is what we mean by saying that what appear to be the anti-nomian values implicit in welfare mesh with the nomian values found in the law and the market.

PARABLES OF LAW AND LOVE

We begin our explanation with the parable of the Good Samaritan[54]. The context of this parable is that Jesus is seen as consorting with those, such as publicans and sinners, who stand outside the Law and in doing this putting himself outside of the Law. It will not do, as we saw, to say that this is precisely what is intended and that Christ came to overturn the Law with love. But nor does it mean the opposite. The story starts off with a lawyer asking Jesus what he should do to gain eternal life and Jesus gives an answer impeccably in terms of the Law - 'Love God and thy Neighbour as thyself'. For Jesus came to 'fulfil the law' but that does not mean that the arbitrariness of love or welfare is left out. Were that the case, it would mean treating the parable, as Ld Atkin did (see chapters 4 & 8) as supplying a definition of neighbour which can then be applied to other cases. But one can also look at the parable in another way - not as laying down a definition of neighbour but saying that that person is your neighbour to whom you act in a neighbourly manner. You constitute the relation of neighbourliness by your actions. The

---

[54] 'On one occasion a lawyer came forward to put this test question to him: 'Master, what must I do to inherit eternal life?' Jesus said, 'What is written in the Law? What is your reading of it?' He replied, 'Love the Lord your God with all your heart, with all your soul, with all your strength, and with all your mind; and your neighbour as yourself.' 'That is the right answer,' said Jesus; 'do that and you will live.'

But he wanted to vindicate himself, so he said to Jesus, 'And who is my neighbour?' Jesus replied, 'A man was on his way from Jerusalem down to Jericho when he fell in with robbers, who stripped him, beat him, and went off leaving him half dead. It so happened that a priest was going down by the same road; but when he saw him, he went past on the other side. So too a Levite came to the place, and when he saw him went past on the other side. But a Samaritan who was making the journey came upon him, and when he saw him was moved to pity. He went up and bandaged his wounds, bathing them with oil and wine. Then he lifted him on to his own beast, brought him to an inn, and looked after him there. Next day he produced two silver pieces and gave them to the innkeeper, and said, 'Look after him; and if you spend any more, I will repay you on my way back.' 'Which of these three do you think was neighbour to the man who fell into the hand of the robbers?' He answered, 'The one who showed him kindness.' Jesus said, 'Go and do as he did.' Luke 10: 25-37

parable says that neighbourliness is something that you actively do rather than a definition that you passively apply. But surely this begs the question? You still have to know whom it is that you have to be neighbourly to before you can constitute the neighbour relation by your act. That is true, but we must not see them as separate elements for they are in reality two sides of the same coin.

Let us take an analogy from cosmology. On a version of the 'big bang' theory of the universe, one might say that the universe starts from the explosion of a singularity. That explosion is arbitrary - there is no reason for it. Yet that explosion carries within, in its unfolding, rationality in the shape of time and scientific laws. For causality and all of scientific rationality are inscribed within that explosion and unfold in it. Scientific rationality might stem from an arbitrary act, the explosion, but that does not make it irrational for the rational is inscribed in the arbitrary and vice versa. Take a more prosaic example: people ask if they can stay with you to visit the Edinburgh Festival. You offer them hospitality and invite them to stay and use you home as a base. If this is not too pretentious, you have given out of your love something that they need. But that, as we know only too well, is not the end of it. For your guests then ask if they can take you out to dinner, and though you might not want to go, your obligation as host makes you do that. But it does not stop there. Because you know the town, and they do not, then you have to find a restaurant which will be appropriate, in the right price range etc. etc. So the first act of love (there was no particular reason why you should let them stay in your house) carries inscribed within it the bonds and the rationality of the host relation. The law is already inscribed in the act of generosity and one cannot escape it. A useful, though not full, analogy would the rescue cases in English and Scottish Law[55]. Roughly, though there is no duty to rescue, once someone starts trying to help another the law relating to negligence applies. The arbitrary act of rescue comes within the realms of the law; it has the law inscribed within it and one cannot get away from it.

In the parable, the lawyer asked the question to catch Jesus out by getting him to say that the law does not matter. This Jesus does not do - on the contrary, to gain eternal life one must follow the law. However there is more – this does not exhaust the question. One must go further than applying the legal definition, one must connect with those who in terms of the law are not your neighbours (the Jews and the Samaritans were enemies). One makes that connection by one's love in acting in a neighbourly manner. The Good Samaritan applies the rule 'love thy neighbour' to someone who only becomes a neighbour in that application, and thus by that loving act within the purview

[55] See Menlowe and McCall Smith (1993)

of rules and rationality. The application, as a mysterious explosion of love, carries within it the bonds of rules and rationality. The loving act was part of the lawful act. And it is the intertwining of the two that make the act appropriate – not one or the other.

If we look at the parable of the Labourers in the Vineyard we will see that it is not so simple either. For the Master, in replying to the Labourers also uses pro-market terms. For he asks them why they are complaining when they have all contracted freely with him. And yet at the same time that is undercut when he says, 'Or do you begrudge my generosity?'. For the market principles of the rules of duty and obligation only operate because of 'my generosity'. Put less parabolically, liberal societies like ours, which rely on the close intertwining of the Rule of law and of the market, can only be kept going by institutions which are not of that kind. The market and legality are not self-generating and depend upon institutions which are not like them. They depend on acts of love and generosity. The trust and love necessary to keep the system going cannot be generated internally since this is precisely what the market eschews[56]. It is however a dialectical process. In terms of our previous imagery: we need the big bang and that big, arbitrary explosion is the obverse of the system rationality which both needs it and is sustained by it and, lest we want to throw system rationality away altogether, is sustained by that very rationality. Let us return to cosmological theory again. To explain the beginnings of the universe is not just a matter of explaining how a string of black paint came to be on an empty white canvas. We have to explain how the canvas and frame came to be there as well. And one of explanation of that would be that the explosion of black paint creates the frame and canvas which then also creates and determines the paint. But for society a one off explosion is not enough. Society can only be sustained by a continuous explosion of acts of love which both sustain that society and determine the acts of love. We turn now to explore this.

MARKETS, LOVE AND COMMUNITY

We now turn to the interconnections between the market and love and what that means for community. Part of the problem is that those who follow Hayek forget that at some level the market is justified in terms of outcome. The trickle down effect is supposed to make everyone better off. It seems illogical to say we cannot intervene because we do not know individual preferences but at the same time when we know general outcomes, and they are not what we claimed the system would generate, to refuse to intervene. If the justification

---

[56] See Fukayama (1996)

for doing nothing is because we cannot *know* then, when we *do* know, we should do something.

The problem is that in some respects the internal workings of the market, that way of getting rational outcomes through individual selfishness, carries over to the reason we might have had the market in the first place, that is to produce a sort of collective love (contrary to some of the social contract and possessive individualistic stories). We can see studies[57] that show how the market production of the notion of equality enables us to produce intimacy and friendship that is no longer dependent on power relations. Thus we can now be enjoined to love not merely through helping the poor. And we can produce the collective security that enables us to deal with poverty and we do not need it to practise our love. In recent times Scandinavian systems, especially the Swedish ones, have been leading examples of that.

Now this might be seen to be attacking the image of the parable of the Good Samaritan with which we started. For that seems to depend upon a pre-modern conception of community where people needed love because they were poor and thus were dependent and vulnerable. And the rich needed the poor to save themselves through practising acts of charity. 'Give us this day our daily bread' is now, in the West at least, replaced by love and intimacy which are based on equality and respect. And this enables us to have general love in abolishing the poor and creating collective security which partly comes through the manipulation of the market. But it would be a mistake to think of the parable as enjoining us to practice charity through helping the poor.

But the relations portrayed in the parable are deeper and more profound than merely an injunction to love the poor. They have much to say about the profound interconnections between law and love. Firstly, as we saw, the answer given in the parable is impeccably within the law but is not thereby privileging it. Nor does what is said amount to the idea that sometimes law is not enough and that love is necessary. We can see this if we look at a second point. The parable is given in answer to the question put by the lawyer: 'Who is my neighbour'. The lawyer is asking from the security of the law a question as to whom should one extend the comfort and safety and privilege that exists in the law. Jesus turns this upside down and looks, not from the point of view of the law, but from the point of view of need. His question becomes something like; 'to whom should one turn when in the direst need, thereby extending the hand of brotherhood and community?' The answer that Jesus gives is shocking and challenging. For the one you are to love, to make your

---

[57] See Wolfe (1989)

neighbour is not the 'man fallen among thieves' but the Samaritan. So you are not meant to love the poor but the rich![58]

What can this mean? This is not part of the master/slave dialectic nor are the poor being asked to love those who help them because they help them. It is a much deeper and profound relationship than that. What is being said is that one should not think of the law as providing safety. The man fallen among thieves was a Jew and in possession of the law but that did not thereby guarantee him safety. He needed someone outside the law to sustain him in the law. Law is not enough and you need love to sustain it. But that gift of love itself cannot be seen as the strong helping the weak. For in that act of giving the Samaritan makes himself weak (helping the injured traveller was dangerous for the Samaritan – it could have been a trick to catch him unawares and rob him as the road from Jerusalem to Jericho was a mugging opportunity for some) and he depends upon the law to make him strong.

And so, as we saw at the end of the last section, law and love both need each, are both locked together. Moreover, Jesus is speaking to the lawyer and is asking him to consider this. So he is asking the lawyer to think of himself in need and dependent and to seek from those whose response might be unwelcome and unexpected. And what that is saying is that we should consider community not as a group of autonomous self sufficient individuals but as people who are vulnerable and need each other. And even if we consider ourselves autonomous and self-sufficient, we are to consider ourselves in need. Finally then the lesson is that no-one is strong and that we must all consider ourselves equal in our vulnerability.

Why is this apposite to the Swedish case? Part of the Swedish system in relating benefits to work gives everyone an incentive to stay in state systems of insurance and not opt for private ones. So giving benefits to all in work or not and not just targeting them to the needy means that there is an incentive to keep these benefits and the state care systems that they engender. Thus collective security enables poverty to be dealt with. Targeting to the 'needy' gives those who have the money and influence no incentive to fight for state benefits and therefore they tend to be lower in those systems. But does this collective security mean we no longer have to love? Thinking that we do not is precisely what the parable warns us about. We can accept that it was ideas of equality produced by the market that generated the acts of love necessary for producing the system of collective security. The parable warns us that its strength and security is an illusion. There will be a problem if that is to be

---

[58] See for similar readings of this parable Davis (1997) and White (1989)

sustained by the system rationality of self-preference. A paradox is thereby generated. For that also does away with the individual acts of love that are necessary in a system where there is no collective care. For now people might begin to think that they no longer need to care since there is a collective security system - I no longer have to care because we have produced a system that will care for all of us. It is much easier 'to walk on the other side of the street' because we know that the system will care. But the more that happens and the less we individually care, then the less will we see the need for the collective system which is in the end paid for by institutionalised generosity, our taxes. For we will see taxes not as the 'gift of welfare' for all but as an imposition. Paying taxes will be a burden and 'forced labour'[59] and not an act of love and so systems of collective security will begin to collapse[60]. People do not care because they care collectively but they only care collectively because they care individually and so we have a vicious circle. The explosions of love which are needed to keep re-inventing the rationality of the system in general are missing. In organising in terms of the system rationality of self-preference we loose the need for them. And that is where the point about equality in vulnerability comes in. For it is in that that we recognise our fragilities no matter what system we design and that which can spur us to perform the individual acts of charity (love) that sustain the collective system. This points to the need for a thriving voluntary sector in care and welfare, and also to a thriving civil society in general. And this is not to replace collective security nor to give people the opportunity to salve their consciences but something that is necessary to keep the collective system going[61].

THE MORALS OF THE MARKET AND THE MORALS OF WELFARE IN INSTITUTIONAL PRACTICE.

We now turn to some of the effect of these points in institutional practice. Let us look more closely at the law and the trial. What are the implications of some of the points I have been making? Within the trial, we might say that this process makes the defender invisible. What does this mean? Chesterton (1960)

[59] See Nozick (1975)

[60] In this sense one might say that Thatcherism was generated by the Welfare State.

[61] People fail to see this point when they castigate individual acts of charity as doing nothing since they do not get at the real problem - they only alleviate the problem of poverty and do not look at its causes so that it can be cured. But people need to recognise that there is poverty and that people are poor or there will be no incentive (or indeed point) in devising a cure. We have to see someone as poor and reach out to them, at one in our vulnerability, for us to begin to try and work out systems of preventing poverty. People do not often say they do not want to help the poor they deny there are poor – they are invisible to them. Unless we, or some do this, we walk by on the other side of the street and deny the problem and so do not think of the cure. We need both the individual act and the system. One might say this is why people such as Mother Teresa, and Princess Diana, are necessary.

in his detective stories makes this clear. In one he gives us the classic locked room mystery. Someone is murdered in a locked room, the sole entrance to which has been kept under observation. No one was seen. Who did it? The answer is the postman because no one noticed him. Since he was always there he was invisible. Think of the way some people have treated, and treat, their servants. They are people who perform certain functions and who never get in the way - never appear to be there. People would say that they were alone when in fact surrounded by servants. Indeed this ability to treat the servant as invisible was seen as a mark of the upper class[62]. The trial process is analogous. The defender in the trial is not the concrete human of the concrete world. He is, as I described above, a legal person, the abstract bearer of rights and duties. This means that nothing is relevant in the trial except those things which are relevant to proving liability. Political, moral and social opinions, particular concrete circumstances that the person finds themselves in are excluded. He has no history because the only thing that is at stake is liability in respect of the rules. The things that he might see as important are often ruled as irrelevant because they do not determine liability. That is all that is at stake. The trial becomes what Garfinkel (1955) calls a degradation ceremony. What this does is strip real persons of all their concrete humanity so that they become literally invisible, unnoticed and irrelevant. The classic examples of this are in 'closed institutions' such as mental homes. There the inmates might just as well not exist though they are the *raison d'etre* of the institution. Some research in the courtroom has been struck by the almost literal irrelevance of the defender. The trial could go on just as well without him or her (Bańkowski and Mungham (1976).

The above is one way of describing the trial process. But another way would be to say that this invisibility protects the defender. Because it prevents prejudice as to the particular sort of person they are from determining the result. The defender is not subjected to a humiliating trial where all aspects of their life and history are looked at and exposed to public view. Indeed, if we look at rape trials, the complaint has been that there is not enough of this indifference which above was seen as morally questionable. Here the moral question is whether an innocent women's sexual history should be paraded before the world and all sorts of erroneous inferences drawn from it. The trial process is aimed at preventing that happening. And that is the down side of caring. In the trial context caring can too often degenerate into a journey to the inmost soul of those involved.

[62] See Bańkowski and Mungham (1976: 87-104)

Let us now turn to health provision. In the Gift Relation, Titmuss (1980) compares the free donation of blood with the selling of blood and what consequences it has for welfare. For him the turning of blood into a commodity means that nothing is sacred and that

> 'All policy would become in the end economic policy, and the only values that would count are those that are measured in terms of money and pursued in the dialectic of hedonism. Each individual would act egoistically for the good of all by selling his blood' (p. 12).

The implications of this are that the relation between doctor and patient would change if the system of health care were market-based. Treating someone as a customer rather than a patient will have certain consequences. The relation changes from 'caring' to 'providing services for a client'. 'Defensive medicine' is more prevalent in a market system. Here, treatment is not merely dependent on the doctor's judgement of need but also in order to avoid law suits in the future. Litigation is much more common in America than it is here[63]. Medicine is pushed into areas where money will be made rather than where there is real need. Cosmetic surgery becomes more important. The relationship of trust disappears to be replaced by the wary relationship of the man of business.

Should the health service be like that? We might think not, but are we not being naive when we think that in the non-market system we will always be able to trust doctors. Here, all the problems of professional power are raised again. We must bear in mind the fears, raised by Hayek and others, that we discussed earlier. What will happen in a society where those who think they know best dictate to others? True, the actual structure of the relationship will change. But is that necessarily bad?

One final example. Lawyers are often held to make the painful process of conjugal separation worse. One reason for this is that they will practise 'defensive lawyering'. The parties might come to an informal and amicable arrangement where one gets less than they are legally entitled to. Defensive lawyering means they will be advised of the full extent of their rights. This might create suspicion and tension. It might produce a fight where before there was agreement. Is this bad? We might not want to make divorce harder. But how do we know that the informal arrangement is truly acceptable if both sides do not know their real rights? In the long run, it might make matters worse.

---

[63] We can see this changing as the British NHS changes in a more market direction

In the former societies of Eastern Europe, non-market principles were applied everywhere, including economy and law. In the West, there was, and indeed still is, an attempt to marketise all fields of social life, including the 'caring' institutions. For the Marxists, the commodity form (the market principle) tended to spread and infect all forms of social life. For the liberals, command economy principles tended to spread and drive out the other forms. This might be true as a matter of sociological and historical fact. Powerful institutions in society do spread their values and their ways of going about things. But it need not necessarily be the case. Society is not a site of logically contradictory or counter principles where the one drives out and hides the other. To the contrary, social life and its institutions are based upon a mixture of principles which are in tension, one with the other. Particular social institutions will resolve this tension in different ways. They will balance the principles in particular ways in differing concrete circumstances. But this will not be a compromise in the sense that more of one will mean less of the other. The point is that this will not be a compromise in the sense that having more welfare means less legality etc. When we come to looking at political institutions we will not necessarily justify them by the grand and abstract principles of 'freedom' or 'welfare'. Thus the market definition of absence of coercion will not be the one always applied. Freedom from poverty, freedom to organise, etc. will also be in play. These particular freedoms will be pursued at particular times and places and will be weighed against each other. Likewise with welfare, this will mean different things in differing circumstances and differing concepts will be balanced against each other. State intervention in declining areas no more breaches the market principle than does aspects of the market in health and education. The problems of choice that arise in political life will not be susceptible to reduction to one principle or another[64].

When we look at institutions in our society then the question is not the abstract one of whether market or welfare principles are best. We cannot rule out market or welfare principles per se. The solution to problems of professional power will depend on the particular circumstances involved. Solving them by marketisation or 'customer power' will not be appropriate in all cases. Compare students, patients, passengers and prisoners. Should all the areas involved, education, health, transport and the prison system, have customers instead? Do market principles for the distribution of goods necessarily detract from the principle of care? Is it the same in health and education?[65]

---

[64] see Hindess (1987)

[65] see Le Grand and Estrin (1989); Dworkin (1985); Raz (1986)

Legality will not prevent child abuse, but it might prevent social workers abusing the rights of children and their parents. Legality and the welfare principle are both necessary. Legality is not compromised by the introduction of lay justice and welfare principles, rather the institutions of social regulation are thereby made stronger[66]. Both are necessary.

JUMPING OUT OF THE MACHINE

One can put this in another image. Law and love articulate together in such a way that one can say that their articulation brings something else into existence. We may call that legality which consists of the articulation of legalism and [love]. In that articulation both lose their negative aspects by being dependent upon each other. This is what I meant earlier in the book when I said the law should not be seen as heteronomous and morals as autonomous but rather law and morals should both be seen as a mixture of heteronomous and autonomous aspects. And that is what I meant by lawful, used in the connotation of *Recht*. Thus legality consists in the articulation of autonomous and heteronomous systems. We need heteronomy as well as autonomy. We cannot collapse the one into the other. We need to be dependent upon people, we are beings that need other people and cannot live without them. But this dependency means that we must not think of ourselves as wholly autonomous, dependent upon our will alone. Nor does it mean that we have to surrender our autonomy and live a wholly heteronomous life. We are neither slave nor lord of all. The law seems to have a universality that takes it away from that concrete case into a system rationality of its own. Here we are concerned with how the autonomy of the concrete case can break into system rationality and not be swallowed up. How we can look at system rationality and concrete autonomy without downgrading either.

Take marriage as an example. We can, according to Luhmann (1986), oppose marriage with love or passion. Love is spontaneous and always questions itself. It is always in the present, the future does not exist for it. It operates in the now. It is uncoupled from external relations, it is contingent and a matter of fate. The lover does not ask how or what it will do or where it will lead. It is a grace and those questions are irrelevant. The lover is just grateful for the love. He or she does everything because of love. There is no need for duty or obligation. At the same time love consumes everything, it thematizes the whole relationship. Everything that the lovers do, all the everyday decision that they take, even the most banal (should we have corn

[66] See Bańkowski, MacManus, and Hutton (1987)

flakes for breakfast?), is taken as going to the roots of the relationship and questioning it. Marriage, on the other hand, loses passion or love. Marriage wants to make something eternal, not something in the present. Marriage wants to reduce spontaneity and make things simpler. It operates to 'calm this grand passion', to reduce spontaneity and cut out chance. To make it possible to live because every decision does not thematize the whole of the relationship. It thus denies love. Marriage then routinises. It is boring and lacks the warmth of love. Love often transforms itself into marriage because this is the way love stabilises itself. But in so doing it loses that love and is no longer connected to it. We are doomed to be slaves or lovers.

This way of looking at it seems precisely analogous to our problem. It appears that we can be heteronomous or autonomous but not both. I want to argue the contrary. Love comes not from autonomous passion but from the articulation of that passion with the heteronomous nature of marriage. It is then that we can say that there is love. It is the way in which we join these strands. In a marriage or a long term relationship we can recognise certain phases. Sometimes at the beginning, people are so 'in love' that they do everything together, operate as a single unit. Then, realising that this is not the best way, they act autonomously but as though they were completely separate - one would be amazed to find out they were married. They only realise the relationship properly when they come to some way of yoking these together. When they move from the first stage of 'undifferentiated unity' and the second stage of 'differentiated disunity' to the stage of differentiated unity'[67]

Let us turn to the cash machine again. I put the card in and it tells me that I cannot get any money out. I start to argue with the machine, for my need is pressing and urgent. I beg the machine to give, out of its love, money for my need - but to no avail. Then, hearing my desperate pleas, the teller comes out. But, as we have seen, that is also a machine. He says no for that is the way the law must operate. The teller never gets beyond the smart card. But what, if no matter what decision he comes to, he considers the matter? Then the converse is the case. For then he is jumping beyond the smart card and reaching me, the concrete voice crying out of need for love. He then breaks through the smart card. For the decision he made is particular, at a particular time in concrete circumstances. Even if he says no, he has lost touch with the smart card and is only in touch with me. On the one hand he is locked in the universality of the smart card and on the other he is locked into the particular case.

---

[67] See Cohen (1974). See also Hegel (1948)

We might say that it is better that he be locked in love for that at least is better than the machine. What is so restrictive about being locked in the particular? Surely the point of love is that it knows no bounds; that it is always ready to move beyond and help? Surely it is better for the teller to be there? But we have to be careful for there is also danger there. There the teller can become restricted by the boundaries of his will and not see beyond it. There he can become locked into a private realm, that of his own experience. This precludes the rational discussion of any moral or political arguments for there is no public space where we can discuss our disagreements in some articulate way - they are nothing more than disagreements. He becomes solipsistic in the sense that there is no access to any, in this case moral, reality outside of what he wants - that becomes the sole defining feature of his love for there is nothing else. Worse, the realisation of this can work in the opposite way and thrust him back to where he started - the law[68]. Scott Veitch (1997) in talking of the retreat into particularity puts it like this.

> '...the effect of this retreat is most profound where the viability of meaningful agreement or disagreement is seen to have been largely excluded because of the way that moral expressions have been conceptualised. According to Alasdair MacIntyre, for example, such "emotivism" works to preclude rational discussion and resolution of ethical - and to the extent that this includes questions of social justice, political - controversies which liberal societies face.' (p. 98)

Veitch goes on to argue that for MacIntyre this implies that moral conflicts get referred for their resolution back to law - back to the secure way out. For MacIntyre this means that in such societies, and by this he means liberal societies, there is not the possibility of rational philosophical debate about what to do. These societies are thrown back on to the law, whose point its precisely to cut off debate, as the only means of resolving such disputes. That becomes incoherent in its own terms precisely because it cannot cut across all these private islands. The communitarian answer to this, that MacIntyre and others tend to, is to see rational philosophical debate in the context of a tradition and thus get the universalism that way. In some ways, this answer merely, as we have seen, replicates the problem. For the community itself becomes one and the state of being locked in one's own desires, the "emotivism" that MacIntyre speaks of, is transferred to the community. Politically that leads to a form of homogeneity and denial of the pluralism that liberal societies want. 'Rational' philosophical debate becomes locked within the context of the community which all too often becomes identified with the

---

[68] One merely has to look at the careers of many of the 60's radicals to see this.

leader or leaders who are in power - for they and the community are one and when they speak in its name we also speak.

To see more concretely what this can do, and what harm it can cause both socially and personally, let us go back to the bank teller again. Consider Hamish X, a bank manager on an island in the Scottish Highlands[69]: Hamish has worked in his branch of the bank for many years and becomes a much loved and well respected figure in the community. Over the years he begins to care deeply for the customers he serves and wants their well being. So much so that when they come to him asking for loans for various ventures, he is willing to lend them money even though, strictly speaking this is going against the rules of the bank's small loans department. He does it because he feels for the members of the community, which he has now become part of, and wants to give them success. He does not want to let what he thinks of as the petty rules of officials in Edinburgh prevent his making life better for his people. Here then is a bank teller/manager who cares; who metaphorically steps out of the cash-line machine into the world of the particular; who touches with his love the need and welfare of the concrete customer.

What then, can we make of the inevitable failure of Hamish's mission? There are three aspects to consider. Firstly, one can see it as a scenario rather like that of, something common in recent years, the 'rogue trader'. Someone who uses the bank's money, unauthorised, for purposes of his own - only in this case not for themselves and not for personal gain. However, if Hamish goes too far we might extrapolate a similar sort of outcome; the collapse of the bank through unauthorised exposure of funds. Here then love destroys possibilities of distributive justice for it is loaning all the funds in one way without looking at the whole picture. Thus it makes it impossible to distribute any more funds (the bank collapses) and treat the other customers equally -it destroys the universal. However that is not all; for if that alone was the case then the argument would be circular - after all, the point of the exercise is not to apply equality as a form of universality (see chapter 5). More seriously, it precludes the possibility of treating the others at all - there is no money left. And this is not the Thatcherite version of the parable of the Good Samaritan, that the only reason the Samaritan was able to help was because he had money. The point here is that unless you employ some universalist criterion, then your love shown by noticing and responding to one concrete particular means that you will not be able to respond to any others.

---

[69] I owe this example to Neil MacCormick

This leads to a profound problem. For one could argue further that the love that leads me to include the concrete particular within it, necessarily leads to the exclusion of some other particular. My love is always turning inward. This is not just a moral point about the danger of love turning into mere self-love but rather one about love as a form of inclusion being necessarily a form of exclusion. I cannot love everyone for giving myself to one person, in this way, means not giving myself to another. In social terms this can also be applied to national identity and what has been called by Nussbaum (1996) patriotism. The fact that people are my co-nationals is morally relevant in my dealings. My love of country and therefore of them excludes others[70].

So far we have looked at it from the point of the bank and thus, in terms of our metaphor, as a destruction of the universal which thereby destroys other particulars not touched by the love. Even here some hard headed people might say that this is just life; that we can pick and choose whom we love; there should be nothing more. Notice that this is not like the views of the market-right that we saw before. For though they might hold to the view that love is arbitrary in this way, they would also link people through the universalism of the market and law. What I have in mind here is a form of brutal anarchism. But ironically, one can also see that form of selfishness, love turning into self love in forms of the communitarian alternative - in the sense that the community, as we saw above and as we shall discuss later, becomes the all-embracing final context, only those within count and everyone else is excluded.

I now turn to the second aspect that we have to consider in the story of Hamish X. Here we deal with the problems for the concrete particulars that have been included in his love. Things are not so simple for them either. They have been given the money but for some of them it has not been very helpful - for the schemes that they had in mind were very risky and not really likely to be successful. They were ways of getting out of what seemed an impossible situation, to try and recover themselves and save the community which otherwise would be in danger of dying out. Hamish did not apply the rules which had been given from the centre - the community and its people had touched him and he had responded to their concreteness. The result in the end was that their plans failed, they ended up in a worse position than they had been in before and the community was even more devastated. So everyone was worse off. To take a more actual example, sometimes there is no point in funding a co-operative run by the workers of a failed industry when the reasons for the failure of the industry are not to do with the mode of ownership

---

[70] I deal with this in terms of the European Union and European Identity in chapter 10 where I look at the possibility of inclusive identities.

but general and global conditions. They will not only be worse off but they will also lose their meagre redundancy money.

We now turn to the third and final aspect of the failure of Hamish X. There is a parallel with the rogue trader to be made. Hamish is not using the money for personal gain in the sense of wealth but he is using it, in a certain sense, for himself. What he is doing is feeding an image of himself, that of the benevolent carer and helper of this Highland community. He is so locked into that vision of himself that he is trapped in it and will not listen to reason. He will help them not so much because he cares for them but because he cares for his image of himself as a kind and caring man. In the end he is deeply selfish and his actions destroy the community and himself.

CONCLUSION

We saw then in the last section how unless we articulate the spheres of legalism and love we run the risk of being stuck in one or the other. Neither prospect, as we saw, being particularly attractive. The problem is analogous to the marriage example. What counts as 'differentiated unity' as opposed to 'differentiated disunity' to the stage of 'undifferentiated unity'?

The link is the risk that we take in moving out of both of those spheres and dealing with them 'in the middle' and it is that that creates the unity. We shall see that the unity is always there but it is always being remade. In a sense we might say that the middle is the unity for it is the space created by the moving out of self contained spheres, and where seemingly opposed principles are held in coherent tension. It is there that we can live in and out of law and love. Before we examine this further, we turn to look at rules and the machine more closely.

CHAPTER 7

DON'T THINK ABOUT IT

INTRODUCTION

In Kafka's story *In the Penal Settlement* an explorer chances across a prison camp far away. There, one of the instruments of punishment is a machine that works justice by inscribing the punishment on the body of the convict. Things are changing but the custodian of the machine still fiercely believes in it, patching it up with makeshift parts. He is so in its thrall, that when it appears to be breaking down, he submits himself to it to show its purity. It works on him and falls apart, carving out on the body of the unfortunate custodian, the phrase 'Be Just'.

This is a particularly brutal version of the machine image running through the book; one that appears to inscribe justice on the body politic and ethics on to our personal lives. The image with which the last two chapters ended was that of the cash-line machine and the teller might be that custodian. He submits himself to the machine for that encompasses his world and gives him safety and security. So much so that he does not notice the damage that it is doing to him until he is dead. The machine cannot exist with anything else, either its answer works by imposing itself on the world or it falls apart and perhaps takes the world with (see the automated sell orders in chapter 6).

But we saw that the teller who saw and wanted to 'jump out of the machine' was not particularly successful in his attempts – he jumped out only to be locked into the other sphere. All that that can be done, it appears, is a never ending cycle of law and love with no connection between the two. To the contrary, I suggested that there was in fact a connection which was, in general terms, a risky articulation of love and law; risky because one can never know where that might lead to. I look at the mechanics of that in later chapters. In previous chapters I have concentrated on images of love. In this chapter and the following two I look more to the image of the universal rule in terms of the metaphor of the machine. In so doing, I hope the articulation that I referred to will become easier to conceive.

LIVING WITH THE MACHINE

I) Judge Dredd

I have so far given images of what it appears to be locked in on either side of the dichotomy. But the image I have been using for rule might be thought to be unfair. For I have been likening rules and their all encompassing universality to machines, as though living the life of rules is entering into the machine; in my metaphor, the cash-line machine. This seems to be a very negative way of looking at it. I am painting the picture of a society that we are accustomed to, one with rules, as one to be likened to a machine. This brings to mind Hobbes' vision of the machine-like society of the Leviathan and its seeming totalitarianism and, nearer to home, a common Marxist vision of capitalist society; that of a locomotive running along with the safety valve jammed unable to stop. An image of something uncontrollable crushing all before it.

What I want to do now is to explore the metaphor of the machine a little further; to see in what sense the machine image is appropriate and how, exploring this, the machine and love fit together. Through this examination, I hope to come to a clearer view of what is important about rules, and their relation to love, for our life. The last chapter looked at this from the starting point of love. In this chapter I want to start from the other side, from the machine. In doing this I will make the machine metaphor more specific and concrete and use, as an image of the machine, that of the computer. This is not only because the cash-line machine is a computer but because the use of computers in law is a topic of academic and technical controversy. Through an examination of that we might get a better idea of the place of rules, and a particular image of rules, in our society.

Why then does the prospect of computers doing more and more things in our society and especially in law scare us? We get the idea of computers gradually taking over the world, all decisions having to go to the computer that runs the world. When we apply this to law, we have images of some Frankenstein-like machine taking over; one which is programmed rigidly to apply the law - only caring that it is technically correct and not caring if the decision that it enforces and applies is manifestly bad. We see this in a genre of films such as 'Cyberborg' and 'Robocop'. 'Judge Dredd' is an interesting film in this genre where the 'machine' is actually human. Here we have a dystopia and a cadre of police (judges) enforcing a harsh law in a breaking-down society. One of these appears too fanatical and rigid in his enforcement of the law . At the same time he is admired and seen as something of a role model. He is framed. It transpires that he was the result of a secret cloning project which structured him genetically with a love for justice and right - but this ended up as a fanatic love of the rules and application of them. Nothing else gets in the way - not even the love interest! His discovery of the secret of his creation leads not only to his being cleared but also to his being offered an important position in the reformed organisation. He rejects it and goes back to being a policeman enforcing the law. He rides off to enforce the law. But the ending is ambiguous. We are not sure if he has left the woman behind and how he will now enforce the law. Here we have the conflict between love and rules. We will see how this story mirrors some of our problems and the solutions I propose. When we think of applying computers to the law, something like the above scenario occurs. We worry that computers will take over; that things that seem to define humans like creativity and love will not only be downgraded but sacrificed at the altar of rigid rule application. We will be held in the machine's grip, unable get beyond its parameters. We will become like it rather than it like us.

ii) Expert Systems

I now turn to another example connected with the idea of expert systems in the law, which I hope will make the above clearer. The idea here is that through the formal representation of law, one will be able to programme it into a computer thus facilitating legal reasoning. There are those who think we can achieve computer driven systems of working out legal problems or minimally playing a great role in helping legal experts to solve them. They believe that there are computer programmes '..capable of functioning at the standard of (and sometimes even at a higher standard than) human experts in given fields'[71]. Crudely, the main argument being that law is in principle calculable and the difficulties, albeit great, are in essence technical. Much of the argument against this view comes down to a claim that this view of law is false. It is only because the computer enthusiasts see law as reducible in some way to rules that they can make the claims they do. If they were not fixated by rules they would see the deep conceptual problems with their enterprise. I do not want here to take part in that jurisprudential debate. It is clear that rules play some part in law and there are expert systems being constructed that seek to take non-rule parts into account. The main point to note is that the systems, whatever they are using as their data base, are trying to formalise it and to that

[71] Susskind (1987)

extent introduce more certainty, predictability and transparency into the system.

Expert systems are designed, according to Zeleznikow and Hunter (1992), for three main types of users; for lawyers, in which case it is a form of 'advanced interactive textbook' (p. 96) since it assumes the lawyer will still do much legal interpretation with what she gets out of the system. Secondly; for paralegals and administrators as, for example, helping social security clerks advise their clients. This does not go into complex answers but deals with most enquiries in a more certain and less time-consuming fashion. At the final level, for the general public, they say that no such system yet exists. Here we have to deal with much more open ended enquiries and no expertise - which means that there will also be the grave problems of translating from natural language into legal language.

Much of the criticism of legal expert systems can be summarised by the argument that the world is a complicated place; law is just to complex to be able to capture it accurately into a legal expert system - it will necessarily simplify the law. Why? Because rules are vague and ambiguous; they are concerned with value and interpretation at all levels; there are just too many of them; they are to been seen holistically (you cannot just take a particular portion of the law for the rules are all interlinked); some systems (as common law systems) are particularly insusceptible to being captured wholly in rules[72].

One can agree with much of this but the argument misses the point. Because you can recast and reconstruct legal reasoning in the form of deductive logic as an expert system, does not imply that this will now exhaust the whole of law - it is the frame of the ultimate decision that can be seen in deductive form. To be sure, only to see it in that form is impoverished and simplificatory. For it sees the simplicity of rigid rule following as all there is. It collapses legality into legalism. But legalism, or this form of simplification is necessary as well. The argument of this book has been that one cannot throw away legalism; that it is a necessary part of living the life of rules; that in articulation with love it is not impoverished at all but rather is what legality really is.

So, in the context of legal expert systems, in answer to the cry that the world is complicated, we can say that it is precisely one of the jobs of law to simplify it[73]. So our answer to the criticism that legal expert systems make a complicated thing simple would be that at least there they are doing well!

[72] See Twining (1986)
[73] See Luhmann (1985)

Legal expert systems then, might be said to close down the world. We might say they make simple that part of legality that is, in essence, straightforward and easy, legalism. This might be boiled down to the claim that legal expert systems will be all right since they need only to apply to easy cases - we can leave hard cases alone. Against this however, it can be argued that potentially everything is a hard case. The argumentative structure of the law (cases depend upon arguments being made and arguing is in some respects confrontational), as Moles claims[74], means that each case is potentially open to challenge, when someone finds it useful, for various reasons, so to do. Given the difficulty of pinning down precise meaning (as we saw above and discuss in chapter 8), this is always possible.

In general that argument says that the meaning comes from the instant case; all cases are constructed and so there can be no easy case. But this argument, carrying with it the assumption that the only construction we make is to turn something into a 'hard' case has the implication that, in a sense, things do have a straightforward meaning but it is always possible to overturn that. Thus in a sense the critics fall victim to their own argument since they do assume at least some taken for granted meaning, albeit it possible to overturn.

An example might make this argument clearer. Doreen McBarnett (1981) argued against the claim that one could use lay advocacy in the lower courts because cases there were relatively easy and thus one did not need lawyers[75]. Her argument was that constructing a case was something that was not to be found in the 'raw event' but was a specific legal skill. It is from the activity of the lawyer in laying out (constructing) a case that 'easiness' and 'hardness' came. But if this is the case, one might ask why should what lawyers decide is hard hold sway. In our research on Lay Justices[76] we frequently saw, in these low-level courts staffed by lay people, different constructions of what was easy and what was not come into play. Lay Magistrates were clear as to what the law said but felt that lawyers were 'bamboozling them with legal stuff'. Lawyers countered this by claiming it is the Justices who were threatening justice by just processing these cases without 'thinking about them' and that they (the lawyers) were serving justice by problematising and making it harder to convict. But at the edges of this it as an open question as to whether justice is best served by the 'hard' or 'easy' route. The breathalyzer legislation, though it appeared simple, and was designed precisely to make the definition of drunkenness something objective soon fell into an almighty tangle. The problems of legal aid, of the spinning out of cases to make money; of cost

---

74 Moles and Dayal (1992)

75 See Thomas and Mungham (1979)

76 See Bańkowski, Hutton and Macmanus (1987). See chapter 7 for this argument in context.

chasing are well documented. It is clear that lawyers have a vested interest in making things harder[77].

What lawyers are here doing is in part 'desimplifying' the world. Why is that just? Perhaps the world in these cases is easy after all? Moles says everything is hard because it is always possible to construct things as hard - but you can construct things as easy and make it impossible to subvert them. My argument here points two ways. I am claiming that in parts (see chapter 8) the world is simple in the sense that one can have plain meaning. Secondly, even in cases where it is not that clear, it might be morally and socially correct to ensure that it is so by applying closure in the sense of rigid application. Part of the reason for that must come from an idea of what the rule actually said. If it is all constructed then what can the no criterion for saying the 'hard' route is better than the 'easy' one - surely the easy route is to be preferred, it is quicker, cheaper and more transparent. Against this the argument for the hard route might be that this at least defends people from false convictions . But how can one know that there has been a false conviction? If all is constructed then why should the 'hard construction' be more accurate - the fact that more people are acquitted will not do - all it might show is that the justices have been 'bamboozled with legal stuff', contrary to common sense[78].

As against this 'desimplification', how do rules make the world simple? Moles (1992) argues that rules are like a shorthand:

> 'When unsure about what to do we consider many factors - when we have weighed them up, and decided what to do, we attempt to encapsulate the approach in a shortened form which we can remember - and we call that brief account a "rule". If a similar occurrence occurs we can refresh our memory about what to do by looking to the "rule". But if someone else should question the suitability or adequacy of the rule, then we have to put to one side our shorthand form and consider the full range of factors which are pertinent' (p. 195).

His argument is ambiguous. On the one hand we can take it as saying that rules formalise a complex world. My argument in counter to that has been that this is not necessarily a bad thing. On the other hand, the argument touches on

---

[77] See Bańkowski and Mungham (1976)

[78] In fact the argument is somewhat circular for it assumes that the fact that more acquittals are gained by the hard route, by 'desimplifying' the world, is evidence that the easy route is wrong. But why should that be unless one assumes that the point of the criminal justice system ought to be to acquit (a point of view which some activists seem to hold) - and a good one is where this happens more often. But one should not, even in the light of all the terrible miscarriage of justice recently, make that mistake - the point of the process is to make sure the guilty are convicted and the innocent acquitted. See Smith (1994) for a similar argument in respect of the police.

another point that Moles makes. He argues that we should not fall into the trap of thinking that the law is something that is to be mechanically applied. There is much that I agree on with him here. We might say that whatever the *meaning* issues involved (can you have clear and unambiguous meaning), there is still the question of whether or not the rule is to be *applied*. There is then a difference between the meaning and application. Klaus Günther (1993) makes a distinction between justification discourse and application discourse which we can adapt by saying that to get the meaning of a rule is one thing and to get its application is another. Much of the book so far has implicitly assumed this sort of distinction and I deal with it more explicitly in chapter 8. For Moles, application cannot be straightforward and mechanical and my argument has been and will be that in certain instances that is precisely what it has to be. In this context Moles could also be taken to be attacking the idea that law might be though of as a species of 'exclusionary reason'[79]; a view that I will argue precisely supports some of the mechanical and machine analogies that Moles attacks. In chapter 8, I adapt the idea of law as 'exclusionary reason' to develop my argument about these issues in the context of legal reasoning.

My argument so far has been that some of the things that scare us about computers are precisely things that we want in our daily lives. So in a sense we should not be so much scared that computers/machines take us over - but in part we should be like them, and certainly law should. This does not sound very encouraging if in the first place it is precisely that image of them, and so of law, that scares us! To elucidate this further I now turn to a study of our interaction with machines, computers and legal expert systems in society.

iii) 'The machine and I

Harry Collins[80] looks at computers, artificial intelligence and society in a way that illuminates our problems. He also asks the question as to why we are we afraid of computers and their supposed intelligence. After all, we are not, he says, afraid of books which do much the same thing. Thus one might look at books as encoding human knowledge and, by putting them in this rigid defined written form within covers, they rigidify knowledge and creativity. The book defines what we can do and we do not go beyond it. Plato, he says, was deeply suspicious of the written word:

> 'It shows great folly.... to suppose that one can transmit or acquire clear and certain knowledge of an art through the medium of writing, or that written

---

[79] See Raz (1975)

[80] Collins (1990)

See also Bańkowski, White Hahn (1995: introduction, esp. pp52-61) where I made this argument.

> words can remind the reader of all that he already knows on a given subject.....The fact is Phaedrus, that writing involves a similar disadvantage to painting. The production of painting looks like living beings, but if you ask questions they maintain a solemn silence. The same holds true of written words; you might suppose that they understand what they are saying, but if you ask them what they mean by anything they simply return the same answer over and over again. Besides, once a thing is committed to writing it circulates equally among those who understand the subject and those who have no business with it; a writing cannot distinguish between suitable and unsuitable readers. And if it is ill treated or unfairly abused it always needs its parents to come to its rescue; it is quite incapable of defending or helping itself.' (Plato 1973: 1. 275)

We talk of someone who 'gets all their knowledge from books' and not from 'real life'; someone who is only guided in what he can do by what books tell him The American Realists made great play of looking at the law as it happens and not 'the law in books'. We all know people who turn to the nearest library to solve any problem and who will not be satisfied that they are right until they read it in an authoritative book. We can see how easily this applies to law or ethics; people find the answer by turning to the relevant book. This is not just a point about the rule-book method of solving disputes, though obviously that is highly germane to our topic. It is also about the idea of formalisation. One can think of the book as an encoded version of human knowledge put in the form of writing. In this sense it can be treated as a formalised system for encoding the results of the experience of human interaction (see Plato above). Parts of the claim of formal systems will be that they encapsulate knowledge in a particular area and to know how to operate there you do not need to go outside that system - they will provide all the expertise necessary. In the 19th Century this idea was seen in the encyclopaedia[81]; that book which would codify all human knowledge. Hence the idea that the library, through its books, will contain all human knowledge.

Now this is not all that different from the machine/computer horror stories we saw earlier and yet it does not have such a hold on our imagination. We do not think of books taking over the world. We do not immediately want to burn all legal textbooks and get rid of the statute books. We do not see the book as taking over the role of the lawyer, or in my metaphor, swallowing the bank teller into the cash-line machine. We have become comfortable with books and we do not fear them. Because we cope in our social interaction with books we do not see that the machine like metaphors applies to them as well; we do not look closely at the fact that we already deal with that sort of activity; we do not throw up our hands in horror at the idea of law being in part like that.

[81] see Macintyre (1990)

The whole thing becomes clearer if we explore the analogy more directly. Let us then look at the way Collins pictures our interactions with computers. For him, it is helpful to think of the computer as social prosthesis. He takes the analogy of an artificial heart. Medical science might not be able to replace hearts perfectly but it can do things that are acceptable enough. Even if it did not work exactly as the human one, we would think of it as satisfactory. Why? Because the body would be able to function in more or less the same way as if it had a human heart. I might have to change my behaviour patterns somewhat to cope. It would not however, be such a change that I could not be considered to be living a human life anymore. We might not know, in looking at such a person, that he had an artificial heart. If we forced him to do hill running or see him taking his pills, we would of course know. By and large however, the heart would perform satisfactorily enough to be able to mimic the human heart and thus mimic human activity.

We are here then thinking of the computer replacing the human being in the social organism - it is a social prosthesis. The analogy is not with the brain where the computer replaces the brain. On this social view of it the question then becomes, if it cannot quite do it, what adjustments do we have to make to make it appear acceptable. The analogy in terms of the heart would be more or less immuno-supressive drugs. The level of acceptability would of course depend upon how far we wanted to make it appear artificial.

How then should the computer fit into the social organism? What should we expect of it? Collins claims, we should not expect intelligent behaviour. To illustrate this he considers the Turing Test, an operational definition of intelligence proposed by Alan Turing. The test is based upon the ability of a machine to fool an interrogator, in a series of type written exchanges, that it is a human, i.e. the responses of the machine will not be differentiable from those of a human. Turing's' original version of this was based upon an imitation game which was common at the time. A man and a woman went into a another room and were interrogated by written questions. They both answered as women. Turing proposed that the man be replaced by a machine:

> 'We now ask the question, "What will happen when a machine takes the part of the [man] in the game?" Will the interrogator decide wrongly just as often when the machine is played like this as he does when the game is played between a man and a women? These questions replace our original, "Can machines think?"' (Turing 1982: 54, quoted in Collins 1990: 181)

What is important here is that the machine is asked to mimic someone who is mimicking someone else (a man mimicking a woman). Now this is much easier for a machine to do. Just as it is much easier for me to pretend I am someone who is pretending to be someone they are not. It is much easier for me to pretend to be someone pretending to be a native of Fort Augustus than to pretend to be someone who is a native of Fort Augustus. In the latter case a native born inhabitant would almost certainly catch me out, while in the former it would be much harder to differentiate between the impostor and the one pretending to be the impostor.

Collins' argument is meant to suggest that, whatever machines do, it is not to take over human activity. Machines rarely do the same work as humans, they interact with humans who make good their deficiencies. Humans sometimes behave like machines and machines can mimic this perfectly. What is it they do then? We can see this by looking at the difference between action and behaviour. Machines behave and thus operate in the world of cause and effect, whereas humans act in the world of intentionality. It is this that machines cannot mimic. What can be distinguishable between acts and behaviour? The notion of 'machine like behaviour' is a good metaphor here is. It is something we sometimes want humans to perform and if they do not we count as a defect. Collins calls these behaviour-specific acts i.e. those that humans always try and instantiate with the same behaviour. An extreme example of this might be in the military where we sometimes want soldiers just to make automatic responses; to ensure they obey an order and act automatically 'without thinking about it'. One of the reasons for the seeming pointless drill exercises is to produce that effect. Repetitive action is something that we make the same; try and reduce it to causal laws as in science. These sort of acts, Collins says, can be described by their 'behavioural co-ordinates' without loss of meaning. The past is, in a sense, like this. It is already fixed and can be described without loss of meaning in terms of behavioural co-ordinates. This makes us think that the future, where it is not past behaviours that are important but future actions which have to be described in terms of intention, can as well. However, just because you can retrospectively analyse behaviour as rule governed does not mean you can predict future action unless you see society as a machine like repetitive behaviour.

In certain instances that is what the dystopias that we looked at above foresaw; a society ruled by machines reducing people to acting like machines. However we do not have to look to science fiction to see this. For part of the point to law was to create the 'automatic man' necessary for the production processes of capitalist societies.[82] The management theory of 'Taylorism' is a particularly good example. Here work is split into smaller units and tasks so that in the end each worker is left with only a small repetitive task to do. This did not require much skill or thought and so the worker could act more like a machine or robot (significantly 'robot' comes from the Slav root for work). Though this sort of management theory has gone out of fashion, 'deskilling' is clearly a feature of much of today's production processes[83]. But there are other activities where this epithet, 'machine-like' might apply; activities whose significance comes from the possibility of their being done in a regulated way. Here we can include counting and calculating which are mechanical even when done by humans in a conscious way. So a machine merely mimics, in many instances, more efficiently, the mechanical procedure followed by a human being. It is a machine imitating a human imitating a machine. At the same time in society in general, we saw in Chapter 1 how Max Weber saw this as part of the general process involved in the rise of capitalism through what he called 'rationalisation'. There we saw how, just as modern science takes away the magic of the world, so the 'machine' of formal rational law takes away the magic from the normative world. It makes that world and those subject to it rational and predictable.

LIVING IN THE MACHINE

In using the metaphor of the machine so far, I have been arguing that contrary to much of the narratives about machines in our society, we do not have to postulate that the machine will take over humans. Rather we might see the machine taking upon itself one activity of humans, that is humans when acting in a 'machine like' way. Therefore we do not have to worry for machines are a prosthesis for only that aspect of humanity - they will not become better humans and freeze us out. We also saw that I used this metaphor of 'machine-like' behaviour to explain what I meant by being trapped in the cycle of universality and rules. I have also hinted how to some extent metaphor and reality are much closer, especially when we deal with the use of computers in the law. But before we get to that, I want to explore further the notion of 'machine like' behaviour. What has that got to do with rules and the problems of legality and legalism; about living the good life in and out of the rules, that I have been trying to explore in this book?

---

[82] Kinsey (1979)

[83] An example one might take is repairing various appliances or even cars. Much of the work now involves not so much repairing as exchanging one sealed module for another!

i) The Library

We might think of machine like behaviour in this model of a library system and its rules[84]. This would be a system where there are rules which specify 1) how many books each category of user might have, 2) for how long they might keep them out, 3) which forbid exceeding the allowance of books, and 4) which forbid the loan of books to anyone in breach of the regulations. We could imagine this as an automated system. Everyone would be issued with a card which would be inserted into the computer system. The system would see if you were in good standing in respect of the regulations. Only then would it let you borrow an electronic copy of the book desired which would self-destruct after the loan time allowed!

All of the above is technically possible. But we are not interested in technical possibility here. What is important is that it has transformed what is happening. Before, there was the possibility of choice. But now there is none. Once within the library system, the pathways that the rules set are followed. This gives us a model of machine-like behaviour. There is no room for thinking about whether it is right to do so or not. The rules are applied. They are applied because what we have here is a species of institution and once you fit into its categories you are swept along in its tide. Thus once you are a defined as a postgraduate student, for example, it will be seen that you can only have x number of books. You will not be allowed any more because the machine will see that you have exceeded the limit. What is important here is that the deontic modality is being factored out - the normative rules have, to an extent, become descriptive. The rules and the system work better when we do not have to cater for the deontic. Why? Expressing that one 'ought' to do x cannot represent and specify with the certainty of predicate logic. This is because it deals with what people 'ought' to do and what they 'ought' to do after the violation of a conditional obligation might vary depending on the circumstances of the case[85]. That is why there is always a push to, as Sergot

---

[84] I take this example from Jones and Sergot (1992)

[85] This is expressed in logic by Chisholm's paradox. I take an example from Bańkowski, White and Hahn (1995: 661):

1. If Mr C dies, then it ought to be that Mrs C receives a widow's pension.
2. It ought to be that if Mr C does not die, then Mrs C does not receive a widow's pension.
3. It ought to be that Mrs C does not stab Mr C.
4. If Mrs C stabs Mr C, then he dies.
5. If Mrs C does not stab Mr C, then he does not die.
6. Mrs C stabs Mr C.

The following forms of inference are taken to be valid:

(i)If P, then it ought to be that Q.
P is true.
Therefore, it ought to be that Q.
(ii)If P, then Q.

and Jones say, ' to force actuality and ideality to coincide'. If what you ought do is what you actually do then it is much easier to represent it. And this is what has happened in the library. For all practical purposes most of the rules in our simplified model have become redundant in their normative form - they now describe what is the case. We have achieved this by machine, by automation. But that is only because it is harder to achieve it by just having the rules without the automated system. Though there will be slippages in both, the automated system is more capable of achieving ideality - but that is at least part of what we want (the legalism part) with humans obeying the rules.

One of the important things in this process is, as we have seen above, the idea that one can think, in certain contexts, of the law as for all practical purposes a definition. Once we have that then things just follow from it for the individual is, as we shall see in chapter 8, subsumed under that definition. What this leads on to is the notion that many laws, though they appear to be expressed in deontic form, can be expressed by what they call 'qualification norms' or 'definitions of the legal term in the consequent by means of conditions in the antecedent'[86]. Thus, as we saw, the library regulations become in some instance descriptions which qualify the essence of a member of staff, a student, a postgraduate etc. And in this way we know that the system is following the old normative rules which have become by and large redundant. It makes no difference to say that a postgraduate can only have x number of books - that will always be the case.

It ought to be that P.
Therefore, it ought to be that Q.
(iii)It ought to be that if P, then Q.
It ought to be that P.
Therefore, it ought to be that Q.
Now from 4 and 6 it follows that
7. Mr C dies.
And from 1 and 7 it follows, by virtue of (i), that
8. It ought to be that Mrs C receives a widow's pension.
But from 3 and 5 it follows, by virtue of (ii), that
9. It ought to be that Mr C does not die.
And from 2 and 9 it follows, by virtue of (iii), that
10. It ought to be that Mrs C does not receive a widow's pension.
So Mrs C ought and ought not to get a widow's pensions.
If, instead of 2, we put
2a. If Mr C does not die, then it ought to be that Mrs C does not receive a widow's pension,
then from 1 and 7 we still get the conclusion that
8. It ought to be that Mrs C receives a widow's pension.
while from 2a and 9 we now get the conclusion
11. It ought to be that it ought not to be that Mrs C gets a widow's pension.
So Mrs C ought to get a widow's pension, but it ought to be that she ought not to.
(A version of Connor's case)

[86] Bańkowski, White and Hahn (1995: 41)

We can view parts of the law, in effect, on this model and this brings much of it into a form which can be utilised for modelling by computer systems. Thus in their work on the British Nationality Act Sergot *et al* (1986) claimed that the main point of the Act was to spell out the conditions under which an entity qualifies as a British citizen. Much work has been done in this vein in what is known as logic programming which aims in this way to set out the law in a clearer form. I am not here interested in the political and sociological objections to this[87]. What interests me here is the general point that, where legislative texts are taken to produce qualification norms, then for all practical purposes the deontic modalities can be ignored. In fact whole categories of law can be, and are, expressed in this way. As Honore (1986) points out, much of English criminal law can be viewed as a definition of the notion of offence. Statutes are commonly in the form that 'doing x in y manner shall be an offence'. The deontic modality comes in the general assumption that one should not commit offences - which is by and large assumed and not questioned. One might say that this dynamic is inherent in the law since, once the ideal becomes the actual, things get more predictable and that is part of the point of the law. That is why definition is good - once you know what something is, you know what follows from it.

ii) Situational Crime Prevention

The above example has been one where the messy law, with its variable paths, is taken, and by factoring out the deontic, regimented and channelled down one (hopefully straight and narrow) path. Situational crime prevention is a good example of all this in action[88]. Situational crime has been described by Ken Pease as an aspect of 'primary crime prevention'. This concentrates on the 'crime event', on why and how the crime was committed. 'Secondary and tertiary crime prevention' look to the changing the person who has already committed a crime; secondary looks to measure in the community in general, concentrating on those perceived to be 'at risk' of falling into criminal behaviour while tertiary looks to people already in the criminal justice system - those imprisoned or on probation or doing community service orders and so on.

We are not here so much interested in debates as to its genesis or effectiveness but with the way it raises the very issues that I am discussing in this book. Pease says that the idea was first thought of when it was noticed that when natural gas, which was non-toxic, was substituted for town gas which was, then the total suicide rate went down. This implied that when the preferred

[87] For those see Leith (1986)

[88] See Pease (1997) and Clarke (1992)

method of suicide was unavailable (putting one's head in the oven was relatively simple and painless), then people just did not try to kill themselves. If the disappearance of the opportunity worked for suicide, might it not work for crime as well? In fact evidence did become available that the compulsory fitting of steering column locks to all cars in West Germany reduced auto theft and their compulsory fitting to new cars in Britain reduced the proportion of those cars stolen (Pease 1997: 669). The ideas of the architect Oscar Newman on 'defensible space' also played a part. He tried to utilise design of buildings and the environment in order to protect crime - designing buildings and areas where it was not so easy to commit crime, there being less escape routes, less hiding places and the like. The spirit of situational crime prevention is summed up by Clarke (1992:14) in a 19th century Italian example where there was a problem of persistent urination in the streets. Lombroso suggested imprisonment for offenders while his pupil Ferri thought more in terms of the provision of public urinals!

Clarke (1992: 13) recognises twelve general categories of situational crime prevention. These comprise many different approaches from what he calls increasing the effort, through increasing the risks and reducing the reward. At one end of the spectrum we see things that are analogous to my example of the library regulations; automatic gates as entry points into certain facilities, mostly libraries, which begin to prevent theft (Scherdin 1992) and rapid transit facilities which tend to cut down fare evasion (Deschamps and Bratingham 1992). Again 'target hardening', another of Clarke's categories, works because you cannot take the thing that you want so in the end you will stop trying. Thus we saw the case of the car locks, but there are also examples from making card-only telephone boxes, to vandal-proofing in general - making it harder to inflict actual damage.

One aim of situational crime prevention one might say then, is to organise the world so that the crime does not occur, so that behaviour which causes the crime is deflected. Thus the all-automatic ticketing and entry on insertion of valid ticket through difficult-to-climb-through gates has the effect of producing predictability - you can predict that by and large those on the system will be in possession of a valid ticket. Here also we can see the introduction of computer systems into hotels with computer controlled locks which can be individually programmed. We can see the relevance to our themes. For what is being attempted here is to produce in people the 'behaviour specific acts' that we saw described above. What is wanted is for people to react to without having to decide what to do. Collins uses the example of a rock. When we stumble against a rock we do not have to decide not to walk through it.

> 'It will give us guidance about where to walk in its vicinity whether we think about it or not. We may walk besides it or away from it but not through it [we should not take our science fiction metaphors too seriously - we are not superman!]. We do not have to decide *not* to walk through it. Our actions are caused directly by the rock rather than our interpretation of what the rock is.' (1990: 52).

Obviously this is not true of all methods of situational crime prevention and it may also be characterised, as Clarke does, as stemming from rational choice theory; the actor makes a rational choice not to do something because of the costs to themselves of doing it[89]. But what is happening here is the attempt to make that a choice more and more a bounded one; to make it more and more constrained by his *physical* environment into a situation where he has no choice. But the rules can be looked upon as part of the physical environment themselves. They constrain the choice because they are the rules and since they say, 'do x', there is no choice. We can see them as a sort of symbolic physical environment. The move from physical to symbol is on a spectrum. For example; the methods of crowd control of football matches which involve the segregation of supporters, the marching of fans from the train to the crowd in column, the insulating of them from everything, are all ways of channelling behaviour. The police who do it are, as it were, part symbol part rock[90]. So situational crime prevention is in part to make the rules like what, in part, they should actually be - to instantiate the repetitive and mechanical behaviour demanded of them more obviously.

iii) Learning virtue

We can see then, that some of the ethical problems that attend situational crime prevention will be analogous to ones we have been discussing in this book. These have been recently usefully summarised and explored by Von Hirsch, Garland and Wakefield (2000)[91]. The sources of difficulties, they show, comes from the broadened impact of these measures - they operate without suspicion of wrongdoing whereas traditionally only violation or suspicion of violation is targeted. This leads to a more 'flexible' approach to rights. Thus CCTV cameras survey everyone regardless of whether there is reason to be suspicions of their activity or not. Since surveillance is a large

---

[89] This is, of course, a traditional way of arguing for deterrence.

[90] As an illustration of this, a friend once told me the story of the time he was a student in the Soviet Union and went, in while in Moscow, to a footballmatch between Dynamo Moscow and Dynamo Kiev. This was a major confrontational event, involving differences of nationality, religion etc. He remembers leaving the ground with everyone quiet and well behaved. This not being his normal experience at 'derby' matches, he was amazed until he looked around and saw militia men with fixed bayonets lining the streets!

[91] I am grateful to Anrew von Hirsch for letting me have sight of an unpublished paper of his on the subject.

part of situational crime prevention, there is an impact on privacy (see von Hirsch (2000). Strategies of exclusion (keeping people out of certain zones) exclude whole categories of people rather than actual suspicious characters from public or quasi public space (shopping malls), thus having an impact on liberty (von Hirsch and Shearing (2000). Issues of distributional justice also arise in questions of 'target hardening' for they might make certain facilities (e.g. 'phone boxes) less available in poor areas. We can see here, as they show, the way in which situational crime prevention produces regiments people in certain areas and thus controls them. We can see this in the library and the subway, in the entrance and exit screening at airports and other places. The full force of this sort of regimentation, and the Foucauldian properties of 'micro control' that it brings, can be well seen in Shearing and Clifford's (1992) study of disciplinary control of the customers at Disney World.

It is that final issue of regimentation that is important for our topic here. We have seen many different sorts of scheme which are gradations on a theme; the aim is to produce some predictable and thereby controllable behaviour. But when we look at it like this then we see that all that we might call preventative action is trying to produce that; the policeman waving you down on the road; the book of rules being waved at you. They all try to get you to react in one particular way to something which can be likened to a rock, the physical barriers of a subway system to the physical barrier/symbol of the fixed bayonet or policeman's hand, to the symbol of the code book. And we saw how the library example and its representation in law effectively tried to make law this kind of barrier. We want to make them act without thinking about it. Here then we come to the ethical problem that is at the heart of this book and at the heart of situational crime prevention. Is situational crime prevention immoral because it makes people less moral in the sense of making them heteronomous and not thinking about whether they are doing wrong or not?

What we appear to be wanting, in these situations, is not really so much reflection on what is being done but rather the actual specific behaviour. And this is why situational crime prevention has become popular. One of the reasons, according to Clarke, was the perceived failure of the rehabilitative ideal. 'Prison did not work' in the sense that it seemed to be failing in changing a person's heart and mind. This being the case - why bother with trying such measures, in prison or out of it? Let us just get them to do what we want. But if we go down this road, what do we do? All we will do is to control behaviour in the particular locations that we have set the schemes up and merely displace the criminal activity elsewhere, we are not getting people to address the issues of right and wrong. And this 'displacement' of crime is a problem for situational crime prevention, as Clarke admits.

Let us start with that final point. Displacement is not necessarily a bad thing. Transferring crime to another locality might add to our quality of life. It all depends on the particular case. Pease (1997) gives a good example. If we have a piranha infested river and manage to effect it so that all the piranhas are only located in one stretch, then that will aid river crossing in general. We might think of the same with, for example, transferring street prostitution to regulated saunas[92]. It all depends on where the transferred areas are and other such factors. In that sense then, regimentation or channelling is no bad thing. But still; doesn't that fail to make people good? For, since what it does is merely ensure that they react to things in a machine-like way, it does not teach them what virtue is.

Aristotle thought that part of the way that one learnt virtue was by doing virtuous things so that in the end one just did them. We live in a world where to develop we have to recognise certain sorts of inductive similarities and differences between actions and activities and *respond* to them in order to develop and progress in our life (Collins 1990). The same would hold true for our moral life. We might say that the potentiality of responding in this way, this mysterious facility that enables us to jump forward in this way, is one of the things that makes us human. But this situation of *response* is something different from the *reaction* that we have to objects as rocks in our example. There we cannot see beyond to respond - we see straightforward similarity and we react to it by doing the same thing in a repetitive manner. That is what Collins called the world of 'behaviour specific acts' and is the world that machines inhabit. The key element here is what Collins calls 'digitization'.

> 'Digitization is the method by which the invariance of tokens in such a system [a formal one] is preserved, and digitization is what makes the value of such pieces unambiguous.' (p. 23)

Once we transform the world into something like that, then we can react to it in repetitive manner because everything is made similar. The computer will react in an invariant way to the pulses 1 or 0. This makes it much easier to manipulate the world. Take an example from arithmetic. When we grade the overall performance of a student what we are actually doing is taking a set of finals papers and judging their quality, - good, bad indifferent - and then trying to get an overall result. This is obviously quite hard for how can you get an

---

[92] As has unofficially been done in Edinburgh.

average of, for example, three good, one indifferent and two bad ones. To make this easier, what we do is digitise the process by giving numbers which stand for these quality judgements and get an overall result by performing arithmetical operations on them and getting a digital answer (numerical average or total).

We can see the behaviour engendered by situational crime prevention on this model. Much of our own mental life is in fact on this model. Thus calculation is machine like activity. We might have to interpret the results but the process of getting to that stage (acts of calculation themselves) is machine like; in principle the same if we do it ourselves or we let a calculator do it. We can see writing as an act of digitization in the sense that the alphabet enables us to manipulate and make simpler speech. The written page is

> 'merely the behavioural counterpart of the act of speech, but a behavioural counterpart that corresponds to a central feature of the human use of language.'(Collins 1990: 61)

We do not think of these actions as machine-like until something goes wrong and then we have to correct for them. Quite often we do that automatically - we quite often never see misprints when reading a book - we automatically correct for them. But take an analogy that Collins uses. A robot production line programmed to spray paints would work perfectly until a shape that was not in the programme came up - it would just carry on spraying in the same patterns. It is then that we could distinguish it from humans because they would see the difference.

On this model situational crime prevention would indeed not be able to teach virtue. However humans have this facility, as I said, of not only reacting but of correcting - and on this analogy we might think of that as jumping beyond, learning virtue and thus being able to be virtuous in other circumstances. How do they learn this virtue? Well one way is precisely through this form of machine-like activity. It is through the repetitive action that we see and learn the similarity that enables us to respond when necessary, when we see that it is not quite like that, that the shape is different. So it is doing the machine-like acts that helps us to see and respond beyond them. We humans do have that ability and that is how we morally develop. Central to this ability though, is that sort of machine like activity that feeds the response and drives it on. Think of this example which I adapt from Collins (p. 71). Ballroom dancing might be though of as a stylised activity which, in principle, we could get machines to do - there is only one way to waltz and the machine could in principle do it with another machine. They might not do it with the same flair but it would still be recognisably a waltz. However what the machine could not do is build on these steps and, in an appropriate situation, change them and form another dance but still based on a thorough knowledge of the waltz[93]. In the next chapter we see how legal reasoning can both give us the flair and take us beyond.

The creative then, depends on the machine-like. However, even though we have this ability to go beyond which comes from our interaction with our machine-like capacities, we always have the danger of being locked in the machine. For it is a fragile line between response and reaction. Here ideals come into play. It is always necessary to have ideals but the problem is that one must not, as I showed in Chapter 4, think of them as something that one can attain. They are there to guide and if we think we have reached them, we risk converting the morality of aspiration into the morality of duty. This is always a tension in the deontic; it always tries to achieve ideality; to convert the actual into the ideal as we saw in our discussion of the library. But the paradox of that is that its (supposed) attainment does away with the ideal and leaves no room for creative jumps. I will deal with the ideal as something not attainable but a sort of horizon in the final chapter. Here, we can notice that the ideal has, in a sense, a capacity to lock us into the rules just as the machine. For there is this push in the normative to achieve ideality and dissolve itself. Ideals, as we shall see, have to be both present in the rule and beyond it. Part of their presence is the giving of the possibility to move beyond without disturbing the smooth running of the present rule system.

CONCLUSION

We have explored the relation between law and love, between autonomy and heteronomy in many different ways. This chapter has looked at these relations focusing on the heteronomy of law. It has extended further the analogy of the machine that I have been using throughout. The idea of the machine metaphor is to explore how it would be to live a life of heteronomy; of being in thrall to the law and rules. Since I have characterised this as, in part at least, machine-like behaviour then it is appropriate to explore this by looking at the way we interact with machines in society and attempts to introduce machines (computers) into the law.

We have also looked at situational crime prevention because it shows up these problems at a policy level. Here we appear to be getting an attempt, in

---

[93] See the film, 'It's only Ballroom' which is a witty exploration of this point. One might also say that this is how rugby developed. 'He picked the ball up and ran'

some instances, to do away with autonomy - we are not so much interested in people 'thinking about it' as just reacting and doing it. My argument here has been that the worry of those who think that the introduction of these, and similar devices, risks turning the world into a machine like dystopia needs to be unpacked a bit more. Firstly if they think they will turn us into machines, then that is ill founded because in part of our activity we are precisely like machines (the machine mimics a human mimicking a machine). Thus in part of our rule following activities we just follow the rules. And this is no bad thing - simplicity and predictability are things worth having in both social policy and personal life. So being in the machine, locked into the universality of rules is no bad thing if kept in its place. The metaphor of 'machine-like' behaviour is thus not necessarily negative. In the law it is useful because there we often expect this machine-like response. At least part of the point of law is to create some form of order out of a chaos of particular instances, and, in so doing, create the possibility for prediction. And that in itself is creative. It carves out of the chaotic world an order that we can follow. But our creativity is wider than that and we must adjust to a particular situation when it becomes necessary. We saw that we have this ability, in our interaction with machines, automatically to correct when things go wrong because of their mechanical behaviour. We can ignore the misprint, stop painting the wrong shape.

Two questions need to be asked here. What is that ability and wherein does it come from? I pointed to some of the answers in my discussion of the ethical problems of situational crime prevention and will deal with them further in the next chapter. Secondly, will not the machine like activity negate it? It might indeed. Throughout the book I have pointed to the way that it might do so - in converting legality into legalism, into overreliance on the market and so on. And herein lies the tension; for our ability to jump from the machine-like order when necessary rests, to an extent, on our following that order. But at the same time following that order is also the condition for our sinking into it with no life-line out. We need to be machine like because that helps us love - at the same time that can be the agency of preventing that. To go back to Judge Dredd again. He needs to be the enforcer of the law and he needs his lover; for she is able to mitigate his rigidity and allow him to jump. But his skill in enforcing the law which gains him his lover could also be the condition of his losing her.

CHAPTER 8

REASONING IN THE MACHINE

INTRODUCTION

So far I have been using the images of jumping out of law or jumping out of love. This way of putting it implies that we jump from the one to the other. But I do not want this to imply that that we must make this an 'either/or choice'; that principles or reasons hunt in pairs and, because there is no rational principle of choice from the one to the other, we are doomed to an eternal oscillation. Either/or is still the safe choice for it is at least jumping into something that is clear, even if getting there might appear irrational. Love can also be the safe choice. We saw how Hamish X could in certain instances be seen as selfish, locked in his own desires, certain that this is the right thing to do, unable to see beyond. Recall how Antigone transforms love of the family into a righteous certainty; a certainty that in the end, confident of its rightness, does not care for others. The urge for that form of certainty transforms itself into law and rules (thus Antigone transforms the *philia* of the family into the law of the gods). Even love can be transformed into legalism, into the rationalism of a coherent and consistent system which can inform our decision-making. But that is not to say that legalism is something perverted - just that in this case it was not appropriate. Let us follow rather, Nussbaum's reading of Antigone, and say there is no haven and that we have to move into a zone where we cannot be sure that the answer will come out right, where we are holding all reasons and principles in tension, not taking one on board to the exclusion of all others and this includes legalism.

The zone that I have in mind, is analogous to what Gillian Rose (1992) calls the 'middle', where the contingency of love breaks through the secure frontier posts of the law and yet, as we have seen, only makes sense because of the law itself. The contingency of love finds its expression and its meaning against the certainty of its law. Think of this in the context of creativity. If love's transgression is a form of breaking and going beyond the law, it can be characterised as the creative breaking of the law rather than a destructive nihilistic sort of anarchism.

This (see chapter 7) does not mean the doing away of reactive, repetitive actions but stems from and only makes sense in their context. Take an example from art. If we go to certain art galleries we can see rows of Madonnas with Child. This might appear rather boring since they all tend to be similar. However it need not be if within this mass of paintings we can see a few brilliant and original ones that stand out from the rest. They are related to them but they stand out from them and we can see through them, and the mass of copies, how the style developed and what is good about it. These few stand out because they are situated within the context of a mass of copies that are not so good. But that mass of copies is also enhanced thereby because of the master-works - one can see their origin and appreciate the difference. Thus they mutually reinforce each other. One can see this in the experience of going to a gallery. One full of brilliant works can be curiously unsatisfactory. All that genius overwhelms and it is impossible to take it all in - one just randomly picks out certain works. The exhibition of the entire oeuvre of Picasso illustrates this. If all his work was equally brilliant it would be impossibly overwhelming. But what you get from that exhibition is an idea of how his work developed and the brilliant works stands out from many more ordinary works. The brilliant works stand out in the mass and the more ordinary are also enhanced by them. An old master is enhanced by being showed with several works which are in that style by pupils and followers, and, at the same time, they gain in a way in which they would not shown just by themselves.

You cannot just have a steady line with no peaks - you need peaks and troughs. It is this that makes the peaks so good. A game of football played by two competent teams is extremely boring because there is no brilliance. But a game played between teams of brilliantly skilful players is also unsatisfying since it stops being a game of football and becomes just an exhibition of individual skill. What one needs is high level competence enlivened with flashes of brilliance. For that is what makes it a game of football, the highly competent play suddenly and unpredictably erupting into brilliance - the two elements enhancing each other and making a better whole. It might also explain why top level basketball is curiously unsatisfactory. The players are all too brilliant which makes the game, paradoxically, routine and boring - there is nothing to stand out.

In the context of computer aided design in architecture, it has been argued that architectural precedents destroy creativity since all they produce is copies of existing styles - we lose originality and get a mass of second rate material. But one can apply my argument about painting here also. A city based just on these precedents would not be so splendid as one which was not. What makes the difference is that a city have some wonderful original buildings as well. But it is not just those buildings that make a city - it is that they are set in this mass of very good copies which both makes them and the city stand out. It is the interaction of the copies and the originals that is important. A mass of original buildings would not, it seems to me, make such a splendid city. Why? Because while each one would be beautiful in its own right, it would be too much as a whole. There would be overload and the whole would be worst than the sum of the parts. But the buildings have to be in a context - they cannot just stand alone as though in a desert. For in that case they might be beautiful buildings, but they would not be a city. And it is a city that we are talking about. The context also cannot be dismissed as not worth bothering about. Those buildings which form the context will not be bad, just not works of brilliance. And they need to be like this because the city would not be so wonderful, if it were just a random collection of arbitrary buildings - mostly bad with some brilliant ones thrown[94]. The jewel in the crown is set off by the crown and makes the crown more splendid.

But there is another problem in this middle zone. For here the presence of law as a reason for acting along with other reasons generates a special problem. For it appears that law cannot be just a reason among many. The point of it is to be a rationalising and totalising force; to make things coherent and consistent; precisely to get away from the arbitrariness of different incoherent and crosscutting reasons. We have see, in various ways and in various contexts, how this can be both good and bad. This problem is best expressed in the exclusionary nature of law; a formal reason that excludes substantive considerations. Law's reason for doing 'x' is because it is the law[95]. This gives strong force to the 'thin end of the wedge claim' - for as soon as you look at it as one reason among many to do 'x' you start to destroy its exclusionary and formal nature. So law's essential claim acts to make the middle zone impossible to inhabit, from the point of view of law at least. We go on, in this chapter, to deal with these problems in the context of legal reasoning; to see if we can look to ways of dealing with these problems without destroying the point of the law.

---

[94] See Tzonis and White (1994) for a discussion of this in the context of architecture.

[95] This fits in well with the Weberian view of the formal rationality of law (see chapter 1)

THE TIGER

Part of the aim of the book is to explore what social theory means for the individual ethical life and *vice versa*; in that sense to incorporate the personal and the political. Here also, I hope to make clear some ethical problems involved in living in and through rules, and indeed some general ethical problems, through the optic of the theory of decision-making and reasoning in law.

There are two broad points involved here. First of all, we can say that legalism is ethically important *per se.* It is something that Neil MacCormick calls the ethics of legalism

> 'that stance in legal politics according to which matters of legal regulation or controversy ought, so far as possible, to be conducted in accordance with predetermined rules of considerable generality and clarity in which legal relations comprise rights, duties, powers and immunities reasonably clearly defined by reference to such rules and in which acts of government however desirable teleologically must be subordinated to respect for such rules and rights (1989: 184)

But there is something more than just that broad ethical point at stake here. For the justification of legalism on this view (and, in its appropriate place, correctly so) is that rules are there because we need, in situations of differing and partly irreconcilable moral values, to regulate the borders of conflict; that they are devices that we use to patrol those areas where values conflict so that we have clear answers to them; we use them as co-ordinating mechanisms, not only in situations of practical need, such as in Road Traffic control, but also in normative and moral need. This implies a certain lack of faith in people's ability to come to the right decisions in any particular case of conflict without pre-regulation. This is not necessarily to impute to people malevolent motives for co-ordination needs rules no matter how good people are. Even a society of angels would need rules[96]. What is necessary however is that the method of coming to a decision under the rules must be pre-regulated in some way. Decisions are then legitimate if they stem in some fair and rational manner from application of the rules we have all accepted in the first place. And that is why legal philosophers busy themselves with, among other questions, how judges do and should reason in order to have rational and just determinations from the rules. Though we rely on a particular cadre of people to make these determinations and insulate them from the political process, the rules still in a sense control them. That latter point is deeply contentious as we have seen.

[96] See chapter 5; also Finnis (1982).

There are those who argue, as the American Legal Realists did, that legal reasoning is by and large a sham; that one cannot get through it the coherence and consistency necessary for formal rationality; that things are just too vague and indeterminate for that. There are those who argue against this view and say that, granted that there must always be some form of indeterminacy in rule-based systems, this does not mean that in the end one cannot produce a rational, coherent and consistent rule-based structure[97].

But even if there were to be the case (and I will argue that it is the case) then problems would still remain for us. For even though we could produce a rational, coherent and consistent rule-based structure there would still remain the problem of the 'middle zone'. For though the system of law might be internally coherent, it would give us no principles or criteria as to when to step outside of it. It would give us a way of solving the problem of the meaning of a rule, an important advance given the reason advanced for rules, but it would not tell us whether and when it is appropriate to apply it. The judge has to ask not merely what the rule means but whether it is right to apply it to the case before him. If that question is answered by saying that it is the meaning which will determine the application, then we will have preserved the law and its rationality but at the cost of ignoring the particularity of the case up for decision. Like the cash-line machine we ignore the pleas of the customer and follow the fixed meaning of the programme. It is a well known legal maxim that 'hard cases make bad law'. But we sometimes find that unsatisfactory, it ignores the real pain and hurt of the particular case. But, if we move to saying we will know when to apply the rule by looking at the circumstances of the particular case, then we start to lose connection with the meaning of the law and thus negate the point of legalism.

What we are also talking about here is the relationship of formal and substantive justice. In the former, there are general categories by which particular cases are decided. Here, there is clearly a distinction between adjudication and legislation. But there is something more. For the implication is that the decisions made under the rules must be capable of justification independently of the rules. In other words, if you are arraigned under a rule, you must show that that is correct independent of the goodness or badness of the rule. For example, if I am charged with tax evasion, then I cannot escape

[97]The *locus classicus* of this is in MacCormick (1994). We see here how MacCormick's book also gives one solution to the 'England problem' of Max Weber. Why, he asked, in the first country that developed a capitalist system, did formal rationality in the legal system not obtain? Weber had this problem because he thought that the common law was not a formally rational system. MacCormick shows how it can be reconstructed as such, and does in fact operate so. Dworkinian theory, though ostensibly against rules, could also be seen in this vein. For ultimately he makes law a tight and coherent rational system with right answers, albeit 'interpretative' right answers.

the charge by arguing that taxation law is immoral and unjustified and that the economy would improve if there were no tax. I must show that my particular activity in this line is not covered by the tax laws and thus not forbidden. Likewise a prosecutor could not argue that the reason you are guilty is because not paying this particular tax is immoral as not honouring obligations to the community. He must show that what you did is an example of tax evasion.

The other model is something rather different. Here, we determine the goals independently of the rules in some respects. We decide cases by what is most likely to achieve these goals. We call this a regime of substantive justice. Here decisions are those that are best calculated to achieve the purposes and law becomes a kind of technical thing. On this view of it, the policies and purposes that the law serves are the most important consideration. And whatever values are (radical) justification of laws, are also justifications of the application of the law. The distinction between the law maker and the law applier is minimal - they act in concert. Quite often these goals are things that might change for the overall purpose of the law will be to serve the needs and welfare of each particular individual in that society.

On this standard account meaning and application are somewhat conflated. On the one hand, the complaint of substantive justice is of lack of flexibility in determining what the rules mean, something that can then go on to cause injustice because an inappropriate decision was taken. On the other hand it could be something that leads to a deeper ethical problem, that the particular is ignored and that the action of rules makes the concrete individual disappear (recall the cash-line machine). The claim here is something more than a problem of the generality and vagueness of the rule. The problem is that it *is* a rule and therefore universal, implying that it must be applied in all the cases where the conditions for its application are met.

But there is more. This brings up again the ethics of alterity which we briefly mentioned at the end of chapter 6. Why is the particular is so important? Why does it seems to stand against the rules? Part of the argument is summed up in Detmold (1984)[98]. He claims that only particulars give reasons for action and that rules (as universals) can never capture the particular since there is always a level of description underneath them. Particulars are a mystery, they are what makes the world mysterious. Rules try to appropriate the mystery of the world by forcing each particular under their aegis and thus denying its particularity. They are a cowardly way out of decision-making. They mean that I no longer have to make up my mind in the

[98] See also his unpublished manuscript 'The Law of Love' where the argument is developed.

encounter with the awesome mystery of the particular before me. The answer is given by a rule which in describing that particular necessarily misses something and thus tames and domesticates it.

What does all this mean? [99] Two ideas are important and germane to our discussion. Firstly, that particulars are a mystery. Detmold says this is a mystery of our daily life rather than some deep cosmological question. A flower or the tiger or you or I just *are*. The question is not how can something come from nothing but rather the deeper question - why does something come at all? Why does it not just remain nothingness? In principle one could ask that question of God. Science might explain the first question but not the second. The mistake we make is thinking that the explanation will get everything about it. But it just will not capture the mystery of its being – indeed for Detmold it would be something like blasphemy to try and capture that mystery in an explanation. An analogy here would be one argument against zoos. This argument says it is wrong to keep animals therein, because they lose the grace and beauty that they might have had in the wild. It is cruel in two ways. Firstly it can cause the animal suffering. Secondly, it destroys the animals in the sense that the zoo takes away the particularity of the actual animal in the interests of giving us an example of the species. In so doing, the particular tiger is lost; it no longer displays the beauty and grace it did in the wild. And this is precisely because it is no particular tiger, but stands for all tigers - I no longer show any awe and respect for that tiger because I no longer confront *it*. Now it is not the particular (the tiger) that gives me a reason for action but the rules (the tiger in the zoo).

Secondly, what this appears to be saying is that the only appropriate response to the tiger is to confront it and stand in awe in front of it - something like the 'ethics of alterity' and, as in some parts of Lévinas, complete submission to the 'other'[100]. But we must stand against this and think of the real and cogent reasons why rules are adopted. Think of the tiger again. We cannot just encounter the tiger and stand in awe of it. Tigers are dangerous and they are liable to bite or eat you. We need to lose the tiger in the rule so that, in our defining it, we can approach it with some degree of safety. Risk is important but we cannot be completely irrational about it. The particular needs to be mediated through rules in order for us to approach it. It might not have to be the zoo, it might be a safari park or some large national park but we must still attempt to lose some of the tiger's particularity. The particular (the tiger in the example) is not rational - it is contingent and arbitrary and we do not know what it will do. We take precautions precisely by

---

[99] See Bańkowski (1998) from where this argument is taken.

[100] See Veitch (1998)

capturing and constraining it in rules and, by bringing it under the net of rules, we lose, for our benefit, its individuality. In the same way, what we were faced with in the beginning of this book were many different and diverse voices to bring together, to co-ordinate. They too are arbitrary in that, with their diverse and diverging values, we do not know, and cannot predict, what will happen next. This is dangerous and liable to cause damage unless to some extent we capture, and bring them, under rules. For love is a dangerous and powerful force - one has to be strong in order to approach it or it will destroy[101]. We need mediation to stand up before it.

We have made throughout this book the connection between 'love', 'discretion' and 'arbitrariness'. This makes love powerful as well as potentially dangerous . We have seen how, once set in motion as a principle of government, it can eat a society up (I might not like you). We need to have the strength to trust to make it work and that in part will be established by structures and codes. The problem is, as we have seen, that this is also dangerous – it has the potential to abolish love and leave only the rules.

These ethical issues will come up throughout our study of legal reasoning itself. We saw how we needed to be in the middle, in the space between law and love. We also saw how that middle did not preclude the use of rules, what I have called the machine mode. For, in fact, we need to be in the machine mode, be able to operate within it and move beyond. The problem is that operating in the machine might keep you there and make you unable to move beyond. In chapter 7, using an analogy with artificial intelligence and computer systems in law, we looked a the 'machine' and saw how the base for moving beyond the machine was reasoning in the machine.

DEDUCTIVISM AND ANALOGY

We now turn to study reasoning 'in the machine' and more specifically legal reasoning therein. It is here that we get the 'behaviour specific acts' of Collins, the repetitive behaviour that guarantees predictability and certainty. The machine-like behaviour analogy best fits in with the views of legal reasoning that see it, to some extent, deductive in form. This is the universalistic answer that, for example, MacCormick (1992) takes in his controversy with Jackson as to whether or not one can see law as a deductive system. The computer analogy is important here as well. For Jackson (1991) sees McCormick's approach as being one where expert systems could be used precisely because the predicate logic that the system of deductive reasoning

---

[101] Thus, in the Old Testament, the love of God is represented by a burning bush in front of which few are able to stand.

will operate is well suited to their use. Jackson accuses MacCormick of thinking of law as in principle calculable; as a large machine-like system which always churn out the answers that its programme ordains and will admit of no exceptions. This is realised in the deductive form simply put for MacCormick as:

i) in any case if p then q
ii) in the instant case p
iii) therefore q

This is valid by the inference rule *modus ponens*[102]. There are many problems about the logic of such matters and this is not the place to go into them here. What is important for us is that the implications of this claim, as Jackson notes, tend to this machine-like calculability (whether possible to realise perfectly or not). Seeing deductivism from within this decidability perspective means we do not need to take the strict view of deductive reasoning that some such as Atria (1999) do[103]. He bases his argument on the claim that Macormick's thesis does not map on to Alexy's distinction between internal and external justification in law. Internal justification is

> 'concerned with the question of whether an opinion follows logically from the premisses adduced as justifying it; the correctness of the premisses is the subject of the external justification' (1989: 221)

What Alexy is claiming here is that to justify fully a legal argument you need non-deductivist criteria to justify the premises and then it is a matter of formally deriving the answer from those (externally justified premises). MacCormick's claims do not, says Atria, appear to map on to this distinction. His claim, says Atria, does not seem merely to refer to internal justification. If it did, then it would be false for you would always need non-deductively established premises to start with. But, if we see his claim as being that deduction plays some part in legal reasoning, then that would be merely trivial - because of course it does. In the end, for Atria, MacCormick wants to have his cake and eat it. He wants to say that there is deductivity but that we cannot use this fact to produce absurd results. This being so, he has for Atria, to claim that deductivity occurs only in normal cases. This is not for MacCormick the claim that all legal cases are by definition normal and it is only when they produce absurd results you might have to go outside of it (a sort of Kelsenian and Hartian view *per* Atria). Rather he is, as Atria says,

---

[102] MacCormick 1978: 24. Technically, as MacCormick admits (1992), this should be expressed in predicate logic - but this does not detract from the main argument and I will, like him, stick to expressing it in propositional logic.

[103] I wish to thank Fernando Atria for the countless discussions we had around these points when he was completing his thesis in Edinburgh.

'committed to claim that, as a matter of law (and not as a matter of ideology or morals) legal rules apply to normal cases' (p. 141).

But this is only a problem if we take, as Atria does, deductivism *stricto senso*, i.e. that reasoning applying logical inference rules. But MacCormick extends the idea of deductivism to encompass Alexy's external justification so that for him it is a mixture of both the internal and external justification of Alexy. In this way we do not get absurd results because deductivism is broad enough to cover it. What is important is not whether deductibility will work in this way, but the whole project of characterising legal reasoning in this image. This image persists even though one might discard the strict logic. Seeing deductivism from within a decidability optic means that it is part of the image of closure, of legalism in a system of rules - we do not have to argue as though it might work literally as my machines in chapter 7. But the system will be a system of closure, rather than one that can also move beyond. MacCormick wants, in the end, closure in order to encompass things within the law albeit with frontiers less clear cut than we might think - but broadly within the law as it is[104].

I turn to look more closely at this broadly conceived deductivist way of looking at it. We start from the way that seeing law as to all intents and purposes a definition (see chapter 7) in some respects effects closure. It makes it easier for a deductivist system to work for once you establish what something is, you give it a predicate, and from that you know what the consequences are to be. Once you know something is an offence, it follows that you do not do it. You do not have to work out what to do when faced with a particular - you have to work out what it is - once you know that everything follows. Thus once you know someone is a neighbour then the question what to do is easy for we know how to act in respect of neighbours, that is understood.

Analogy could be looked at in roughly the same way. You get something defined, compare other things with that definition and you have an easy answer. The tricky part might be establishing the definition but then everything follows. We ask a descriptive question rather than a normative

[104] This makes him similar to Dworkin even though Dworkin (1977) is the *locus classicus* of the attack on the positivists. Dworkin complains that the 'strong discretion' of the positivists means that they 'run out of rules' and have no legal answer in hard cases, whereas for him (Dworkin) that does not happen since principles, by which the law makes decisions, are in fact *legal*. If we look at MacCormick's theory however, we see that implicitly and explicitly he answers that point. When he talks of the limits of deductive justification and what goes on there (the external justification of Alexy) we see that ultimately that is also *legal*. So both Dworkin and MacCormick are trying to effect legal closure. In fact their theories of legal reasons, when unpacked, have strong similarities (see also chapter 4 'Responsive Autonomy').

question. How does this work in cases of reasoning by analogy? Firstly, you take a case and define it, effectively by deciding what the essence of that case is. Once that is done, it is a matter of seeing if other cases match up and then applying it. Thus though analogy appears to mean moving from case to case, it can also be seen in a deductive way. For the definition of the essence of the baseline case then becomes the principle from which we deduce the consequences. Of course it does not work out quite as simply as that and the formalisation becomes pretty complex. Here I adopt Martin Golding's (1984) formalisation as a way of showing how *Haseldine v Daw*[105] was decided by analogy with *Donoghue v Stevenson*[106]:

1. A provider of ginger beer is one who produces a product which is intended (i) to reach the ultimate consumer (ii) in such a form as to leave him with no reasonable possibility of intermediate examination;
2. A provider of a lift is one who produces a product which is intended (i) to reach the ultimate consumer (ii) in such a form as to leave him with no reasonable possibility of intermediate examination;
3. A provider of ginger beer is one who (iii) owes a duty of reasonable care to that consumer notwithstanding the lack of contractual relationship;
4. Being the provider of a product which is one which (i) is intended to reach the ultimate consumer (ii) in such a form as to leave him with no reasonable possibility of intermediate examination is relevant to (iii) owing a duty of reasonable care to that consumer notwithstanding the lack of contractual relationship;
5. Unless there are other countervailing characteristics the provider of a lift is one who (iii) owes a duty of reasonable care to that consumer notwithstanding the lack of contractual relationship;
6. There are no countervailing characteristics;
7. The provider of a lift is one who (iii) owes a duty of reasonable care to that consumer notwithstanding the lack of contractual relationship;
8. A &P. Steven Ltd. is the provider of a lift;

---

105 [1941] 3 All E.R. 156. Haseldine was injured by a lift in a block of flats. This had just been serviced by a company, A.& P. Steven Ltd., who had a contract to service the lift and report any problems to the owners of the block of flats. This they did negligently and did not give a report to the owners. They were found liable.

106 Here it was held that Mrs. Donoghue, who was made ill by starting to drink, in a cafe, a bottle of ginger beer in which she claimed there had been a decomposing snail, had a remedy in negligence against the manufacturer with whom she had no contractual relation. Lord Atkin said:

> A manufacturer of products, which he sells in such a form as to show that he intends to reach the ultimate consumer in the form in which they left him with no reasonable possibility of intermediate examination, and with the knowledge that the absence of reasonable care in the preparation of putting up the products will result in an injury to the consumer's life or property, owes a duty of care to the consumer to take reasonable care. ([1932] A.C. at 599)

9. A&P. Steven Ltd. owes a duty of care notwithstanding the lack of contractual relationship.

But of course, there are problems here. For we must decide, having established this, whether or not to apply the analogy. One might say that here we have the problem of application[107]. But it is not quite that for the deductivist/closure type thinking. What is important in the end is whether the analogy is correct in the sense that the instant case is correctly subsumed under it, whether the definition of the essence of the base case covers the problem here. It is now no longer merely a cognitive problem (of course this case is the same) but an evaluative one - we move from cognitive sameness to evaluative sameness, MacCormick says. This done, as MacCormick (1978) brilliantly details in his book, through a complex interlocking of principles, practices and rules which inform and create the instant particular[108].

All of this is a question of what to do when the case is 'hard' in the MacCormick sense, when strict deductive reasoning runs out; when, in Alexy's terms, internal justification gives way to external justification. But, as discussed above, they are inextricably connected. We can see this when we see how the decision making when we move from the internal to the external which seems to be particularist and without control is in fact brought into the fold of the internal. MacCormick tries to show how formalism, broadly conceived can mesh in with substantive reasoning in law, thus acting as a constraint. So in that sense deductive reasoning never runs out. For him the essence of justification is in universalizability (which here is part of the idea that like cases are to be treated alike) and is the most important of such constraints. For judges to justify a decision, they must be able to show how that decision falls under a general rule which implies that similar cases have been so treated.

How does one do that in these 'external' cases? MacCormick here suggests that one looks at the consequences of the decision that is proposed. But that would appear to make it merely substantive reasoning. So what is important is not that one looks at the consequences of the particular decision but at the consequences of the decision in general or universal terms. Thus in *Donoghue*

---

[107] This would be Atria's view.

[108] In that respect the particular is already something that is abstracted - notice, for example, that when lawyers are asked for the facts of the Donoghue case they give a story about neighbours and almost never talk about a separated lady who was fed up with the scandal her estranged spouse was causing her and who in talking about the possibility of divorce with her lawyer also happened to mention the incident with the ginger beer etc. etc. And MacCormick says, in his discussion of analogy, that you cannot easily separate arguments of principle and analogy.

v Stevenson, the judges are not interested in the consequences for that manufacturer but for 'all manufacturers' and 'every article':

> 'I think that if the appellant is to succeed it must be on the proposition that every manufacturer or repairer of any article is under a duty to everyone who may thereafter legitimately use the article. ... It is logically impossible to stop short of this point ' (at p.57, per Lord Tomlin)

So consequentialism, as a form of substantive reasoning, is brought under the web of the universal for though the court looks to the consequences of a decision to justify a ruling, these consequences will be general and universal. So we have both general and particular, substance and form. The formal taking note of the substantive but making sure it does not get out of hand. In this sense, substantive reasoning is constrained by the testing of the universalisable rulings of the courts against their consequences.

But this brings in the problems of rules that we talked about. Take one of MacCormick's examples. In the case of *Ealing London Borough Council v Race Relations Board*[109], the question was whether discrimination 'on the grounds of colour, race, or ethnic or national origin' includes legal nationality. Of course, this is not the actual problem before the court. The question before the court was whether one Mr Zesko, a Polish ex-RAF pilot, who had remained in Britain after the war because of the political situation and had never taken British Nationality, should be given a council house. Ealing Borough Council, the relevant housing authority, did not do so on the grounds that he was not a British national and they made them a priority. But to bring the case one had to move beyond that and see it, not in terms of whether an ex-Polish fighter pilot should have a house, but as generalised to all people in that situation and then ask what the consequences would be if all were treated in this way. MacCormick says that the question asked is not a particular question, rather Lord Dilhorne

> 'conceives it necessary to decide whether any act of discrimination by *anyone* against *anyone* on the grounds that he is not a British subject constitutes discrimination on the ground of 'national origins'. That is not a question about a particular act of discrimination: it is a logically universal question.' (1978: 78)

But notice what happens. Zesko is now out of the picture and the judges talk of classes of people who might or might not represent him who is no longer there. We saw when we noticed what had happened to the 'facts' of *Donoghue v Stevenson.*

---

[109] [1972] A. C. 342

What is important to note about the MacCormick method is its deep Popperianism. It is the legal version of the hypothetical/deductive scientific method. It involves a procedure which tests competing hypotheses about the interpretation of legal rules by seeing what their universalisable consequences would be within the context of the coherency of the system as a whole. In its Popperianism, it suffers from the same difficulties. What guarantees that the hypotheses thus to be tested are reasonable and not completely crazy? They must, says MacCormick, have a legal warrant , which means that they must have some coherence and consistency within the system. Judges are required to decide cases only in accordance with rulings which are coherent with the existing body of law, and supported by it. Hence the importance of reliance on principles in legal argument. The ruling in a hard case must be shown to be justifiable by reference to some legal principle, and thus 'coherent' with already settled law. Rulings must also not be inconsistent with pre-existing laws, in the sense of not directly contradicting some binding or authoritative rule. If that were not so, the idea of legal systems as being or including systems of valid, binding rules would be necessarily false. When unpacked this comes down to postulating some kind of fit with precedents, statutes and the like which are themselves to be judged in terms of consequentialism.

So what we see is a sort of circle and the ultimate guarantee is, as in Popper, the fact that we trust the experienced scientists not to come up with completely crazy hypotheses. So in a sense we might say that the integrity of the law rests in the fact that there is a cohort of judges organised and socialised together whom we can trust not to come up with crazy ideas. John Bell (1986) shows how the constraints within which legal reasoning operates are defined not merely by the logical structure of the logical procedures adopted for performing the task but also by the socially developed criteria of what is acceptable. Canons of acceptable argument embrace both rules defining the logical character of legal discourse and standards of acceptability developed by the principal group within the audience to which reasons are addressed.

This is an important point because in part we can read Bell as an answer to those who attack deductivism and think of it as a way of formalising and losing the social context. Their argument is that the body of knowledge is divorced from the teacher and given in formal bodies of knowledge (rules) thus doing away with the craft and apprenticeship system[110]. They claim that in the end rules will not work because knowledge has a social base and so the law, like any other branch of knowledge is ultimately instantiated in the form of life of those who practice it. This argument is used to say that rules can

[110] See my argument in chapter 7. See also Collins (1990) and Leith (1990).

never work because they infinitely ramify and you can never capture that by rules which will only serve to simplify, give a shorthand or just get it wrong, overlooking some vital fact[111] which has been missed out in the rules because judged irrelevant.

But one can use some of this argument against its proponents. Accepting that knowledge is instantiated in a form of life, there is no reason to suppose that this cannot be seen as a sort of formalist way of life. A formalist way of life at least in the sense that rules do matter; that we do refer things back to rules which are known and published beforehand; that ultimately we have to refer back to the meaning of the statute or law. There might be different levels of this in different systems but ultimately formalism will matter in all systems of law. By this is meant not formalism in the sense of clarity but the idea that finally you have to refer back to the promulgated law and 'not think about it'; what determines what is correct to do is the law[112]. One can see this in a comparative study of statutory interpretation which aimed rationally to reconstruct the method of reasoning involved in this context[113]. A large typology of argument forms was identified and then a model, thought to be valid transjurisdictionally, was promulgated:

> (a) in interpreting a statutory provision, consider the types of argument in the following order:
>
> (i)linguistic arguments
>
> (ii)systemic arguments
>
> (iii)teleological-evaluative arguments
>
> (b) Accept as prima facie justified a clear interpretation at level (i) unless there is some reason to proceed to level (ii); where level (ii) has for sufficient reason been invoked, accept as prima facie justified a clear

---

[111] A very vivid example of this is given in Collins (1990) where he tries to operationalise that point. He conducted an experiment in seeing how you can pass on the knowledge to grow crystals. His research assistant, trained in chemistry, would talk to the technicians in the lab where they were made, and try to produce rules for growing crystals. Collins would apprentice himself to the technicians. The rules the assistant made were not as successful as the apprentice method at passing on the knowledge. A crux in the process was in fact a manipulative trick (ostensibly nothing to do with growing crystals) for the easier pouring of liquids from one flask to another without spilling them. It was only after reading Collins book that I realised why it was that I could never repair my motor-bike even though I seemed to be following the manual perfectly!

[112] see Atiyah and Summers (1987) for a detailed examination of this point.

[113] I realise that we run the risk of trying to codify socialised knowledge - but what is important here are the general and approximate results.

interpretation at level (ii) unless there is some reason to move to level (iii); in the event of proceeding to level (iii). Accept as justified only the interpretation best supported by the whole range of applicable arguments

(c) take account of arguments from intention and any other transcategorical arguments (if any) as grounds which may be relevant for departing from the above prima facie ordering MacCormick and Summers (1991: 531-2).

What we can see is how the emphasis is on that of meaning (i) and coherence and consistency which is expressed within the system of law itself and how even when we look to (c) meaning, in terms of intention, plays a large part[114]. This then is clearly a formalist way of setting out legal reasoning, combining, we might say, Alexy's internal and external justification. The values that underpin this formalist approach are, as we saw, in large part very important and, as we saw, we need a group of people socialised together, i.e. a 'community of interpretation', to be able rationally to sustain them.

But for legality we also need something more - we need to be able to move beyond while sustaining the formalism. To say, that the judges participate in a formalist way of life and practice is no bad thing but this can be only part of the story - there must always be mechanisms in that context for going beyond. There is always a strong tendency to closure which produces one of the paradoxes of democracy that we have been looking at. For though we need to have this relatively tight knit group to produce that formalism and rationality that is required for legality, this in itself produces a dynamic of social exclusivity which is arguably not only wrong in principle, but which fixes meanings in particular ways and works for a particular class[115]. The project of Bentham, and the formalists that followed him was to use codification (and this would now also include computers and legal expert systems) in order to break the power of 'judge and co.' and thereby have transparency and democracy. The paradox (see also chapter 1) is that rules, the means chosen to do so, necessitate both some group exclusivity and, ironically, loss of transparency since rules also lose the particular (see chapter 11).

In general however, the reasoning examined above is a subtle way of finding out the meaning of the rules when they might be vague and unclear[116].

---

[114] This is especially clear in the UK. See MacCormick and Summers 1991: chapter 10.

[115] See here Griffith (1977). I have used Marxism to show how the structure of law is tied in with, and to an extent constitutes, capitalism. But this is not to deny that an instrumentalist view of Marxism might not also be true -'Your jurisprudence is but the will of your class made law'.

[116] It is in this sense that MacCormick (1978) dissolves the 'England problem' for he shows how that reasoning can and does have connection to prospective rules. For his reasoning envelops the seemingly particularistic case by case reasoning of the common law as well.

Rationality, predictability and accountability are instantiated within criteria of what is acceptable, socially developed by the 'community of interpretation'. Thus there is an interlocking network of reasons, principles, rules, standards, analogies which go to make up the tradition. Quite often the process of justifying a decision at law will be a mixture of articulated and unarticulated arguments and assumptions which constitute the tradition and thus give coherence and rationality to it. But in doing that, in terms of our analogies, we are still in the realm of the computer; in the realm of meaning. We do not ask whether it is appropriate to apply the rule by reference to the particular instance at the time; even analogous reasoning seeks to produce a definition and then apply it. So for MacCormick the decidability thesis is maintained and closure kept because the law still applies *meanings* that stem from the rules. These meanings are more elastic and flexible but still refer back to the universalism of the rules. Jackson's image of the machine like quality of MacCormick's theory is still right. For though the substantive comes into the picture it is, as we saw, lost and engulfed in the universality of the system.

LEGAL INSTITUTION AND EXCLUSIONARY REASON

The closure I have been alluding to is best expressed by seeing law as what Raz (1975) calls an exclusionary reason. The following is an example adapted from Raz. Someone is phoned up late at night by a friend and offered the chance of a speculative but potentially highly lucrative investment. The only drawback is that they have to make up their mind immediately. Knowing he is a bit drunk and tired, and thus not trusting his judgement, what should he do? He could make the decisions on the balance of all the reasons *pro* and all the reasons *contra* including the reason that he is tired and a little drunk. He could, on the other hand say that he makes it a rule not to take investment decisions late at night. The former way of doing it would be to make the judgement on the balance of reasons. The latter would use the rule 'Don't take investment decisions late at night' as a reason for excluding consideration of the investment decision on the balance of reasons, even though that decision might be to make the investment. His decision would operate at a second order level in respect to the reasons of substance as to whether to take the investment decision or not. It would thus be an exclusionary reason or a content independent reason. We would have a reason for not thinking about the substance of the case because of this second order reason.

The exclusionary reason summarises, as it were, all the reasoning that one would have had to go through before making one's mind up about the investment decision and then excludes them from consideration because they are contained in the rule. In that sense the rule is, as Moles says, a sort of shorthand and that is its *raison d'etre*. For Raz, it is this sort of schema that makes sense of our practical reasoning. Let us take promise keeping to make it clearer. It is a way of conceptualising promise that prevents it from collapsing into Godwin's renewed utilitarian calculation every time a new fact comes up[117]. We follow the promise because we have made a *promise* - it enables us to ignore reasons that might come up later. For example, I promise to go drinking with a group of my students. On balance the reasons for going (I am thirsty, I have good relations with the students, I am lonely) outweigh the reasons for not going (I am tired, they could be boring) and so I promise to go. On my way to the pub I meet my professorial colleague who asks me to go to dinner with her. I regretfully say I cannot go because I am on the way to fulfil a promised engagement. I don't go because I have promised the students. Had I known this fact when my students had asked me to go with them for a drink, that fact would, on balance, have disinclined me to have promised to go with them. The promise gives us a reason for not recalculating - going to dinner with the professor is not a bad thing *per se* and likewise going drinking with the students is neither good nor bad.

All the above is not to say, according to Raz, that there will be no revisability. The reasons for my wanting to break the promise will not be the same as the substantive reasons that I adduced to make the promise in the first place (including new reasons of the sort that the professor invited me to go with her to dinner). They will be second order reasons (different from the substantive first order reasons that made me make the promise in the first place) and I will have to balance them against other second order reason like the general justification for promise keeping.

Let us now transfer the analogy and turn to law. I walk down the street and see some money lying there. What do I do? There are many things I can do with it. I could keep it, give it to the poor - but which poor for there are many deserving causes to choose from? However I realise that in law the money is not a *res nullius* and since it is not mine I am obliged to hand it in to the police. This I do - the law acting as a second order reason prevents my consideration of what substantively to do with the money. What if I do not know of this law and phone to promise to give it to Shelter? On my way to the Shelter office, I meet collectors for Oxfam who ask me for the money. I say I cannot give it them because it is promised elsewhere. Here I cannot recalculate for my promise gives me a reason for not putting Oxfam into the equation. I do not do so because the Shelter is more deserving than Oxfam but because my promise gives me a reason for not having to make that calculation.

[117] See chapter 1

But the Oxfam collector finds out how I came about the money and mentions the law on the matter to me. I can now break my promise and give it to the police. Not because giving it to the police is better than giving it to Oxfam or Shelter but because I now have a reason to break my promise that is not a first order (substantive) reason. It is one that goes to whether or not I should break a promise and not what I should substantively do with the money. So I now balance, at the second order level, keeping promises against keeping law. The criteria used here (it is important to follow the law or else society will break down etc.) will be different from the criteria used as to where the money should be located in the first place.

It is through this idea of closure, of law as exclusionary, that we should consider legal institutions (and in fact law as an institution). Law as an 'institutional fact' is a way of ordering normative activity. It creates new facts. Recall how in chapter 5 we viewed the market as something existing by virtue of its being constituted. In the same way we saw that 'contract' and other legal facts are also what McCormick and Weinberger (1986) called institutional facts by virtue of being constituted by the institutive facts of the law of contract. There are two other sets of rules; consequential, those that deal with the consequences stemming from a contract that has been constituted by the 'institutive' rules; and terminative, those which say such a contract ceases to exist. These institutions have a capacity for creating long term linkages and thus creating what he calls 'diachronic practical information' (or, rather, given what Weinberger calls 'practical information' a diachronic quality). This becomes relevant when we wish to stabilise the momentary practical information (the information relevant for action at any particular time) that we receive and reduce chance in our acting. Thus the institution of contract will link together the diverse actions of many actors. The facts thus generated will enable practical decisions to be taken about one's activities and enable reasoned long term decisions as to what has to be done to be made. MacCormick says:

> '[a]t any given moment, one can then survey the terms of specific existing arrangements interpreted in the light of consequential rules, and, taking account of events and circumstances interpreted in the same light, one can derive the momentary consequential duties, liberties and powers one has in respect of a given arrangement. This indicates how it is possible for practical thought involving law to be, not a chaotic moment-by-moment response to normative requirements or their absence, but at least partly a stable and predictable business in which a measure of secure planning is possible.' (p. 79)

Now we can see much of this on the model of exclusionary reasons. Once you enter into the institution you create what MacCormick (1992) calls a 'normative predicate' and your activity is channelled down predetermined pathways. The institution creates the legal facts precisely because it wants that sort of behaviour. I will take two examples. My first example is from the work of Sandra Dewitz (1995). She has attempted to design a system for an electronic contracting network. The aim here is to automate the generation of bills of lading involved in the carriage of goods for import and export. What she proposed was that the system itself would generate the documents. The model she used was the MacCormick and Weinberger institutional model where, for example, a contract exists as an 'institutional' fact, generated and constituted by interpersonal dealings interpreted under certain rules. But the computation just transforms raw facts into institutional facts according to its program. It does not itself apply a rule. We see here the automatic quality of what happens when we enter the institutional rules of the system. Once there we don't think about it since the performative network, being the medium through which the acts are performed, can observe acts and assert successful to a legal data base. It makes things much more convenient to all parties because this reduces the risk of error and also makes disputes less likely since the institutive rules, as the 'umbrella contract' make things explicit.

My second example is taken from the work of Atiyah (1986). For him formal reasoning is seen much as on the model of Raz's theory of exclusionary reasons. He uses the example of marriage to show the point behind formal reasoning. He confronts the argument proposed by certain legal scholars that it is not necessary to introduce the formal status of marriage in order to make decisions about property rights, custody etc. when cohabiting couples break up, since these decisions are already made, to some extent at least, by having regard to all the circumstance of the case. Since marriage is no longer a good formal reason for recognising the rights and obligations of cohabiting partners, why bother with the institutional fact of marriage? Atiyah goes on to discuss some issues arising from this. What happens, for example, if we look at rights to action under the Fatal Accident Acts and similar legislation? Though it might be said that we can base this on simple *de facto* dependency it does not seem clear, according to Atiyah, what sort of dependency would found an action of *solatium*. Again how would the law in respect of intestacy work, having regard to cohabitation rather than the status of marriage? There would be problems because it would not only be the length of cohabitation but the quality of it that would be important. It would not be easy to draw up a simple tariff giving a proportion of the estate depending upon length of cohabitation. The intentions of the parties ought to be taken into account. Surely a relationship entered into with the intention of its being a lifelong one, ought to be treated as grounding, in the event of death, rights to a large proportion of the estate, even if it had only subsisted for a short time? Though this could be effected by testament immediately upon entering the relationship, this ignores the fact that marriage enables one to do this merely by the fact of entering into marriage. Again, what counts as cohabitation is not something that is easy to define, as we can see in social security decisions on the matter, or the immigration 'primary purpose rule', and the problems that arise from the old Scottish form of irregular marriage where the marriage was constituted by 'habit and repute' (i.e. in part by cohabitation).

The validity of the particular arguments is not important for our purposes, what is important to note is that in these discussions Atiyah is showing, if not the utility of the legal institution of marriage, at least wherein that utility would lie. For an easy and practical solution to the problems Atiyah raises is after all by having the institution of marriage. This, once entered into, guides reasoning about what to do into particular pathways and makes more coherent sense out of a potentially chaotic aspect of social life. The introduction of the status of marriage insulates us from many of these problems and gives us clear definitions by tying co-habitation to marriage.

Atiyah says that the reason we feel that our formal decision is right is, in the end, because we are satisfied and certain in our substantive decisions. The implication is that at some time the substantive problems were solved rationally and thus we can now afford to use formal reasoning. The institution comes about because gradually a practice grows up where, for example, we do something we say we will, not merely for the substantive reasons we had in saying we would do it, but also because of the reason that we said we would do it. At first that is one among all the reasons but gradually it excludes the other and so we might say the convention of promising grows up. We do it because we promised and the other reasons are excluded. Thus the institution grows up on the back of the substantive reasons since the reason that it is a promise can be seen as a universalization of the substantive reasons. This both gives us a democratic, autonomous, input and machine-like heteronomy.

CONCLUSION

I do indeed think that one should see law as exclusionary reasons instantiated in institutions. But is this a solution to our problems? In a way no, for we still have the institution as a template which imposes itself on the 'raw events'; my helping of a friend becomes, for example, a contractual obligation to the mortgage lender with whom I stood guarantee. The ethical problem of getting to the particular still remains, for we still appear to have lost that particular in the universality of the institution. Substantive reasons might have founded it - but where are they now? They are lost in the template which imposes itself on our particularity. The decidability thesis and closure of MacCormick still apply. It is to these problems that we turn in the next chapter.

CHAPTER 9

REASONING BEYOND THE MACHINE

INTRODUCTION

In this chapter we again look at some of the ethical problems involved in legal reasoning. In the last chapter we saw one way that the law might be said to stay in touch with the particular. This was through seeing the law as composed of institutions whose formality and exclusionary nature rested on the fact that they rested upon acceptable substantive reasoning. But what can we do when the substantive reasons on the back of which the institutions rest are no longer so? What happens to the institution then? We ended the last chapter by saying it just kept the machine mode, imposing itself on 'raw events' and making it impossible to unpick them. In this chapter we start from the other end, as it were. One might argue that ultimately these machines collapse into substantive reason, into particularity – even though we might hide this from ourselves because we want to live like a machine and not take responsibility. We always have the choice but we do not take it because we are blind to it.

We can see this collapse into particularity if we go back to exclusionary reasons and my example of promising and law. Our example produces a problem. I decide to hand the money to the police because I balance keeping promises against breaking the law. But is that the correct balance to make? Is law perhaps a third order reason to be balanced against other such reasons? How do I decide that is the case? I can only make that judgment and act for that reason if I balance all reasons including the ones that I excluded in the first place. Thus, it might be argued, because that judgment reaches down into the substantive particularity of the problem, one can always re-conceptualise the system of exclusionary reasons as one taken on the balance of reasons.

But need we make that judgment about the law here? Surely the law excludes my making that judgment (that I should balance the law against promise-keeping) as well? I follow the law without asking the question of whether it can or cannot be balanced against promise keeping. More generally then, we have to ask if the exclusionary reason excludes itself. Sufficiently complex ones will, Detmold (1984) argues. Thus, if one of the main points of law is to produce a system of authority which will enable us to have a common way of settling things which might otherwise be continually disputed and thus harm the society, that is in itself also a reason not to ask questions about law itself. This generates a paradox. If law is excluded as a system of authority from being questioned, then it does not count in practical thought and we are left with the substantive reasons. But if we say that we cannot exclude it, then it generates an infinite regress of third order, fourth order reasons etc.

What Detmold means here is that we are always trying to get to the 'raw moral data' and the exclusionary reason is a way of trying to prevent that. But the reason we give for whether it excludes or not in any particular case, tries to burrow down into the 'raw moral data' - that judgment will partly be based on the result we expect from excluding or not. In other words it will be based on the result we get from looking and balancing together all the reasons, including the exclusionary one. To avoid that we go up a level and say the balancing is done not at the 'raw data' level but at the second order level - in our example, balancing the general reasons for keeping the law as against the general reasons for keeping a promise. But there we can, as we saw in the example with Shelter and Oxfam, perform the same operation again thus going up to a third level and so on in an infinite regress.

Essentially his claim is that the rules are not self-applying. We have to decide whether to apply them and we can only do that by looking at the situation in all its uniqueness. Part of the meaning of universality then, that the rule is always applied when the conditions of its application are met, presents us with a problem. Since the rule is not self-applying we have to decide each time whether the conditions of its application are met. This is not necessarily because the rule is general and vague. It is precisely because, as Detmold says, each situation is unique that we cannot just let the rule apply itself and have to decide, at each putative application, whether it applies. In so doing, morality and law are inevitably and necessarily conjoined since I must decide whether it is the right thing to do and think that it is the right think to do. Part of Detmold's argument rests on a posited distinction between justification and application. It is one thing to determine what justifies a norm and another to see whether it is appropriately applied in any particular case[118] and the criteria for the latter will be different. The meaning of a rule is

[118] Günther (1993)

something different from its application. And it is from the fact that the criteria of whether it is correct to apply the law will differ from the criteria as to its meaning, rather than vagueness or ambiguity that the indeterminacy of the law comes.

Take an example from Private International Law. A marriage contracted in Germany comes for divorce to the Scottish courts. It is decided, that under the conflict rules prevailing here, the law that is applicable is the law of Germany. The court might have no problem in applying these laws. But if it is unclear as to the German law on the question, then it will take expert advice as to the meaning of the German Law. That advice will be a matter of German law and the criteria for determining that will be different from the criteria for determining whether German Law applied in the first place - that will be a matter of the Scottish conflict rules. We might say then, that every rule has a meaning element and a jurisdictional element and the criteria for each element will be different.

In Detmold's view the refusal to accept that and merely treat the rule as containing the conditions for its application would mean that we would be acting as computers, programmed to apply the rule without thinking about what is actually happening; we would just follow the rule blindly; we would no longer show respect and love for the unique mystery of that particular's existence. This would be against the ethics of alterity; it would deny respect for the other. But this also leads to a final problem. Don't we need criteria to 'think about it'? If we do, will they not become a meta-system of decision making which could reproduce the legalism that we want to avoid in the first place? These will be the questions of this chapter. I turn to see look at the meaning-application distinction and the ethical problems it raises for legal reasoning in the context of Bernard Jackson's (1988: 37-60) discussion of the normative syllogism.

REFERRING TO THE PARTICULAR

Here, he looks at the problems of seeing legal reasoning as a deductive process for the rule of law. He gives the example of a deductive syllogism:

All persons who blaspheme the gods are liable to be executed;
Socrates has blasphemed the gods;
therefore Socrates is liable to be executed.

A number of links have to be established, he claims, if this is to work. Firstly, we have to show that Socrates did in fact say something. Secondly we have to qualify the facts - his saying what he said in the way that he said it - as blasphemy. Finally we have to make sure that the words used by the legislator 'cover' the case. But because legal doctrine lacks the temporal dimension which necessarily exists when in the process of adjudication, deductive reasoning presents problems for the law. For in doctrine one might say that the syllogism is temporal in that it is either hypothetical;

if it is true that 'all persons who blaspheme the gods are liable to be executed'
and if it is true that 'Socrates has blasphemed the gods'
then it must be true that 'Socrates is liable to be executed'

or to be expressed in an indefinite present.

But the problem with adjudication is that temporal relations come into it. Witnesses have to establish that something happened in the past and, in very general terms, they have to say that a law was made that covered the case. This is important because the point of the rule of law is, that in being prospective, it enables us to predict what will happen and thus enables us to organise our lives in advance. So when we are judged, whether criminally or civilly, it is important that the situation and event happened after the law on the basis of which the adjudication is made. If we look at the typical law, 'if someone has done y then...', this is ambiguous for we have to know whether or not it precedes 'x has done y'. If it precedes the action, 'x has done y', one cannot punish since the law, 'if someone has done y then...', refers only to acts committed before its enunciation. If the law comes after the action, though we might think that the case is covered or referred to by the law, it would be retrospective and thus against the point of the rule of law. Thus, Jackson claims, we need a major premise which has 'eternal' or 'omnitemporal' force even though the minor premise, the event, is 'time bound'. We cannot get rid of this temporal dimension and we have to show how the atemporal law covers or refers to the particular case.

The problem here is how the judge can, in adjudicating the case, link the atemporal law with something that happens at particular time; with something that exists in time and space. Can the law pick that event out? Can it have it in mind? In the syllogism we started with, can it be said that the major premise refers to the actual time bound Socrates? Can the judge so conclude by deductive reasoning? MacCormick says that it can and thus legal decisions are capable of being justified in terms of that form of reasoning.

Jackson's argument against this is that the Rule of Law is prospective but the normative syllogism must be atemporal. It thus cannot 'cover' the particular events in time and space that it is alleged the general rule covers. Laws expressed in universalistic terms do not refer to particular cases, they merely link universally stipulated legal conditions to universally prescribed legal consequences (MacCormick 1992). They cannot thus get at the event in a trial; cannot be said to cover the actual Socrates in our example because they merely state what would befall someone who fulfils the conditions that a Socrates would have fulfilled. This cannot be said to pick out the actual Socrates in the trial. And that is what deductive reasoning purports to do. But we plainly do say that people are liable under laws. How do we do so? How do we link the law to the particular event?

Jackson goes on to claim that even within the tradition of analytic philosophy, the way we do this destroys deductive reasoning as a model of justification. When we say that a law covers the particular case, what we do, says Jackson, is say that it refers to that case. But reference is not an attribute of the meaning of an utterance but something that we do. Jackson uses Strawson (1950) to make this point clear. The problem in Strawson's famous paper consisted in what to make of sentences like 'The present King of France is bald'. They are clearly not nonsense in that they appear to mean something but it seems difficult to call them true or false. Strawson's answer is that the sentence can be used to mention or refer to someone, but since in this case that person does not exist, the reference fails and one cannot say that the sentence is true or false. The sentence is intelligible however and does have a meaning. This is not to be conflated with mentioning or referring, which is something one uses a statement to do. The point is that it is not the words that refer but the use made of them. It is not the words of the sentence (the meaning), 'All those who blaspheme the gods are liable to execution' that refer to the actual Socrates but the use (application) we make of them. Thus an argument has to be made to say that the major premise does in fact apply to the Socrates actually on trial and this has to be done at the trial. The fact that the major premise has meaning does not mean to say that we can take it that it automatically applies to the actual Socrates. This is not a point about vagueness and lack of clarity in the law, though of course, that might occur in practice[119]. The claim here is that even when a situation falls within the general sense of the rule there is nothing inevitable, speaking psychologically, sociologically or logically, that it should so refer to that event. This could be seen as another way of saying that there is a difference between the meaning of a rule and its application in a particular case. And to say that the rule applies

[119] So in the law we might adopt the tactic of saying that the minor premise does or does not fall within the words of the statute.

has to come from an argument that takes account of the particular case and that can only be made when confronting that case. For the application of rules lies in human hands. It is in this way that the rules break away from their self referential cycles of moving from universally stipulated legal conditions to universally prescribed legal consequences and back again and get into the world.

The implication of this is that universal abstract rules cannot hit the target they aim at, or rather, they do not aim for the target one might think. Think of our running analogy of the cash-line machine. The machine will understand the rules in respect of when you are enabled to get money from it. It will know who is to be defined as one-who-cannot-get-money. But say nevertheless, for grave reasons, you want money. In this case it would not be able to do anything about it because the rule cannot tell it that - under it you are defined as one-who-cannot-get-money. What would be necessary here is a teller to see you in pain and decide that it is appropriate to give you money (the act of reference). That can only, on the Jackson view, be done at the moment of application and would deny the prospectivity of the Rule of Law.

But this is not a just a parable about an uncaring machine. For the reason that the machine does not give you the money is because it does not 'see' you. What it does is read or 'see' the card which perhaps (as many modern ones do) has a laser embossed picture of you on it. So it sees that picture and not you. In a sense you are that photo which is part of the card. There is a gap between the photo and you, the living being standing there with that card. The machine sees only the card with the photo. Why? Because the machine's programmes, the laws, cannot hit you for that is not the target they aim at - they are aiming at the card which is representing you. The universal rules can only hit another universal, the card, which represents those that look like it. Remember the tiger and how, in putting it in the zoo and trying to see it as representing all tigers, it lost that grace and beauty it had in the wild. We might say, to carry the analogy further, that the photograph on the card is rather like the tiger in the zoo. It now represents the class of all those that are entitled to use the machine and so you have lost the beauty of your particularity. The effect of that is the machine no longer cares about you but only about you as represented in the rules. So it is now no longer interested in your actual needs and wants - it is only interested in that representative of you, the card. Again, think of the tiger. The zoo feeds and cares for the specimen in its keep, that imitation of a real tiger. It does not need the same care that the real tiger, the one that is no longer there, would. Some animals in captivity cannot even be set free, for they would die, their wonder has been destroyed for ever. And so for Detmold, it is vital that we do not lose sight of the person behind the photograph.

The analogy shows that the dynamic of rules seen in this mode (of law like exclusionary reasons) is to close the gap between meaning and application. This comes out if we pursue further Jackson's (1991) controversy with MacCormick (1991). MacCormick's view is that the question is not of reference but of sense; in other words, meaning determines application. For him, our task is to see if the minor premise instantiates the major one; if the actual Socrates instantiates the norm 'all those who blaspheme the gods are liable to execution'. But how do we know that this is the actual Socrates? Does that come from the meaning of the words or a story about how words are to be used at the time of adjudication? MacCormick argues that the Rule of Law would indeed lose its force if we could not say prospectively that the words of the legislation covered the case. We therefore need, he goes on, sound interpretative arguments (not all of them deductive - but deductive in our wider sense) to show that this is the case[120]. But Jackson claims that MacCormick's rebuttal would only work if we thought of the original sense intended by the legislator who utters the law. On Jackson's view, MacCormick is ambiguous here because he tries to rescue his argument by going to the sense of the proposition given by the legislators while denying that this has anything to do with what the legislator actually had in his mind (he attacks the argument that interpretation only has the function of finding out what the legislators actually intended). That latter is of course a perfectly correct argument but it loses the prospectivity of the rule of law. For the sound interpretive arguments have to be made by the judge in the case, who claims that either this is what the actual legislator or some 'ideal rational legislator' intended. That claim would be made, as Jackson says, by the judge at the time. So even if one accepted the instantiation version of it the point of the reference story would still hold. And the prospectivity of the Rule of Law lost.

What is important here, claims Jackson, is to distinguish between doctrine (meaning) and adjudication (application). At some level of abstract doctrine MacCormick's points might hold but when it comes to adjudication one can say that something else is going on. That is why the computer analogy is important for Jackson to use - for his claim is that the more the answer to his Rule of Law problem is given in MacCormick's way the more you get machine-like operations with no possibility of change.

[120] See our discussion of MacCormick's view of legal reasoning above.

We are still left then with the question of how to have our cake and eat it; of how to preserve that Razian structure of practical reasoning in the law (it seems to serve so many good and useful purposes) and yet at the same time accommodate in that flexibility towards the particular. We saw, in the previous chapter, one attempt by way of what I call the 'wide' view of deductivist reasoning. In a way this is saying that the exclusionary reason is as strong as it was before but flexibility is achieved by the fact that its scope is flexible. But all that does is say that the meaning of the rule might be vague and that once you fix it that meaning applies in the rigorous manner of the exclusionary rule. So it would not really solve the problem we are concerned with for again it is wanting to disguise application as meaning. In the rule, 'you can only marry people of the opposite sex' the question is not whether a male transsexual, after the operation, is a woman and so can marry a man but whether that sort of marriage should be allowed.

Another attempt is defeasibility. MacCormick's says:

> 'The point about defeasibility is that every appearance of validity may attach to some arrangement set up under legal rules or some legal state of affairs ostensibly arising from some set of rules and events: and yet it can happen that this arrangement or 'institutional fact' is subject to some kind of invalidating intervention. That which was initially, or on the face of it, valid turns out to be open to attack, and under attack to lose its initial validity, or be revealed as never having been valid, despite all appearances. That is, the arrangement (or whatever) in question is defeasible, and invalidating events bring about its defeasance. (1995: 99)

Much of defeasibility, unless it is explicit (there is an 'unless' clause), is to do with pragmatics:

> 'Law has to be stated in general terms, yet conditions formulated generally are always capable of omitting reference to some element which can turn out to be the key operative fact in a given case....... So general formulations of rights are apt to leave many background conditions unstated, especially those which arise only in rather exceptional cases. The presence of unstated elements appears to be a general feature of law, albeit different legal systems take different characteristic lines on the degree to which statutory draftsmanship should tend towards completeness in each statutory formulation, rather than giving broader allowance to a reading of statutes in the light of their whole systemic context.' (p. 103)

Thus, if it is explicit, then it can be fitted within the narrow deductivist system and if it is pragmatic then it takes place within the wider deductivist system that I talked about. Much of the argument about defeasibility then is about how to produce a more flexible meaning - but that will always be what determines the application.

But there is another problem[121]. For we might say that there cannot really be an 'exception' to a rule - for all that means is that we did not understand the rule. At the moment of its instantiation with the exception, we see its true meaning. Thus there is no distinction between justification and application - problems of application largely apply to exceptional situations which of course would be merely a way of specifying the rule[122]. But this, though it saves the idea that meaning determines application, destroys the determinacy which is its point. For the dynamic of that argument is to think of the rule being discovered more fully each time it is applied with the danger of falling into the particularistic nihilism of claiming there is no rule. This, ironically, has the effect of transferring the important phase to the application and at the same time loosing all contact with the determinacy of the rule. Defeasibility then either collapses into particularism or rests locked in the determined meaning.

This problem is the one of the application of law and of qualification; the universal normative propositions would seem to be unable to refer to the particular prospective instance and reference by the user would seem to lack universalistic justification. Various solutions take one or the other side of the divide and we are left sliding from an insulated decision where we cannot connect with the substantive to a substantive one where we cannot connect with the universal. One is either locked in the general rules or stuck in particularity. A computer programmed to apply a legal code will do so without reference to the outside. It will only refer to its own internal operations and ignore the reality outside. That will not impinge upon it. It will merely apply the results of its own internal operations to that reality. Rules are like that. To apply to everyone equally one has to abstract from the particularity of each person and make them legal subjects. In doing that, what happens is that the actual person gets lost. The legal subject gets drawn into the self-referential cycle of the law and loses its connection with the real person. One can sum the point up in a phrase that people often use to express a (philistine?) view of art, 'I know nothing about art but I know what I like'. That person just sees the particular. Someone who, *vice versa*, says 'I know everything about art but I don't know what I like' is someone who can't get out of the universal. The former mistakenly thinks that you can know what art you like without knowing about art. The latter mistakenly thinks that knowing everything about art should have determined what you like. Various solutions take one or the other side of the divide and we are left sliding from an

[121] See Atria's careful discussion (*op. cit.*, chapter 3).

[122] See Wellmer (1991) and Atria (*op. cit.*)

insulated decision where we cannot connect with the substantive to a substantive one where we cannot connect with the universal. The one over-ordered and the other, over-chaotic.

Our argument has been that we have to be in the 'middle zone', that gap between meaning and application. It is difficult to keep in this middle because holding the universalism of the law and the particularity of the event apart is not easy and the danger is that we getting locked into one or the other or indeed collapsing one into the other.

THE PARTICULARITY VOID

Gillian Rose's (1992) thesis about the middle[123], to which we have likened our 'middle zone' is a sociological thesis about how modernity theorises the impossibility of creating this space. I want here to adapt it somewhat to the ethics of decision taking, especially in the law. The reason we want to theorise the impossibility of this place, is that it is an anxious place. It is an anxious place because risk always accompanies it. I have to make decisions there which expose myself and I cannot run for cover for the safety of certainty. So we seek certainty either by just applying the law and forgetting about the impulse to love or welfare - thinking that to be dangerous and destructive, or by surrendering to it because that is the only thing that is *real* - thereby giving in to a nihilistic particularism. So for Rose, there is no beginning outside of the middle, it is in there with all its risks that we have to commit ourselves and take responsibility for our decisions. I cannot construct a mythical beginning to give me safety or security (my love or the law). Part of this might mean 'suspending the ethical'; no longer seeing things only as the instantiation of the universal (see the sacrifice of Abraham in chapter 4); not grounding the answer in the foundations of the law and ignoring everything else.

For Rose you have to start from the here and now, you cannot wish away, by imposing a clear system upon them, all the conflicting values, principles, and the tragedies that your decisions might and certainly will cause. We saw in chapter 2 how wishing it away was part of the Kantian project - if I never tell a lie, then no matter what happens, I cannot be responsible. In chapter 5 we saw that the market saw it that way too - I cannot be held responsible for that person's bankruptcy and collapse into penury, I merely followed the rules of the market. We no longer have to commit ourselves.

---

[123] Much of my understanding of Gillian Rose's work was gained in the context of work on Theology and Law which I undertook with Claire Davis and with a reading group on *The Broken Middle* in which she and Fernando Atria participated. I am indebted to them both.

Rose says that we have to commit ourselves to a judgement that will be risky, that ex hypothesi we will not know the appropriateness of until after the event. This is neither a consequentialist nor a Kantian decision, and neither is it procedural. Nor, for Rose, is it something that ignores law. For part of her point is to defend system and universality against those who seek the particularism of, 'All you need is Love'. Law is something that we need in our decision making processes. For Rose, what she calls the singular, is the fruit of the work of politics, of being in the 'middle'. Therefore our decisions will be the fruit of encounter there - with all the myriad reasons, of which law will be one. We need law in our decision making processes but we will never know from the beginning whether our decision is right. Here again we meet the explosion of love that produces and interacts with the law (see chapter 6) and recreates it again. Law is not ultimately, as we have seen, self applying - but that should not diminish our faith in it. We should not believe in the possibility of an error-free society. We can and must always learn from our mistakes and recreate the rationality of the law again. That is part of our personal and political work. That is 'Loves Work'[124].

The above stress on the complexity of things might seem at odds with what I have said in chapter 7 which, in parts, praises the virtues of simplicity. What I mean by complexity though is not that it is never obvious what to do. Quite often it is - what is complex is that even so we cannot be sure that it will turn out right, that you are never sure whither things will lead. What we should not necessarily do in the face of that reality is to say, 'it's very complicated', and do nothing - not taking the risk of going beyond. Doing something safe like following the moral (or legal) rules, a form of Kantianism, is not the answer for that is precisely to hide away from the possibility of error[125].

Looking more specifically to legal reasoning we encounter the 'particularity void' of Michael Detmold (1989). For him it is that space that exists between the meaning of the rule and its application. For him 'reasonable' can qualify either the rule, or its application, it is thus a different question to ask whether a rule is reasonable and whether it is reasonable to apply it. The answer will not be the same in each case. It might be reasonable to apply a unreasonable rule and *vice versa*. Judge 1 makes a decision which becomes a precedent for Judge 2. Judge 2 thinks that the decision by Judge 1 (reasons xyz outweigh reasons abc) is unreasonable (abc outweighs xyz) but nevertheless applies the precedent in the instant case. Why? Because there is

[124] See Rose (1995)

[125] Sometimes it is a risk to choose to follow the law. A radical might sometimes have to risk doing conservative things and be conventional in certain situations even if his colleagues think of him as having sold out.

now another reason v (that the decision was made by Judge 1 in the manner he made it) and xyz *and* v outweigh abc). This might appear to be a universalistic decision (the equality of all subjects under the rule) but the point that Detmold is making is that the decision must be made in that particular instance and the judge must take responsibility for it. He gives a telling example. Suppose you live in a system where you compete for judicial office by exam. You sit the exam and answer a particular problem question. When you get out, you worriedly go to the text book to check to see if you were right. You find you were and so go away satisfied. According to Detmold you are so because you have answered the universal (doctrinal) or hypothetical question. You have not been asked to exercise your practical reason. Now suppose you become a judge and within a few months exactly the same problem comes up. You know the answer so you write your judgement. You then come to deliver it. But don't you hesitate now - even if you know that you have not forgotten everything? You do and you do so, according to Detmold, because now you have a practical question before you. That is different from the universal (or hypothetical) of the exam. Here you have to take responsibility.

Let us put it another way. Say I make a decision, away from all my books on a remote circuit. I get back and worriedly check. I find that I am right. Do I necessarily cease worrying, confident that my decision was after all right? Yes and no. I might feel confident that doctrinally I was right and therefore safe from the criticism of my colleagues. But is that all there is to it? Did I really make the correct decision there? Do I think I treated the defender justly? Now I am dealing with an actual practical decision that I have made and here there is no easy fit between decision and doctrine. For I am responsible for that decision and not the doctrine. That then is the meaning of the argument that Detmold gives for the inseparability of law and morality. In the end the argument is one about responsibility. He says no judge, if he has integrity, can consistently say he is against the death penalty and sentence someone to death. For in the particular situation, in *this* case, in *these* circumstance, he thinks it right that *he* should sentence *this defender* to die. He cannot escape behind the fact that he was applying the law; that he legally sentenced him to die and not morally. That is weaselling out of it. It might be correct as a matter of law and he might have given a correct description of his theoretical moral view. But what he did was cause the defender to die and he is responsible for that. It is easier for him to justify this to himself than an executioner but that is just a point about the banality of evil[126]. The executioner can make the same move too. He can just see himself as an instantiation of the state and of the rationality of law (*I* am not doing it, the

[126] See Arendt (1994)

state is) - but he is the one tying the rope[127], just as the judge is the one with the black hat pronouncing sentence.

The particularity void then is where we take responsibility. Two questions remain. Firstly, what can the particular it be? In what sense can we say that it exists? The epistemological argument we have used so far is two edged. It claims that the particular is always lost in the general. But it can be taken further to say that you can never in fact have a particular because each particular is just a one of a potentially infinite set of descriptions which one can never fully know. They can only be known through the mediation of concepts or laws. This is a variation of Hayek's epistemological argument for the market (see chapter 5), where he argues that we can only know things through abstract categories and therefore there is an infinite amount of facts in the world. This makes constructive rationalism which sanctions state intervention impossible. Strangely, the fact we can never know the particular is accepted by some who are conscious of the ethical problem with which I started this chapter - who believe in the ethics of alterity, in the moral arguments that I have been putting. Observe how Veitch characterises Derrida:

> 'Since [the other] can only be grasped and known through language in and through it is reclassified as other than it was. Justice, for Derrida, is the impossible but irresistible attempt to treat or address that event on its own terms. The event is not in itself justice: "This undecidability 'before the law' is not necessarily (necessary) justice. It is an absolute alterity which is, precisely, undecidable, unknowable before the application of a rule, a norm a value or a decision which would determine it as justice or, otherwise[128]"' (1998:221)

When we do 'justice' to the other, we need law but it will never be sufficient and we will always be fated not to know it. The laws will always be indeterminate and change and there will always remain in them the ghost of the 'other' to worry and drive us on. But where does this get us. For Veitch

> 'The more one hears about "deferring the undeferrable", of "conceiving a justice that cannot but must be conceived" of "saying what cannot be said" and "listening to what cannot be heard", the more one is tempted to produce a charge not so much of relativism (for what values *do* these espouse), but of serious fence-sitting.' (1997: 97)

---

[127] See the memoirs of the English hangman, Albert Pierrpoint (1997) who came to realise this point.

[128] Perrin, C *Breath from Nowhere: Justice and Community in the Event of Human Rights* (1996 University of Kent Ph.D. Thesis 82 (quoted by Veitch)

And if we get off the fence, what do we do then? We just go on and as, Veitch cogently puts it, all we get is versions of Fish's 'doing what comes naturally' which is, not surprisingly, what we do in our society, in our particular community.

Veitch argues to the contrary that one should not conflate epistemology with justice. Because we might not be able fully to know the other, does not mean that we cannot do justice, in the sense that we cannot have criteria and context with which determine our doing of justice in each particular case. His argument is similar to the rebuttal to Hayek's epistemological argument against 'constructive rationalism', - it does not follow from Hayek's argument that one cannot, depending on the circumstances, intervene in certain specific areas.

But can we know the particular at all? The logic of the epistemological argument above seems to imply that as well. And Simmonds (1993) uses this to argue that things like the 'particularity void' are nonsense. For him there is no particular - there are just different sets of descriptions. Veitch (1998) says that Simmonds is partly right. But, Veitch argues, we can see that it is false to claim that we can never speak the particular because it is always expressed in language and thus can have a potentially infinite set of categories if we think of proper names. A mother describes a general category but Danuta my mother, is a proper name that only names my mother and she is unique! Indexicals are not allowed in universal statements. To say this is not to say that criteria cannot be used when making judgements in respect of this particular nor that in some ways she will be captured by them. But it does not destroy the particular.

But accepting all that, the question now remains as to where it is and how do we respond to it. In answer to this question, Detmold takes us to a concrete example of the particularity void. He takes an example from Tolstoy's *War and Peace* and the confrontation therein between Pierre and Davout. Davout has been given orders to shoot Russian spies but he does not shoot Pierre. Holding his rifle, he, looks at him, hesitates and does not fire. Tolstoy says that at the moment of hesitation many things passed through Davout's mind:

> 'Davoust lifted his eyes and gazed searchingly at him. For some seconds they looked at one another, and that look saved Pierre. It went beyond the circumstances of war and the court-room, and established human relations between the two men. Both of them in that one instant were dimly aware of an infinite number of things, and they realized that they were both children of humanity, that they were brothers' (1978: 1141)

Veitch argues that this does not show attention to the particular because what it actually shows is a realisation of Davout's and Pierre's commonality (they were both humans, brothers) - it is the realisation of that context that saves Pierre. So in that respect, it is a form of universalist reasoning for what is happening is that they are both being instantiated under a general norm - All men are brothers and one does not shoot them. And so, though the moment may be for Detmold mystical,

> "I, the judge, and Davout, at the moment of practicality entered the unaswering void of particularity, the realm of love, about which only mystical, poetic things can be said ....: or nothing....Judges enter this realm everyday." (1989: 457)

it is not, as Veitch says, because of particularity but rather because their commonality and universality was recognised. However, there is more to it than that. For it is the moment of encounter and the hesitation that is important. It is at that moment that Davout sees the particular Pierre - he sees through the enemy and he sees not a brother but someone who should be treated as a brother and then he imposes that category on him. He pays attention to Pierre. In that moment of attention he comes to realise that he should not shoot him; he should not be instantiated in the rule, 'shoot all enemies'; that will not be attached to him. This explains why Detmold, who holds that it is the facts of a practical case and nothing else that give me a reason for deciding it one way or another, can still claim that rules are important. For, he goes on to say, the weighing of particular facts implies comparison and, though they are unique, the weighing can only be done by virtue of their attached universals. We weigh particulars with certain universals 'particularly attached' (1984: 179). The attaching of the rule, (the context *per* Veitch) is in the particular encounter and it is the particularity of the situation that determines it. Thus the particularity void is not a mystical situation but rather a statement of the fact that we have to start from a particular situation. We cannot let the rule make us forget that. Davout does not start from 'All spies should be shot'. He starts from meeting Pierre on a battlefield with all the attendant circumstances, including the rule, 'Spies should be shot'. And by paying attention to that he comes to see Pierre's pain. He sees his need and so attaches the universal, 'All men are brothers and should be treated with compassion' to him.

It is true than that in a way it is the 'unknowable particular' that drives us on and so the view that I am putting can be, as Veitch notes in the context of

Detmold, reminiscent of Derrida[129]. However, that is not as important as the paying attention to the facts of the case – and it is that that enables us to do the appropriate weighing and balancing. However here we do not simply abandon the universal for a particularistic decision based on the 'hunch'[130]. What is happening here is that the law is, in a sense, defeasible and a review is necessary (the suspension of the ethical that we talked about). The key point here is that the rule is not necessarily thereby abrogated. We may take an example[131] to make this clearer. A traffic warden issuing penalty notices to cars parked illegally. In one such car is a driver fast asleep. He does not issue the ticket because now other values come into play – but the rule remains. And with this we can turn to our second point. How do we recognise the situation in which the traffic warden finds himself? What do we do in that situation? Where do we go from there? What is important here is *phronesis* and a balancing of the various reasons that we might have of making our decision.

To answer that, I want to start from looking at institutions and their formal or exclusionary nature again. We saw that how for Atiyah these were based on, in effect, a universalization of the many substantive decisions that over the ages people were happy were appropriate and worked well. So in a sense one gets the democratic input. One might say that marriage works as an institution because over the ages substantive decisions that were made when people were in these 'cohabitation situations' crystallised into the formal institution of marriage. People were by and large satisfied with this crystallisation because it continued those substantive decisions. But what it also had the effect of doing, as we have seen, was to freeze the decisions in a particular way. In a sense, the democratic or participatory input that came from these myriad decisions was lost and we just apply that particular status of marriage. But there is scope for change and when, Atiyah argues, we are no longer so happy with these substantive decisions, then we go behind the institution, as it were, and start looking at the substantive reasons again. Atiyah gives the example of contract. He shows how it is that fact that we are no longer sure of the substantive solutions that underpinned the notion of contract that lead us away from what he calls formal reasoning in contract. Thus in some cases it is

> 'hard to avoid the conclusion that the formal reasons themselves have been jettisoned, and the issues treated as though they were completely at large.' (1986: 41)

---

129 One can develop this view theologically - see Bańkowski and Davis (2000)

130 As in the American Legal Realists

131 I am grateful to John Bell for this example

In *Dillingham Construction Pty Ltd. v Downs*[132], the High Court of Australia decided that, even in circumstances where the contract told him not to do so, a builder could still be said to have reasonably relied upon the owner for information and could thus sue him in negligence. The idea that the contract defined everything in advance and that was the end of the matter was rejected, and it was held that a duty of care could arise between the parties. This could be proved by an examination of the facts of the case. Here then, the institutional fact of contract was not seen as an exclusionary reason and the institution was slowly and painstakingly unpicked. We can also see this happening in marriage as an institution. I choose my example here because it shows that formality can be progressive and supportive of human welfare. The tide of anti-immigrant racial feeling has meant that in some cases the courts, and especially immigration officers, now start looking behind the law to see if there really was a marriage. The so called 'marriage of convenience' made to get entry into the UK now justifies, for some, looking beyond the formal status of being married, to the 'dominant purpose', of the parties in making the marriage[133].

What gives us the reason to 'lift the veil', so to speak? Schauer (1991) thinks of rules on the model of exclusionary reasons as 'entrenched generalisations'. Rules pick out a set of operative facts which will always trigger the consequences of the rule. This is done on the base of what he calls the 'underlying justification' of the rule. Like an exclusionary reason this means that one follows the rule because it is the rule, even though the underlying justification might not in all cases be achieved. What makes a rule a rule is precisely that acceptance of what Atria calls 'sub-optimality'[134]. If one refuses to accept that and make an exception then it could not count as a rule. Exceptions are allowed on the model we saw above (a rule with unless.... is still a rule)[135].

But Schauer distinguishes between the idea of exclusion and the force of the exclusion. Sometimes one is able to reach down into the first order reasons and realise that in this particular case you do not need to heed the exclusionary reason. But does this not do away with the idea of exclusion since you are always looking at the first order reasons? Schauer thinks that

---

[132] (1972) NSWR 49

[133] See Statement of Changes in Immigration Rules (1994 H.C. 395). This was suspended by the New Labour Government in 1997

[134] see Atria (*op. cit).* See also Sunstein (1996), especially his discussion of law as incompletely theorized agreement in chapter 1

[135] This however, does not amount to implicit exceptions in the sense of those brought into play at the moment of application. That would deny the rules ruleness - application still equals meaning.

there is a difference between a perfunctory glance at the first order reasons (to see that it is all right to apply the exclusionary reason - for him a perfectly natural thing to do) and a careful look at them – which would indeed be negating the exclusionary reason. It is in this way that the traffic warden in our example acts. Does Schauer's view negate the idea of an exclusionary reason? Atria thinks it does on essentially the argument that one cannot have one's cake and eat it. But this need not necessarily be so for we think of what Schauer is recommending is what we called in our discussions of Gillian Rose and Kierkegaard 'suspending the ethical. Suspending the ethical does not mean you do not apply the rule for you might decide that you must. Reasoning can be thought of as operating in a sphere which is barred by a thick almost opaque curtain. You sometimes dimly see other things that might be important through it. You lift the curtain to look but the curtain is extremely heavy and you cannot stand in this middle zone holding the curtain up for long. You have to drop it and remain on the side you were or move to the new side[136]. Thus the rule works as exclusion but that does not imply that it is totally impermeable - it does not have a 'variable exclusionary force'[137] - it is always heavy.

PARABOLIC REASONING

How do we balance the reasons when holding the curtain ajar? Here one has to be careful, as I mentioned at the beginning of this chapter, not to fold this balancing back into universalistic (meaning) criteria and so construct a new system. Günther (1993) who proposed a distinction between meaning and justification negates it somewhat. For the criteria that for him determine application can be unpacked as broadly the same universalising criteria that he claims characterise justification discourse; that the judgement must fit and be coherent with all similar instances is but another version of the universalisation criterion. Peczenik and Alexy (1990) in their analysis of what

---

[136] One might still use the rule. In *Keep the Aspidistra Flying* George Orwell tells of someone brought up before the magistrate. The judge is about to pronounce sentence when he hesitates and asks the defender whether he has said that he was a writer. The defender says he had. The judge hesitates and then pronounces sentences anyway! (I owe this to Fernando Atria). Think also of the radical who has made decisions which appear to be supporting the law and the establishment. His erstwhile radical friends might have thought that he had 'sold out' and gone over to the establishment. He might however, have paid attention to the case, and considered the law was right. Here choosing the law is a risk - he might be seen as conservative rather than radical. The distinction between the former and the latter is difficult - see some members of New Labour.

[137] MacCormick's solution in recent work is to say that rules can have a 'variable practical force'. There are rules of 'absolute application', 'strict application' and 'discretionary application'. The first is rather like exclusionary reasons, strict application, less so and so on. How does one know which rule is which? According to MacCormick (1998) it comes from 'second tier norms laying down the terms of authorisation or empowerment of the decision-maker' (p. 317) but that merely puts back the problems that we have been discussing to the second tier level.

counts as weighing and balancing reasons, end up with a sort of universalisation criterion; the greater or lesser coherence of logical chains.

How do then we decide? We must go back to Pierre and Davout. It is, as I have said, the encounter that gives us this particularity. We get our results and decision from that encounter by 'paying attention' to its particularity. Where we do that is in the hesitation. It is in that moment of hesitation that we can look and see where the story might take us without assuming that there will be a pre-determined answer or judgement. We let the story lead us on by listening to it. This does not mean that we give up all our faculties to the story - that sort of nihilistic surrendering to the other that Lévinas sometimes seems to advocate. Rather our response is to allow it to speak. Though we have a context within which to understand it, the encounter is a journey which we cannot prejudge, for it can take us beyond. The discussion of the parable of the Good Samaritan can help us here. We saw how that parable was told in the context of someone (Jesus) who was suspected of being outwith the law. But his answer to the question of the lawyer was impeccably within the law - he saw the law as his context. But it did not stop there. Were it to do so, the parable could be viewed merely as something that produces a definition (albeit a more humane one) of neighbour - one which on our model of analogical reasoning can serve as a template which we can impose on the world without 'thinking about it'. However we can also view it as saying 'act in a neighbourly manner to people' On this view it is something that can also move on and beyond - for it is inviting us to begin a journey, constituting neighbours by our act (gift) of connection. It has the potential to go beyond the template, breaking it and creating new modes of being neighbourly (turning the other cheek).

In legal reasoning we saw how analogical reasoning can be something which produces definitions (albeit nuanced ones) and thus in a sense nothing new – as though, in the example of the Good Samaritan, that parable was merely a definition of neighbour and all we had to do was to impose that template on the world without 'thinking about it'. In a broad sense it enables us just to keep repeating our patterns, reacting, as we saw in chapter 7, with behaviour specific acts and not responding but locked into the pattern. And indeed that is what some have thought parables and law to be like – that you cannot use them to move beyond the template.

And certainly this is a view held by many commentators on the parables. Thus Jülicher (1899) fought against an understanding of them as allegories. He saw them as simple stories, complexified by the synoptic Gospels which essentially were there to give a straightforward moral message. We can see here an attempt to reduce them to the working of the sort of analogical reasoning that we described in chapter 8 which we can then formalise, reduce to a template which can then be applied without thinking about it. Here they do not disturb what Donald MacKinnon (1974) in his essay on the parables called 'the cake of custom', there is always an answer that we can read off. But that, as we have implied, cannot be all that there is to parables. Roger White (1989) argues that it would be banal to think that that is all they are; that the dark and complex stories of the parables are just that and something like the parable of the Good Samaritan could be reduced to the principle, 'Love knows no limit'? For MacKinnon also, they are not there to impose meanings on the world, universalised principles to be applied, but an invitation to embark on a journey which might lead to a radically different view of the world - a journey 'beyond'.

What is important then is the idea of a journey and exploration. For, White says, we are invited not just to see illustrations of the Divine - a definition of the Divine and His will which we can then apply - but to take part in an exploration of the Divine which is open ended, the results of which we cannot prejudge or pre-determine. The parables are there to produce something in the hearts and minds of the listeners. To get them ready for a journey which is itself transformed by their response. Hillis Miller says

> 'A parable is a way to do things with words. It is a speech act. In the case of the parables of Jesus, however, the performative makes something happen in the hearts and minds of his hearers, but this happening is a knowledge of a state of affairs already existing, the Kingdom of Heaven and the way to get there.' (1990: 135)

But for MacKinnon the destination is not given - the Kingdom is something to guide and transform the journey and not necessarily a destination. It exists in the transformation of the journey and in that sense is in the 'hearts and minds of his hearers' - the Kingdom is something that transforms our lives (the journey) now and only exists in that transformation, in that opening to the beyond in our day to day lives (see our discussion of ideals in chapters 4 & 10). This is another way of saying that the possibility of creativity, of going 'beyond', already rests in the daily life of analogous repetition. We do this, says White, by exploring in detail, by 'paying attention' to the realism of the stories by being taken through their twists and turns. One can never line up the answers easily, there are too many cross-cutting and even apparently blasphemous meanings. So the parables have the capacity to transform their mundane stories of day to day activity, transcending them and throwing us out and beyond on an exploration of the Divine. But they can only do that from a base in the ordinary world - where to however, we cannot tell.

I deal with this more thoroughly below and in the succeeding chapter where I examine the metaphor of a journey more closely in the context of Europe. What we must note here is that this whole story about how the parables can activate the response to go beyond is done within the context of the inside, the law. Thus parables are where law and love meet - they provide the conditions of existence for one another. Jesus came 'not to destroy the law but to fulfil it' - but the law is tested in the demands of the particular encounter which is able to transform it. The *Lex Talionis*, for example, becomes transformed by the encounter with the enemy. But that is not to imply that we should have no more penal law and regulation. The act of love re-establishes the law anew. So parables define and throw us on to a journey away from the safe definitions - they are the way we talk of the tensions and risks of the encounter of law and love. We might also then think of them as we way we decide in the 'middle' or 'particularity' void.

Let us now turn to legal reasoning and examine it through the optic of analogy and parable. One could argue that reasoning here is also story based. Jackson (1988: chapters 4-5) shows this well. He shows how many of the ancient codes appear to be like fragments of stories. Thus the Roman Twelve Tables, Anglo-Saxon laws, appears to be fragments of what to do in certain situations. Jackson quotes the following verse from the Bible as typical: 'If a thief is found breaking in and is struck so that he dies, there shall be no blood guilt for him' (Exodus 22:1). He says this is not just quaint primitivism, rather is the form in which general guidance was given. It was positivism which formulated these stories into rules and thus lost the empirical detail. Thus rules are really subsumptions of thousands of stories. But, he goes on to say, this form of reasoning is not lost and we can make most sense of some points of doctrine if we look at them in terms of the story and explore the stories in their full complexity

He gives an example of this from the cases on contract where the following situation occurs (1988: 101-106). Someone offers to buy something from a seller while holding himself out to be someone he is not, someone respected and creditworthy. He gets the goods and pays for them with a dud cheque (or something similar) and then sells them on to an innocent third party. The original seller discovers the fraud and wants his goods back. The question rests as to whether title has been passed and that rests on whether the contract was void or voidable. If the latter, it has passed, and the seller is unlucky because the fraudster has passed the title on. The criterion as to whether the contract is void or voidable depends on whether the seller is taken to be selling it to the person with whom he has the face to face encounter or the person whom he claims he is. In the former, the contract is merely voidable and title has passed.

In Cundy v Lindsay[138] the fraud was done by letter. One Blenkarn claimed to be 'Blenkiron & Co.' (an existing and reputable firm). It was held here that the seller intended to contract only with the firm and therefore the contract was void ab initio and title had not passed. This was distinguished in the case of Phillips v Brooks Ltd[139]. There someone went to a jewellers and represented themselves as Sir George Bullough and signed, in exchange for some jewels, a cheque in that name. The shopkeeper checked to see if there was a Bullough living at the address given. Here it was held that title had passed as the shopkeeper had intended to sell to the person in his shop. Jackson now asks us to consider the case of Ingram v Little[140]. Here the fraud was perpetrated by someone who claimed to be one P.G. M. Hutchinson. The sellers checked in the telephone book to see if there was such a person living at the address claimed and when they saw there was, they sold their car in return for a dud cheque. Here the contract was declared void and no title passed.

Now how do these last two cases differ? They both seem to be face to face encounters - both people were wanting to sell to the person in front of them. Jackson goes on to look at the next case in line, Lewis v Averay[141]. Here the fraudster posed as Richard Greene who was a well known film actor. He produced proof of his identity with admission passes to a film studio and a car log book in that name. The car was duly sold for a dud cheque. This time the contract was held voidable and title had passed. This makes the whole thing even more confusing. For one might have been able to make a distinction between Phillips v Brooks Ltd. and Ingram v Little on the basis that a private retailer is different from a shopkeeper, someone in the public market place who must be on the guard for and ultimately accept a level of fraud; 'the consequences of a mistake as to creditworthiness differ according to whether the party is a retailer or a private individual' (Jackson 1988: 104). But then how do you account for Lewis v Averay? It does not appear to be at all different from Ingram v Little. But according to Jackson, if we go deeper into the empirical details of the stories, we can begin to make sense of why the decisions went the way that they did. The key for Jackson are the actual concrete parties involved; a wealthy jeweller, two old ladies of modest means,

---

[138] (1873) 3 App. Cas 459
[139] [1912] 2 K. B. 243
[140] [1961] 1 Q. B. 31
[141] [1971] 3 All E. R 907

and two students. In the first case we had a wealthy jeweller, who could be expected to bear the loss and fraud would be part of the context of his operations anyway. In the second case we had old ladies for whom the loss was great; for whom fraud would not be part of the context of their operations. They would thus not be on their guard and would much more likely be defrauded. In the final case we were dealing with young students, 'on the ball', living in a 'fast milieu'. The student seller, had behaved stupidly (would you, in those circumstances, believe someone who told you they were a well known actor?); was fooled rather than defrauded. If we then think of the judges in the actual case asking how the loss should be distributed amongst innocent parties then we might expect the results that we have here.

Exploring these stories is not so much an illustration of a particular point or principle but a way of pushing you on and beyond it. It is a way of exploring living lawfully. This is not to say that this actually happened in these particular cases or that this how generally narrative is conceived in practice or theory[142]. Jackson himself, though he uses the above example partly to differentiate himself from MacCormick, undercuts the point. For he claims that the example shows that legal reasoning should seen as a process of matching stories, a sort of 'pattern matching'. But this can reduce into the sort of closed analogical thinking that I was describing earlier. For pattern matching itself can be seen as having a template to which everything else conforms. Moreover patterns can be abstract, dress patterns, for example, are abstracted versions of an ideal dress and not an actual dress. Thus in matching to patterns we are matching to abstracted principles, exactly as the way we did in our formalisation of analogical reasoning[143]. When Jackson looks at the pragmatics of courtroom interaction that this is precisely what is at stake there; the constructing of a story of the trial which matches the stock patterns the jury holds. For Jackson, what is happening in our example is that a stock pattern is being imposed on the story (students are clever, old ladies are dim). One can then read Jackson's discussion of the contract cases as a way of producing analytical distinctions through the medium of analogical reasoning - producing principles that will be repeatable. I do not want to deny this happens - indeed repeatability is, as I have argued, a necessary part of the process, but we also want to be able to drive the story 'beyond'. The idea of 'stock stories' could be thought of as what Veitch calls the context of the particular (see above) and thus, as I argued, a version of Detmold's view that particulars all come with

[142] Thus the famous 'chain novel' example of Dworkin (1986) sees narrative as a way of making things coherent - the story feeds back in on itself through the principles and does not breach them. He explores subtlety what goes on within the tradition or story but it is a way of staying within.

[143] This example came up and was discussed in a seminar 'Decision, Reason and Law'. I would like to thank the class, especially for their contributions.

universals (or contexts) attached. But what is important is what context is going to be appropriate in the particular encounter - it is the particularity of the encounter that is decisive for it is in that particularity that we can switch context.

PAYING ATTENTION

But when do we move from applying the analogy, to the exploration of the story, to the unpicking of the institution by delving into the substantive reasons as Atiyah details? My argument has been that we know by paying attention to the story, and letting its particularity give us the sign to move from what I have called the deductivist system outside and beyond. We know this partly through the effects of something happening to us (the story hurls us beyond) and partly because we know when to go with the current of the story. We know that because we are faithful followers of the story in its closed principled, machine like mode because we know the principles that enclose it. That is a way of saying that creativity comes from a structure and that we cannot be creative unless we live our lives in a structured way. Thus the impulse to act in a defeasible way comes from the inside and the outside. We know when to act on the impulses we get from the outside because we live in the structured inside. In so doing we are sensitised to know when to respond from the impulses of love and the like that push us to go beyond it. We recognise them as loving impulses and as something that is appropriate to apply in the present situation. But that living in the inside must be as though there was no outside. We do not actively search outside our tradition, we respond to the impulses when and if they come[144].

The key is to pay attention; to let the story speak for itself and not be too quick to apply closure by imposing a principle or pattern on it. This is the sense behind these mystical post-modern utterances like 'deferring the undeferrable'; of 'saying what cannot be said'; 'listening to what cannot be heard'. Part of what makes a good doctor or lawyer, for example, is the ability to listen; to know when to stop because you know what is before you is a case of x; to know when to continue listening because you see difference. A common mistake is to jump to a conclusion before the story has a chance to reveal itself. In our every day lives we are often so sure of something that all countervailing evidence is dismissed[145]. Doctors might be so convinced that

---

[144] This is the way that one can get over the Jackson argument we encountered earlier. In that argument, he claimed that even when we apply the meaning of the predicate without asking the reference question, we are implicitly asking whether or not we should apply the predicate and therefore everything is in the particular and not automatic deductive reasoning.

[145] A colleague told me of a case in a university where he taught where the teachers on a social work course were puzzled as to why the students kept asking questions in the seminars. They spent a lot of

some symptoms are expressive of psychological problems, that all actual physical parameters disappear from sight until the patient dies!

The trick is to explore the story until you know that it is appropriate to stop and make a decision. This does not make decision making a nihilistic existentialist affair for most of it is done within the machine like mode. Much of our decision making is routinised (or formalised) and necessarily so. We saw in chapter 6 how that structured our creativity. The GP system might also be a good example - much of the decision making is routinised and follows the patterns of closure - so they work inside the story. They are also creative because part of their skill is to recognise when to move beyond; when not to apply the pattern that is all you can do in a say, 5 minute consultation; when to move to a full scale examination at the hospital or with the consultant. The skill to do that is in part gained through 'faithfully following the story', the patterned activities enabling one to spot the anomalies which mean you have to go further. The danger is that like the robot one might just carry on and ignore the anomaly. But that is the point of paying attention, Schauer's peak behind the curtain, the imagination to see whether the infinite possibilities and contexts in *this* case warrant further investigation. The system works because we routinise a complex world and do not allow complexification to get in at the first instance. A system where you have specialists as the first port of call might have two effects. Firstly, even though they are the masters of the complex, they might produce closure precisely because they are blind to any area but their own - so you have to get the right specialist to start with. Secondly, and ironically in reaction to the first effect, they might investigate everything. You go to the doctor with a cold and spend two months in hospital with tests for most imaginable diseases[146].

It is in this way one can understand what I mean by living as though there was no outside. We cannot go actively seeking the outside because that would precisely negate the point of the routinised activity. It is the anomaly and the interruption that sensitises us to the need for action but we spot it by paying attention *from the inside*. I will explain this further in moving from the more individual personal discussion of creativity and decision making to looking at the legal system and how we could operationalise what I have been saying about the outside and the inside.

---

wondering about possible psychological problems. The answer was in fact somewhat different and came out in the exams - they asked because they could not understand the course!

[146] That form of medicalisation, common in the USA, is a product both of litigation culture, and a private medicine and non GP system (see chapter 6).

This might be effected in the legal system by having institutions that are both inside the system and outside of it. They are what I have called 'straddling' or 'bridging institutions'[147]. They are both in the law and have links to the world and the particularities outside of it. Through these the outside filters into the law. I will give two examples of this. Firstly, the jury[148]. It has been said that the jury injects 'lay acid' into the legal system. What that might mean is that what the jury does on occasion is to sensitise the court to other impulses that come into the court, through the jury system, from 'beyond'. The court in being effected by these impulses can reconsider its own system. Thus jury nullification. In the case of Ponting[149] a British civil servant who leaked details of the sinking of the Belgrano in the Falklands War was charged with a breach of the Official Secrets Act. He was acquitted by the jury in the face of his admitting the facts as charged and with a strong direction by the judge to convict. This forced a reconsideration of the Official Secrets Act (though not unfortunately to change it all that much). The Rodney King case where members of the Los Angeles Police Department were acquitted of assaulting King, who was black, in the face of video evidence showing him being beaten up by them, could be seen in this light also. For there one might say that the verdict upset any easy idea of racial harmony and forced the system to think of using federal law in these cases.

Let us look at systems of lay justice more generally. We should not think of them as systems opposing systems of 'legal' justice. Rather that they are an integral part of the system. By and large they work as the law expects the law to work. Much work on the jury, for example shows how they are influenced by the judge and by doing what they think that a judge wants[150]. In our research on the Lay Justice System in Scotland[151] we found that the lay justices did not subvert the legal system and that by and large it operated within its norms and by its parameters (at least no less than equivalent professional judges!). This should not be seen as a subversion of the lay ideal. In general this is what should happen and yet it will continue to send impulses from the outside which might halt the relentless running of the legal machine; to make it pay attention to the particularities of the world; think again and then reconfigure the law.

---

[147] See Bańkowski (1989). This way of looking at has close affinities with systems theory. See Bańkowski and Christodoulidis (1998) where we apply systems theory to the EU

[148] See Bańkowski (1989)

[149] See MacCormick (1986)

[150] See Freeman (1981)

[151] Bańkowski, Hutton and MacManus (1987)

Since these institutions have a foot in both camps the machine is able to be subverted because an act of looking at the particularities can be seen as a legal act as well. The Ponting verdict does not have to be seen as unlawfully 'perverse' for it to effect the rethink[152]. In similar vein we found in our research how lay magistrates made space for themselves to inject what they thought was a distinct 'lay perspective' into the system - but all the time within a system which they saw as 'legal' justice and necessarily so. They saw themselves as basically acting like 'legal' judges except in these instances where their actions helped and enabled officials to reconsider.

Hugh Collins (1986) also shows how the courts might be said to respond 'inside', from the 'outside'. He looks at three aspects of this in the practice of the courts. Firstly the courts seek a climate of opinion, a `dominant informed view'. They are interested in the prevailing attitudes of participants in the activity and test them against the broader climate of opinion found in legal scholarship and professional associations[153]. But, in clashes of opinions with the other informed opinion and the participants, the courts do not necessarily let the opinions of, for example manufactures, set the standard of care in the manufacture of products. Secondly, there are procedural ways of subverting the formal rationality of the law by means of the jury and, especially in a scientific and technologically oriented society, tribunals with various experts. The democracy of these weighs heavily on courts when applying judicial review and their judgements exhibit the tensions in applying democracy and the Rule of Law. Thirdly, the rules governing standing before the courts. In the US this involves class actions and *amicus curiae* briefs and in the UK the situation is edging that way. In Wallerstein v Moir[154] for example, it was the Law Society, not a party to the action, that argued that contingency fees should not be allowed[155]. The Court agreed, relying on the Monopolies Commission and the Law Commission. It is thus misleading to see the judicial system as completely autonomous. Judges consult and restructure their views as against public opinion and this even against an ideological background

---

[152] Neil MacCormick (1986) argues that here we have not a case of a perverse verdict but rather the righting of a perverse judicial interpretation of the law. He argues that the *concept* 'interest of the state' had some part to play in the case. But before we put it into operation we have to interpret it and take the concept 'interests of the state' and formulate some *conception* of the concept fit to be applied in cases arising under *this* use of the concept. This is always contestable, between rival conceptions of the concept. What the judge did was to direct the jury to convict on the faith of a misconception of the concept. If this is so MacCormick says,

'it was the jury which restored sense to the law. The jury's conception of the interests of the state and of what is a person's duty in the interests of the state, it could be argued, was *even in l*aw a better conception of the concept than that expounded by the judge in his direction to it. In this sense, one might wish to argue that the verdict in *R. v Ponting* was a correct verdict'. (pp.172-173)

[153] See f Roe v Wade 410 US 113

[154] (No.2) [1975] 1QB 373

[155] See also Harlow and Rawlings (1995)

where they are proud of their specialised reasoning and lore. This is not like the standard liberal theories which say that when rules run out judges should look for consensus. This does not exist. What happens is that public opinion comes to mean particular organised groups that are able to set the agenda. But we can expand this to give other organisations the opportunity to influence outcomes; to introduce particularities from outside while preserving the system.

CONCLUSION

What is important in these examples is that we should not see these bodies as being inimical to the official legal system; that one must be set off against the other; one or the other chosen. Rather we should think of the legal system, properly so called, as the articulation of the official with the lay, together making one system just as, in our marriage example, marriage was seen as an articulation of passion and routine. One can also apply this to law and say that living lawfully is a system of the articulation of meaning with application, of law and love. It is the articulation of two elements that in their articulation become one system that is the important point even though, for heuristic purposes, it is sometimes necessary to use the language of opposed polarities. In the same way also, balancing in the act of application must be seen in the context of the interlocking of the spheres of application and meaning and these must be seen as a totality. Ultimately balancing is an act that cannot be captured by criteria, it is an act of the imagination. Here lays the germ of truth in Günther's universalisation of the application discourse, for it is an imagination that can pay attention to the infinite possibilities of the concrete particular before it. But it is not an all embracing system, it is not a cash-line machine.

In the final chapters, I will attempt to illustrate the themes of this book with a look at a concrete entity, the European Union. Here we have an entity that is a set of interlocking normative spheres and owes its existence to people with the imagination and hope, out of infinite possibilities, to jump and grasp a way forward. As to whether they were (and are) right - that depends upon what we make of it. It is to the European Union, then, that we now turn.

CHAPTER 10

EUROPE AND THE JOURNEY

INTRODUCTION: THE STORY SO FAR

What we have so far been looking at so far can be illustrated by a story. When I lived in Italy I was struck by the seeming chaos on the roads. But drivers did not go out to kill pedestrians at, for example, pedestrian crossings or at traffic lights. They never stopped but rather tried, with more or less success, to weave around the pedestrians who would be scared out of their wits. I then visited Germany where I was struck by how different it seemed. How at controlled pedestrian crossings, cars, when signalled to stop, always did so. If there were a green light for the pedestrian, one could boldly cross without looking out for cars. One could, something not possible in Italy, cross the road and not fear the cars. You knew they would stop. However, if you crossed the road on the red, you were dead! You would not be seen because you were crossing the road contrary to the rules. You should not be there, therefore you were not there.

That story encapsulates some of the themes of the book so far. What it has been trying to come to terms with might best be understood as 'living in and out of the law'. This is not meant to be understood in the sense of an inquiry as to when it is appropriate to break the law. Rather what I am concerned with is the very idea of 'living lawfully' and what that might mean. We introduced this notion in the general introduction and showed how the rather old fashioned English, 'living righteously' could capture it. We also saw it in a theological image; the fact that the anomian impulse of Christianity does not destroy the law but is rather to be seen in its context. Its impulse to go beyond the law stems from the law and Jesus' breaking of it is his fulfilling and recreating of it.

This brings us back to the theme with which the book began, that of anarchism. One does not have to conceptualise anarchism as being against, and dispensing with, the law; as a sort of nihilism where anything goes and only the individual is sovereign at each contingent moment. Though it is clearly about breaking the law in some sense, it is more helpful to see it as creatively breaking the law. Seen this way creativity becomes a central issue. Here structure and law become tremendously important for, as we saw in the previous chapters, creativity comes within the context of rules and traditions. One cannot be creative unless one takes off from a firm structure. To live lawfully means living a life where the law is constantly interrogated and renewed, it is broken but from within and not from outside. This is why I rejected, in chapter 8, the somewhat positivistic (and Razian) view of Atria where the fact of the application of law always being open to choice means that ultimately the law is about morality. For the way they put it casts it terms of looking at the relations between law and morality and asking which, and at what times, is more important than the other. For on this view living lawfully would be understood in a literal way as following the rules and morality would tell when to break them. Part of the point of the book is to reclaim the ethical but in that reclaiming not to destroy the law. Morality would not be a system constraining the system of law – their articulation would make a unity. What I have called 'living lawfully' would not have the literal sense of just following the law', it means both following and breaking the law as appropriate – thus, at times following the rules would not be 'living lawfully' and breaking them would be.

This takes us to the other theme of the book, the desire for certainty which deforms the ethical and the political life. It deforms legality into legalism; into, as we saw in chapter 3, the rigid following of rules; it subsumes, as we saw in chapter 2, individual moral life under the optic of the rules of the city or the rules of the gods. How does this happen? We saw in chapter 2 how that was in part about the desire to banish contingency from life; to close off the outside and keep everything within the tightly defined circle of the law. What is desired is to cut out risk. Creativity is something that is risky. It is always open to the outside and we can never be sure what the result of our decisions will be. So we try and cut this down by making sure we stick to the rules. Market society, as I have shown in chapter 5, can be something like this. For though it appears to be something about competition and enterpreneurship, it is also, as we have seen, about cutting down moral risk - I am not responsible for your bankruptcy and penury, we both merely followed the rules of the market. Thus Kant's defence of the argument that one should never tell a lie, even when the consequences are clearly bad, applies in both cases (the moral and the social). In both cases there is a fear of the outside; the fear of the contingency of love and passion which has the capacity to drag us forward to places we do not want to go and on journeys we do not want to risk; the fear of welfare arrangements which disturb our peace and prosperity, perhaps making our lives harder and less able to be planned, threatening to tear apart society. We saw what this does in terms both of our moral and social lives . It makes life the same, fixed and repetitious. One does not change or develop - that becomes, as we shall see, merely more of the same thing.

Finally, one has to bear in mind, that the conditions of our creativity are something that can make us fixed and repetitious - that the firm structures needed can also capture us in their cycles and make us unable to see out. We see that typically in those who exhibit, socially or individually, what Judith Shklar called the attitude of legalism - mistaking the repetitive following of rules for 'living lawfully' or legality. We saw how this occurs in present day societies. But, ironically, societies that decide to stand against rules, for example, the 'communist' societies of Eastern Europe, can also go this way. For eschewing legalism for 'welfare' could result in the unmitigated chaos of contingent decision-making or, as happened, in the rule of particular elite of carers who knew what was best (see Hayek). But that latter was also people trapped in their own cycles. They were unwilling to listen to the outside, to what people really wanted and were trapped in the security of their own knowledge as to what was really wanted. They were secure in their own knowledge which they imposed on people and transformed them into images of themselves. Thus, as Skhlar says, this sort of view was the 'first cousin' of legalism and creativity was taken away from everyday life. Antigone, who though appearing to represent love, is in fact trapped in the cycle of the laws of the gods of which she is the sole interpreter (see Hamish X).

What I have argued is that following rules in a legalistic manner or in the chaos of welfare provisions are deformed states of living lawfully; that both take one element of 'living lawfully' and think of it as the only part of it - eschewing all others. Thus legalism, in the sense of the strict following of rules is necessary but it is not all there is. Openness to the outside, to passion and love is necessary but it is also not all there is. The two elements articulate to make one whole. There is a problem here. How does one describe such a process without falling into the dichotomous thinking which I have attacked throughout? Though the description has been of a system, 'living lawfully', which is one and where law and love are inextricably mixed, it appears as though it is composed of the connections of separate systems of law and love in a sort of zero sum game where more of one means less of the other. Sometimes it appears that this complicated arrangement is, as Critical Legal Studies has it, merely a sliding from the one side of the dichotomy to the other without there being any principle of saying, as at least they argue, which side to go to.

The appearance of this is partly inevitable for heuristic reasons. Though I have list of seeming oppositions in this book (see especially chapter 2), part of the way I try to describe them as a unity is by denying that they are dichotomies or contradictions, with the one cancelling the other out. I do this in two ways. Firstly by using the notion of principles in the way that Dworkin does. Principles are not binary like rules, in that they apply or do not apply, but rather that they are always valid in the system. In decision making one weighs or balances them to see which one will be most foregrounded. Part of the problem is that what people do in looking at this complex arrangement is foreground one principle and take it to be definitive of the whole arrangement. Thus legalism, the repetitive and rigid following of the rules, becomes the whole of legality. Or, the plasticity of love and the absolute autonomy of the contingent voice, which some call love, becomes the whole of living lawfully[156]. Secondly, I have tried to show that these oppositions do not map on to neat divides and in fact they cut across each other all the time (see especially chapter 1). This can be seen in the decision-making process described in chapter 9. There I used the notion of the middle as described by Gillian Rose. This is not meant to be seen as somewhere that is literally in the middle of two opposing contradictories. Rather the middle is the position of tension from where decisions are made. Thus the dichotomies are not really contradictory and the 'middle' describes the tension of the principles in the act of decision-making. It is, as Rose says, an anxious place and position because we cannot be sure, although we are located in the law, where our decisions will take us. What this means is that, for example, law and love need each other since that is the only way in which they fully realise themselves. But in realising themselves fully, one cannot say that there is law and there is love, rather there is law-love, 'living lawfully'[157]. The reasoning stemming from this might be called 'parabolic' reasoning. It is the continually misappropriation of that for law or love that brings the problem, especially as that misappropriation becomes the deformed states of love or law that we have talked about.

We see the problem more clearly if we return to our re-conceptualisation of anarchism as creative law-breaking, thus recasting the discussion in terms of creativity. We might see the description of legality and legal reasoning in this book on the 'separate' model - as saying that one is legalistic and occasionally, when appropriate one is not and goes outside to add in the contingency of love

---

[156] Thus one view of deconstruction is that one must excavate the principle (the hidden supplement) that is contradictory to the current one and foreground it. For example, to bring forward solidarity rather than individualism in contract. But once that 'hidden supplement' is no longer hidden, then presumably the previous one is. What is to stop us applying deconstruction to that? (See Jabbari 1992)

[157] See the use made of the parables in this book also

or welfare. So legality is by and large legalism with an added extra which one cannot dispense with. But on the 'holistic' view I am advocating this is not how it should be seen. Rather it is the repetitive actions of legalism which respond outside of their own security, and in doing so transform their repetivity. It is their being open each time that transforms them and that does not mean that the law is changed each time. It is also not to say that the love gets lost in the legalism and the ultimately legalism is most important. Law and legalism are one thing, 'living lawfully'.

There is, however, an important truth in putting it as living 'lawfully' rather than 'lovefully'. We are structured beings who seek structure to make sense of our life. This, as I showed in chapter 1, is both an epistemological and moral truth. Epistemologically, our rationality pushes us into making more of the world than a set of disordered instances . Morally, being a structured being means that we think of our lives as having meaning. This is not to take a position as to whether that meaning exists independent of ourselves. It is to claim we are beings that seek meaning to our lives even if we have to manufacture it. This is well captured in the Dworkinian notion of integrity. In his discussion of integrity in the law, he uses individuals as an analogy. Just as they need to be able to have some idea of the sorts of people they are to be able to judge their actions, fit them into a coherent pattern and be able to predict reactions in certain situations, so also communities can be seen in this way as communities of integrity. The whole parable of narrative coherence and the chain novel is a way of making this clear. But what is also important, and what Dworkin misses in his desire to envelop everything in 'Law's Empire', is the openness of the system. For him this is another way of describing liberal society and reconstructing the best interpretation of it that we can get, so as Emilios Christodoulidis (1994) puts it, it has a 'suspect intimacy'. We can get this openness if we change the chain novel metaphor to that of a soap opera. If we think of it as a soap opera[158], with new episodes being added, then we can think of it as something always in being, as something that has no end and that is always liable to be transformed. In the same way as an important moral decision might be said to transform our lives and make us see ourselves as different from what we were previously (not because we were different but because the decision changed us), then the community and its law is transformed by a decision and, though it stems from the community, will transform it. Later, the metaphor that I use to clarify this is that of the journey without an end. It is this that enables us to see the openness to the outside but at the same time keeping an ordered path.

---

[158] See Smith (1994)

The arrangement I am describing could be seen rather like an atom in the sense that it is made of the interaction of different elements to make one whole. But there is an important difference, the elements do not exist separately as do the other particles of the atom. So though the elements interact with their outside (other elements) there is no outside in the sense that there is only the atom and the true atom is the articulation of all these elements. The atom is primary and when it appears that the other elements exist separately (legalism, for example) they are but deformed elements of the atom - the atom cannot be split. What I am trying to do is to think of 'living lawfully' as something that encompasses its own alterity or exceptions within itself in such a way that it has no problem in seeing itself as both itself and its own negation[159]. It thereby engages in a constant process of transformation.

EUROPE: THE WHOLE AND THE PART

Part of the project of the book has been to develop a conceptual scheme that can make sense of such a system; to set out, in other words, the conditions for the existence of such a system[160]. For this to be successful we need to find phenomena that would make more sense in being seen in this way and which, in their turn would help refine the scheme. I thus turn to look in depth at a concrete example. I have chosen here to look at the European Union because it illustrates some of the substantive points of the book and also some of the methodological issues I have been raising. I do this in two chapters. In this chapter I look at how the issues of sovereignty and identity within the EU touch upon how we can describe as a unity a system which seems to depend upon separate parts. In chapter 11, I look at how problems of governance, democracy and law in the EU help to make clear my enterprise.

I use the European Union for two reasons. Firstly because living lawfully, in the tension between law and love, is meant to imply some sort of unity. A persons who lives like that has meaning in her life - her life has integrity, is whole. It is not fractured because it is torn between these irreconcilable oppositions which drive each other out. Rather life is in experiencing these inevitable tensions and that is its unity and beauty (see chapter 2). Thus we have unity in the diversity that pulls many ways. But it is rather harder to visualise that sort of life at the level of society. This is where the European Union enters the story. For there we can conceptualise the unity of a system

[159] See the discussion on inclusive identity above. See Fitzpatrick (2001)

[160] There is a parallel here with the methodology used in cosmological explanations. Much of it seems to be concerned with using computer modelling to produce the conditions that are necessary for a certain theory to be true.

which is composed of the interlocking of various cross cutting, and in tension, systems.

But where does love come into it? In chapter 11 we look more concretely at a system where love is pulled in. There we see it in democratic governance and in looking at the way we can arrange things so that everyone is heard and their particularity not destroyed. How the individual voice is pulled into the universalism of the law and not lost. How market order and welfare needs are interlocked and how contingency and predictability work with each other. We see this in models which look at the way in which all these functions interlock in differing systems and in that represent a unity.

Love as we have seen is something that is contingent and arbitrary in the sense that it is its own justification and cannot be controlled, constrained or predicted by law, it knows no reason and the demands of law and rationality fall before it. In one sense then, it can be seen as the 'outside' but, as I tried to show in the last chapter, one which is inside. The European Union helps here because we can posit it as a system of interconnecting connections where the outside is at the same time part of the inside. More concretely we will see this in the notion of inclusive or non-rivalistic identity – the way in which identity does not have to build a barrier around itself, is open to make connections, to include and thus transform itself.

All of this shows how exchange and connection are important for, as we shall see, my notions are premised on the openness of the giving and receiving of the units, individual and collective, that comprise the system. Finally, it is in that that we can see love in the European Union for what is important for this to work is that each unit is open to the outside; has the love and trust necessary to give themselves and receive whatever unexpected might come back. It is the denial of this that stops our journey and our love.

a) Interlocking Normative Systems

We start from a study of the problem of sovereignty within the European Union and its relation to the national state. We can take two cases from different jurisdictions to let us see the problem. In the UK, we can look at the Factortame[161] case. Here the European Court of Justice (ECJ), on an Article 177[162] reference, ruled that provisions of the Merchant Shipping Act and regulations made by the UK government under it were incompatible with basic principles of EC law, those of freedom of establishment and free movement of

---

[161] *Secretary of State for Transport, ex p Factortame* [1991] 3All ER 769 (Case C221/89) CJEC
[162] Now art. 234 of the Amsterdam Treaty.

capital. The Act, which restricted fishing against EC fishing quotas in British waters to boats substantially British-owned, was 'disapplied'. But if EC law overrides Acts passed by the national parliaments, then how can they, and in particular the British State, be sovereign? The choice appears to be either Brussels or Westminster (in this case Brussels). One can see this from the other side with a German decision. In the Brunner case[163], the German Constitutional Court denied that the European Court of Justice or any other organ of the EU could be held to have 'competence-competence'. It had the competence to determine the competence of EU/EC organs in relation to Germany and thus it followed that if any matters concerning the rights and powers of Germany were involved, then it would determine competence and would not hold itself bound by the decisions of the ECJ or other European organs. In fact, one might say that it claimed a duty to deny the ECJ competence so to interpret EC law that in it application to Germany it would threaten the Constitution, which was reserved to the ultimate control of the German people.

The British court decided that sovereignty lay in Brussels (was European) while the German court decided that sovereignty lie in the national jurisdiction and not in Europe. The point here is that there were only two alternatives to be seen, since there had to be one monolithic system which encompassed all. Thus sovereignty had either to be national or European. This is, as MacCormick (1993) says, a somewhat 'monocular' view. The traditional theory of sovereignty forces us to look to one sovereign, to view the system from within itself and not look outside. MacCormick claims that this view does not get at the reality of the EU, in the sense that what it is claiming is that there must be one all encompassing system, the European or a collection of independent systems.

If we do not ignore the other forms of normative ordering that occur in our daily lives, then we can see that we do not have to look to a sovereign state, supreme in its own territory with its own people. Instead, we can look to various interlocking systems over the same territory which perhaps deal with the same people. We thus acknowledge different perspectives or points of view. The criteria of validity will depend upon the perspective we adopt. Looking at the validity of laws from the perspective of the UK system, we will come to a certain set of conclusions, as to the validity of laws, including laws that seem to emanate from EU sources. But it will be somewhat different if we look at it from the EU perspective. There, we do not start from the UK parliament or the practice of the legal officials of the UK but from the Treaty

[163] 2BvR 2134/92 and 2159'92; JZ 1993, 1100 cf [1994]CMLR 57

and the ECJ and the practice of EU officials. There we get a picture of what counts as EU law, including sometimes what comes from the member states. No view is thereby privileged. We can thus locate ourselves in different systems depending upon our point of view. No one system will be superior. What we think of EU law *vis a vis* municipal law and *vice versa* will depend upon which system we locate ourselves in - what perspective we take. MacCormick (1995) goes on to look at how this might be seen in terms of the validity of sovereign systems. He looks at models where the rules of validity and the criteria for validity might be different in the sense that the criteria of validity of one of the systems might be that it has validity by reference to another system. Thus in the UK, Parliament might be sovereign but part of the criteria of sovereignty would be that it conforms to regulations set by Brussels. In this way, spread across many legal systems, we can get something of a polycentric system - all being open to the outside and no one being privileged or secure in its own protocols. MacCormick is arguing for more porosity and against a binary all or nothing view. We might say that the systems interact with each other in more subtle ways without changing themselves but not compromising themselves. One must view the EU then, as a set of 'interlocking normative systems'. But with this phrase we can go further than MacCormick. We can look at the whole of the EU and its various systems and try to describe them so as to get a sort of 'view from nowhere' - without looking at it from any one point of view. We can use here the idea of what Boaventura de Sousa Santos describes as 'interlegality'. Sousa Santos says:

> 'Legal pluralism is the key concept in a post-modern view of law. Not the legal pluralism of traditional legal anthropology in which the different legal orders are conceived as separate entities coexisting in the same political space, but rather the conception of different legal spaces superposed [sic], interpenetrated and mixed in our minds as much as in our actions, in occasions of qualitative leaps or sweeping crises in our life trajectories as well as in the dull routine of eventless everyday life. We live in a time of porous legality or of legal porosity of multiple networks of legal orders forcing us to constant transitions and trespassings. Our legal life is constituted by an intersection of different legal orders, that it by interlegality. Interlegality is the phenomenological counterpart of legal pluralism and that is why it is the second key concept of a post-modern conception of law. Interlegality is a highly dynamic process because the different legal spaces are non- synchronic and thus result in uneven and unstable mixings of legal codes.'(1987: 297-298)

We do not have go along with 'post modernism' in the legal world, to realise the usefulness of this concept. For this 'shifting porous world' is precisely the world of the EU and the various actors therein. But there is more to the view from nowhere than that. It is not just a question of describing each system without ascribing superiority, one to the other, in alternatively switching viewpoints from one to the other. It involves a rich skein of interlocking spheres and institutions, not all of which will be necessarily legal ones. The challenge to legal theory is that any such system would be viewed, in the Hartian tradition for example, as a system in crisis. What we, to the contrary, are interested in is to think of that as the normal mode of 'living lawfully', not as something that has the potential to decay or grow into a 'full' system of law. It is not a system in the traditional sense rather it is the articulation of systems that constitutes the whole entity that we are interested in. We must then, look at the way that the various systems articulate, the principles that guide the overlaps and the intersections. In this way we can get a picture of a dynamic and changing entity. The whole point of the 'system of interlocking spheres' is to see the system as stable, in that European Law is recognised within it members states, but also in flux, in that there is no secure end point - the perfect destination where European law will always be applied. Rather the whole system is in a process of negotiation and renegotiation - its identity is in its becoming. The EU then is just to be understood as this entity of 'interlocking normative spheres' (see the analogy of the atom above). In looking at it in this way, systems theory which looks at the world as sets of interlocking systems which are 'normatively closed but cognitively open', can be very helpful and it is to it that we now turn.

b) Systems Theory

In trying to develop a conceptual scheme to make sense of this view of the EU (and of our project) systems theory can be very useful[164]. In its autopoietic form systems theory is a radical theory of legal closure expressed in a sociological way . Law and other such systems exist in a world where they are each the background or environment of each other. They become increasingly isolated from each other as they become more and more self-referential. In an increasingly complex world, this is a way of reducing the problems, such as information overload etc., that come with complexity. One system can never directly penetrate another. Autopoiesis thus explains, in an interesting and useful way, why it is that systems such as law seem such closed worlds and why all attempts at fresh 'social scientific' input into the law fail. It helps us understand why regulation so often fails since everything is translated into legal categories. The same goes for attempts to control other areas in society through law. The other systems just translate them into their own categories.

[164] I have tried elsewhere, and with others, to apply some of the insights of systems theory to studying the EU. See Bańkowski (1977b), Bańkowski and Christodoulidis (1998; 1999). See also Bańkowski and Scott (1996)

Systems theory appears to talk in terms of radical separateness. Recall, for example, how Luhmann (1986) saw our marriage example. There, one was forever moving from passion to routine and back. He did not see the loving relationship as precisely the articulation of passion and routine which transformed each into one[165]. But paradoxically its very radical separateness makes it useful here for it has to include things outside of it as within it and part of the system. It also has to develop a range of metaphors for connection for otherwise regulation and determination by systems would be impossible and this is plainly not the case. But we can take these metaphors rather further. In chapter 9 we talked of the jury and the system of Lay Justice in Scotland and explained how they could be seen as part of the official legal system articulating with the professional judges and system. This can be explained in terms of *unum actum* where one and the same act appears in different systems with different meanings, and the notion of bridging concepts or frontier posts which gives us an image of interlinking and reciprocal influencing. The images are important because they point to how the systems can have elements in them which have, as it were, a foot in both camps and therefore act in both. But that, and the metaphor of structural coupling, where systems become linked and can influence each other in a blind way, can also be seen as binding the systems into one.

Let us take another example. Recall MacCormick's (1995) showing of how the criteria of validity could be taken from another system's; how what is important is what that system sees as valid. This would not be, as in Private International Law, treating that norm as a fact to be taken into account in the national law. For the system is here using as a criterion of validity in its system the criteria of the other system. This can be seen in the relationship of EC law to national law. Though EC law can have direct effect, it does not mean that EC law takes over the state system. It is restricted in scope and it often depends for its effect, on the network of local state institutions and normative systems. It is here that article 234 is important. The accession of a state means that it will regard relevant decisions of the ECJ as valid law in its system and it will refer, under article 234, problematic cases which appear to concern EC law to the ECJ. That court will give a general ruling on the point referred and remit to the national court for decision in the particular case. This ensures that EC law is applied as *national* law in the particular case but using as to the general law, the interpretation of the ECJ and the criteria of validity of the EC system and not the national system. Thus we get an example of *autopoietic* linking. For we can say that the national court in applying the law in this case acts both as part of the EC system and the national system. By

[165] This is like CLS talk of forever sliding from principle to counter principle with no rational criteria of how to do so.

unum actum it joins the two together. Likewise one might say that the ECJ operates both as an EC court and a national court.

The notion of 'communication through mutual misunderstanding' is another system theoretical concept that enables us to make sense of the way we have conceptualised the role of the jury and lay justice. This is another way of trying to understand communication in conditions of radical separateness. Though one system is separate from another it can affect the other in the following manner. The system hears something like 'noise' from the outside and it has to respond to it. In so doing it has to translate that 'noise' into something intelligible in its own terms. But it is not just a question of translating something from the outside into another language, one's own. For the 'outside' is in an important sense 'inside'. What this means in system theoretical terms is that the system/environment distinction is an internal distinction, that is to say that the distinction between outside and inside is already an inside distinction. Taken absolutely literally, and in autopoiesis's own terms, this has huge problems, both epistemological and ethical[166], but taken more metaphorically it gives us a way of understanding some of the issues in chapters 8-9 and in the introduction to this chapter.

Firstly, it enables us to understand more closely the idea of 'paying attention from the inside'. This image was used in chapter 9 as a way in which the system (or the individual) stops and recalculates what is going on. The point was, using the example of lay justice and the jury, to show how it was appropriate to 'lift the veil' of exclusionary reasons; to look behind the curtain before bring it down, the 'raw moral data' having been recalculated. This might operationalise, in the legal system, Schauer's point about exclusionary reasons. He thought it was perfectly possible to have a quick glance behind the exclusionary reason, and see if the answers were not totally ridiculous, before applying the reason without 'thinking about it'. The jury or the lay magistrates in chapter 9 do not necessarily give a substantive answer, though in some cases they do. They also create a 'noise' which the official system has to respond to and then retranslate into its own terms, that is to say into the rationality of the law. Thus the point of the 'lay acid' of the jury or of the lay magistracy is to disturb the system into rethinking the answer - sometimes it will point the way and in fact give the answer - but its primary function is to make the system itself make the answer by recalculating all the options and reviewing the parameters. The lay acid is the 'noise'• that makes the system act because it has to make sense of that noise. As opposed to autopoiesis the noise (the outside) , is not always necessarily opaque since it can sometimes

---

[166] See Bańkowski (1994)

provide its own answers but it is official rationality that adopts the answers and chooses to provide a new lawfulness.

c) Reflexive Law

The noise guides in a way that it does not do in a fully blown autopoietic system. We can develop this if we look at Teubner's (1983) pre-autopoietic notion of reflexive law. There he wants to develop Nonet and Selznick's (1978) model. He thinks that in their notion of responsive law there is a move to a more democratic society but that it conflates two forms of legal rationality, substantive and reflexive rationality[167]. For him the role of reflexive law is

> 'to design self regulating social systems through its norms of organisation and procedure which are centred around communications predicated on a code of legality and illegality which reproduce themselves as legal acts'. (Maher 1998: 241)

For Teubner elements of this can be found in the Selznickian analysis. Thus when Selznick talks of 'institutional design and diagnosis' one finds, according to Teubner, the implication that the job of legal norms is to produce 'harmonious fit' between institutions and social structures; that they do not guide substantively but rather guide procedure and the organisation - trying, for example, to provide mechanisms for self regulation in schemes for the politization of law in respect of social advocacy and class actions (where substantive answers are not necessarily put forward).

Reflexive rationality does not seek to impose its structures on the institution it is regulating but seeks to bend to its logic to allow it to do what it wants. It does not try to identify and deal with social problems but rather creates 'opportunity structures' which do not destroy patterns of social life. It works also in the Habermasian sense of law as an institution (one that produces and guarantees democratic self ordering) rather than as the 'medium' which colonises the life world. One can now no longer have universal legitimation structures and they must vary according to each institution and reflexive law provides this.

> 'Law realises its own reflexive orientation insofar as it provides the structural premises for reflexive processes in other social subsystems.' Teubner (1983: 275)

---

[167] See chapter 4 where the claim is made that at times responsive law appear to be just 'nice' repressive law.

He uses legal regulation of labour relations as an example - it works by shaping legal collective bargaining by creating systems in which the voice of the worker can be heard and is factored into the rationality of the system[168]; how Stephen is heard; how contingency and love come into law. But we can also see how law feeds into contingency and love. We take Teubner's example of consumer protection law. Consumers can be helped by having systems of countervailing power created in the law to put the consumer's (Stephen's) case and feed into the law - the law does not decide what is in consumer's interest but provides means for this to happen. But if these fail because they do not affect the asymmetry of power since they are not able to counteract the strength of the companies, one might try and develop structures which can compensate for this inequality in power. In the case of what Teubner calls 'interaction deficiencies between contracting parties' the law itself steps in and stimulates a self-regulation that will counter that. Though 'general clauses' and standards such as 'good faith' are normally seen as substantive, we might also see them as reflexive in the following sense. When the internal rules of the contracting system such as the prevailing commercial customs and the like are seen as deficient, the legal system steps in and replaces them by judicial definitions of market rules or the judicial process defines standards of public policy in the hope of stimulating them. Here we have not so much the individual's voice coming in as forms of legality, making sure that individuals rights are respected. One can also see this, says Teubner, in the trend of 'constitutionalizing the law of private organisations'. Rather than making substantial interventions in organisations, we can make sure that they have the structures that enable them to take note of the outside; put systems in place which can reach out to 'maximise internal rationality' and the protection of the law. Certain aspects of judicial review work in this way. For what goes on there is that courts take the arbitrary and contingent actions of institutions and judicialise them in the sense of inscribing on them the rationality of the law[169]. Thus they are sensitive to what they are doing internally and not just trample people underfoot in the name of welfare, love and substantive rationality.

Let us turn again to the EU. Thus directives are one mode of the implementation of EC law. Though they might be seen on the model of 'responsive law', with substantive standards being enforced, in fact they are also what one might think of as 'constitutionalizing directives' which enforce

[168] See the discussion of Collins in chapter 9

[169] I am not suggesting that this is what always happens - rather that one can understand aspects of the theory of judicial review in this way.

such standards as equal rights and anti-discriminatory standards[170]. Let us look at them through the optic of systems theory. Thus, as we saw in out discussion of the operations of Art. 234, we do not see here 'direct effect' in the sense of direct EU enforcement - for much of the implementation of EC law is done through local agencies, courts etc. Imelda Maher (1998) takes this systems theoretical approach. She has three conclusions. Firstly that EC law is transposed into the national system via the internal operations of the local legal system which then uses it to regulate social sub-systems. Secondly, though this gives the directive flexibility for it is through the local agencies that it is transformed and used as an operating mechanism, certain parameters are not flexible - thus the time limit and the fact that the court must give it priority against a conflicting local rule etc. Thirdly, since the Community directive is taken into national law and transformed by it, it has to operate in such a manner as will disturb that system's coherency and internal working and the way social processes are already being regulated. So though Community law might have formal primacy in practice, if it does not fit into the local processes easily it might be ignored. For her then,

> 'Formal supremacy means little in these circumstances, with the internal consistency of the social system of law - in particular the need for order on which the whole legitimacy of the system is based [-] will take priority over a rule of supremacy.'(1998: 251)

However, if we do not think of success of specific regulations but of the national legal order in general, then it is clear that its 'internal consistency' does not stay static – the 'opportunity structures' are used. We might not see great and sudden changes but the continuous adjustment and re-adjustment of the order does change it. For example, with the British entry into the EU, we can note the 'Europeanisation' of English law in particular. It is impossible to look at any branch of the law without taking into account the European dimension. European law is no longer an optional extra but is an integral and transformative part of the law. In the methodology of law as well, it interpretation has been loosened up, made more teleological and less formal[171]. In terms of our scheme then we now have a system where the judges are to some extent more flexible; more willing to look to the noise from the outside and use it to re-order their system[172].

---

170 See Craig and De Burca (1998)

171 MacComick and Bańkowski (1991)

172 Atiyah and Summers (1987) saw American Law as less formal and more inclined to lift the veil than English law was - the moment when the institution was unpicked and the raw moral data re-evaluated was sooner. Now it would appear that the distance between the systems has changed and one of the reasons for that is the re-ordering of the English legal system through the noise of EC law.

d) Non Rivalistic Identity

Though systems theory would not have it so, the above way of looking at reciprocal influencing can make us see one system. For in an important sense Community Law and national law, though they reciprocally influence each other and thus can be seen as separate, are one in that the mode of implementation of Community Law makes it one with the national system. Thus we do not have, for example, English law or Community law but rather English/Community law. But we can go further in trying to see this unity among separate spheres when we look to the problems of a European identity , especially the problems of local identities against more universal identities such as Europe. This is linked to the problem with which we started when discussing Europe, that of sovereignties. We can see this linkage in the Brunner[173] case. For though, as we saw, that case decided that ultimately the German constitution overrode EC laws in conflict with it, this was the case only because the Union was not a democratic polity. Were it one then one would be able to say that it had *competence-competence* and so would be able to override German fundamental law. Here the monocular approach is expanded for it is not merely talking about sovereignties, about national law *versus* Community law, but predicating the argument on to states and national identity. Thus what we have is one law and one state, and in the state there must be one people. Thus German law is superior because there is a German state, defined by the German *Volk* whereas there is no corresponding European state since there is no European people which can be identified as such. Were there to be such an identity then the court might decide in its favour. Again we see the binary solution applied, with one identity excluding the other. But it goes further than that. For it sees the solution to Europe as either an arrangement of linked separate sovereign states, on the international law model, or one European super state - the latter solution necessarily excluding other more local identities since it would be the overarching one. So Europe would become one but at the cost of excluding other more local identities by subsuming them under the European. The proponents of local identities make a similar mistake. Part of their argument for the local is that the European is too big to generate the necessary solidarity or glue. Their answer is the local which is just a smaller version of the European in that that also excludes. There is no interlocking of porous normative spheres which in their interaction make one system - there is one system which excludes all else and is not open to the outside.

How can one then construct a non rivalistic system where all these identities will be different and will not exclude each other? Renee Girard

---

[173] *op. cit.*

(1987) claims that at the base of each society there is the scapegoating mechanism which in unjustly blaming an innocent victim bonds the rest of the society together by the continuous ritual performance of this scapegoating. For him Christianity, in the passion of Christ, lays bare this lie at the base of all society and its historic mission is to create a non-exclusionary society. At one level this seems impossible. For the 'scapegoating mechanism' can be seen on the lines of Durkheim as saying that all society needs deviance to bond it together. It is almost a logical truth in that for inclusion we have to have some idea of the excluded. According to Bert van Roermund (1996) 'a whole can only be whole by virtue of being limited, that is to include some and exclude others'. How can we operationalise the contrary to this? Let us recall system theory's claim that the distinction makes between environment and system is itself an internal one. A system to make sense of itself has to make distinctions. It is in the act of making the distinction between itself and its environment that it knows what it is by indicating what it is not. What it is doing there is conceiving of its whole world as consisting of itself and what it is not, making that indication (making the mark) and 're-entering' the distinction on the side indicated. Thus the distinction between itself and the environment is internal for it makes it in order to make sense of itself. This is always, of course, a partial view in that it sees itself in the distinction and with each new distinction it makes its view of itself changes. So its identity is never finished and always in flux (Bańkowski and Christodoulidis 1998). It is in this way of looking at it that we can make sense of the law containing within it its own negation, i.e. enfolding within it breaches of the law. So we can see how 'living lawfully' also includes breaking the law, living in and out of the law.

Let us now put this somewhat abstract way of looking at in the more concrete terms of the way that European identity is formed. Firstly we may say that European identity is always in flux and in the process of becoming. It is 'essentially contested' not because 'European' is a vague concept - rather it is something that is found in the process of the continual renegotiation of European identity (in the continual making of distinctions in system speak)[174]. It is in that process that European identity exists. This conceptualises the Union into a system of interlocking normative spheres whose identities and the larger identity of Europe will not be structured vertically. It will not be a sort of Russian doll model with the smaller identities fitting into, and subsumed by, the larger ones; thus Scottish, British, European. Rather the identities, including the European, one will interlock horizontally. Most important moreover, is that this network of systems will not be seen as static - it will

[174] We can also say, following chapter 9, that the indeterminacy of the concept of Europe stems from its application and not its meaning.

always be in the process of becoming. Thus its identity will be reflexive in the sense that its mode of existence will be the continual creating and recreating of itself anew. The dynamic of this, in Europe at least will be, a tendency to break down the nation state and look more to forms of governance based on sub-national grouping. Thus notions of subsidiarity and the like will start to produce something more like a 'Europe of the Regions', where different grouping at different geographical and functional and status levels will cross and intersect in a 'system of co-operative regionalism with autonomous regions having greater input and influence in EU policies' (Bańkowski and Scott 1996). The European identity will be formed in the intersection of all of this but will be always in a state of flux - exclusion will thus minimised.

Let me amplify the above with a more concrete example. In defining myself as Scots I do not thereby have to exclude because I can say that I am Scottish because I am not English but we are both European. This does not have to be a vertically layering of identities on the lines of the Russian doll model. I do not have to exclude the English for I can see it as part of the way that I define myself. For I bring in Englishness into my identity when I try and make sense of myself as European. But the point here is to see myself as *Scottish* European (and not the other way round) so that the identity is a local one at the start. In starting like this, I realise that my identity now consists, in part at least, of those whom those whom I excluded in an earlier operation, the English. For to think of myself as Scottish European means also that I have to accept that it means that part of my Scottishness is English for they are English Europeans. So my Scottish identity changes as also does my European one. And the English, the French and Germans and so on do this, as do groups at lower levels below the nation state. This means that we come to nuanced views of our identities which in the many cross-cutting intersections and inclusions and exclusions means that nobody is fully cut out. Moreover since this is always in flux - I can never be in a permanent state of exclusion for no one can tell where the next encounter might lead. What we have is a form of localised globalism. Here then we have the idea of a polity which is not vague but is always re-ordering itself. This is because its identity consists in the continual making of distinctions or in the continual re-positioning of its component units. We might call this the process of exchange within its units. This gives a whole that is continually in flux and continually on a journey.

EUROPE IN FLUX: EXCHANGE AND GIFT

One way of looking at this is to say that what we have here is everyone exchanging and it is in this cycle of exchange that we get the polity. In a sense this can be seen as a version of communitarianism. We all grow by exchanging, in the fact of giving myself to others and receiving what I get from them. I give myself to you and receive back you/me which changes me. This is the fundamental for understanding community for it is thus that we build community and solidarity. The gift of myself initiates the relationship and the exchange that flows from it makes it into community. We grow then by this exchange which can be characterised as the encounter with the other which can always produce the unexpected. I do not grow if the return is cut off. This continues at all ontological levels from the individual to the differing collectivities. It is in this way that we can say that everything is in flux and that identity is in the exchange. However some communitarian claims that you cannot have a European state rest on the notion that homogeneity is necessary for the solidarities and glue of community[175]. The mutuality and trust and the conditions under which that can develop is the nation state. Miller, for example, says

> '..it is implicit in the argument that we should aim to create a world that comes closer to the nation state model, partly by encouraging the growth of inclusive national identities in states which do not already have them, partly by creatively redrawing existing lines of political authority so that they correspond more closely to the pattern of national allegiances as we find them.'(1999: 80)[176]

But in doing this they see nothing outside the context of the particular community and thus preserve a stultifying homogeneity. It lets nothing grow and develop because there is no diversity and nothing outside which can penetrate, be part of it, and help change. In some respects the model of single issue groups , groupings around sexual orientation, disability etc. can be seen as a good way of understanding communitarianism. These are seen by some on the post-communist left as the forms of community and communality that are emerging. But the trouble with these, as Millbank (1996) points out, is that they are essentially a utilitarian form of association for the purpose of mutual support and help (which is not to deny that that is a laudable aim). They are not primarily for the joy of association. There is no opening out to the other by which one can develop. For the other in this group is the same as everyone else - a representative of that single issue or status which unites them and therefore not different or diverse. There is no growth because the community sees itself as the final context, there is nothing else, no outside for it to relate to, to include and thereby change. We get something that peers in on itself. The truth of comunitarianism is that we are not ourselves alone. The problem is that they tend to treat that community as though it were a single individual with no context outside - a windowless monad which turns in on itself and

---

[175] See Gestenberg (1998) below

[176] See also Bańkowski and Christodoulidis (1999) where Miller's argument is discussed in detail.

replicates itself. It becomes like a single individual because each person becomes more and more like every other and there is nothing to differentiate between them. Thus we get the organic community where the leader can do no wrong because he (and it is usually a he) speaks in the name of the community and is the community, everyone being united in him (see chapter 1). Thus communitarianism reproduces at the liberal level, the model of liberal theory which for the individual it decries.

Let us develop this notion of exchange and flux. For Millbank the self is in flux through what he sees as a universalised practice of giving. This should be seen, not as the giving 'without want of return', as Lévinas and others might have it, but rather as part of the practice of asymmetric exchange. We do not expect an equivalent back - rather we have to be open to whatever we receive back for that is what changes us. It is because of this continual giving and receiving that the self is always in flux and never fixed. This might be seen as a gloss on communitarianism in this sense; instead of constituting ourselves in others we find ourselves through the continuous process of exchange, that is giving ourselves to others and being open to receive quite often unexpected (and perhaps unwelcome) gifts in return. These we work on and they are the agents of our transformation. For Millbank this happens at all levels, from individuals to different levels of community. Community is thus constituted by exchange both internally and externally at all different levels. It is in this way that we do not hold on to an identity and we can change. Now this implies a practice of being open to the stranger, to a practice of treating, as Millbank says, 'all aliens as neighbours'. At the group level this implies being open to the outside - always being ready to go beyond the limit although that limit is what at the moment defines our existence. In conditions of capitalism, argues Millbank, this exchange gets frozen into commodification where we control what we expect back, that is the exchange of exact equivalents. One can see how, on this way of looking at it then, the community or the individual does not grow at all for all they are doing is replicating themselves. They appear to be open but they are not because what is coming back (and what must come back) is the exact equivalent. Thus there is a lack of differentiation, since all you have is the same thing, sometimes more and sometimes less - there is no transformation. We may take the following metaphor. I want to give from myself and my goods to someone else. To do so I have to open my house wherein these goods are kept and let the recipient in to take them. In that act I am thereby including him and taking the risk that his entry might change me and my house in ways I do not know. To give, I always have to open myself – even locking my house and stepping outside to give is already exposing myself to the donee. On the other hand, fearful of this risk, I might not give at all or might only give on condition I get something the same back - one way I will be able to control for that risk is by making sure the recipient is the same as me and so I can reasonably expect something the same back. I have got so far and I do not want to go any further -from now on progression will be more of the same.

IDEALS AND THE JOURNEY

We saw how Europe can be characterised as an institutional arrangement that is not a state or even a super state but a mass of exchanging units which in their mutual exchange constitute the polity and grow - always being in flux. Part of the point then, as we have seen, is that we must always reach out and, in our encounter and exchange, continually recreate ourselves. But this does not mean we only think of the local and the particular with no thought for universal values and ideals. As we have seen, we can view Europe as in flux, not because it is a vague concept, but rather because its identity is created in its application. This means that Europe is a network of exchanging units and it is in that exchange that European identity is transformed and re-transformed. We examine this through thinking of the EU project as a journey characterised by ideals. In showing how the interlocking flux that is Europe can be deformed into something that seeks security and certainty, we can see concretely, in a particular institution, how 'living lawfully' can become deformed.

Weiler (1994) characterised the start of European integration after the war as a project characterised by ideals. The ideals were those of peace, prosperity and supranationalism. But the scope of these ideals was somewhat larger than might be commonly understood. Prosperity could be understood as something more than just having enough bread or even being rich. What it means can best be captured by the Aristotelian *eudaimonia* (faring well) - a concept which has both spiritual and material qualities. Likewise we can see how peace for him was more than just peace and quiet - the Hobbesian security. It is something that resonates with the virtues of reconciliation and forgiveness and is, as Weiler says, suffused with notions of Christian love[177]- is something about living in harmony with ourselves and others. Peace and prosperity go together in a form of transnational economic solidarity. It is here that the final ideal, supranationalism comes in. This is, says Weiler, to be distinguished from internationalism. The aim of the former is a sort of solidarity among nation states, of what he sees as a form of communitarianism at the state level. Internationalism is much more like liberalism at the state level. Here states become the autonomous individuals of liberal theory, motivated by their self-

[177] This is, as Weiler points out, not surprising given the personal backgrounds of, Schuman, De Gasperi, Adenauer and Monnet.

interest and only connecting in order to fulfil that self-interest. The other task of supranationalism, Weiler goes on, is to patrol and constrain the excesses of nationalism; something which, though important in that it gives people a sense of origin and a place to belong to, and appeals to our sociality, needs to be constrained. For him, ideals have four parameters. Firstly there is the idyllic, the state of affairs that we want. For him this is a state of affairs that is usually, though not necessarily, forward looking. Secondly, they have to have an element of what he calls the demonic; that is, we need to recognise the fault in us that we want the ideal to overcome. Thus we are not looking abstractly at some desired state of affairs but also seeing the ideal as something that confronts us as we are, in our faults. It is those we need to overcome to attain the ideal. So the ideal is not only 'idealistic' but realistic as well since it recognises us for what we are and the appetites we have to overcome. Thirdly, there is the virtuous; that which enables us to distinguish the morally acceptable ideal for ideals can be both good and bad. Finally, there is the idolatrous; that state of affairs which breaks down and corrupts our ideals. We can see the ideal then as something that is both inside and outside (see chapter 4). Something that from the outside converts and transforms our inside and becomes part of it.

We can see the 'European Project' as a journey but one without an end in the sense of a destination - what is important is the journey rather than the destination. This captures the sense of flux that I talked about earlier. You never know what is going to happen next and one must always be open to all twists and turns in the journey. The ideals are not a specific destination - we are not aiming to get *there* - rather they inform our journey. We can view Weiler's founding ideals of the European project in this way. They point us to the future but they never point to a fixed destination. They are then like those signposts on the road from London that point to the 'North'. There is, of course, no such place - we never arrive at a town called 'North'. The North is always further away. It is rather like a horizon. You never actually arrive at the horizon for as soon as you arrive where you thought it was, new vistas and new horizons open up. Ideals, like signposts, point to somewhere further away but to no specific place. They are future oriented but what is important is not some future goal but the here and now. It is the journey that is important and it will not be betrayed if we journey according to its ideals. In this sense, though ideals are utopian they are, so to speak, a practical utopia; something that, though future directed, transforms the present activity - it transforms the journey and makes the way we travel into a future oriented, utopian, activity itself. In this way we bring the future into the present - the journey is the destination. One view of the eschatological consciousness of the early church might clarify this. The strength of this was so great that it transformed the practice of the early church - in a way one might say that they were realising the Kingdom in their practice. The problem came when the Kingdom, as it seemed to them, did not come and so gradually that practice changed and an institutionalised church was built up with the rules as to how to arrive at the Kingdom which was now a far distant destination - the morality of duty had taken over[178]. But my point is that the future is lived in the present through the ideals which make that possible. In this way, one might say that the openness and indeterminacy of the local is preserved but at the same time intertwined with the ideals which are there to prevent our journey going completely off course (North is not South after all!) In this sense then universalism and particularism are combined. For the ideals (signposts) though they do not point to a particular destination enable us to judge the worth of any place where we stop - as on all journeys we have to. What we must not do is devalue any destination by mistaking it for the end rather than just a stop on the journey - the next stage might be completely different. When ideals become idolatrous and corrupting is when we think we have reached the destination and have nowhere to go - we have arrived[179]. We thus freeze the state that we are in, thinking it perfect and not wanting to venture beyond the safety of its walls. We are now no longer on a journey and there is nothing more to do - exchanging has stopped and we are no longer open to the outside or contingent - we are secure in our closed circles.

Part of the problem with the 'European project', says Weiler, is that the ideals have become idolatrous in the above way. It is something that comes, ironically, from a certain seeming success. We appear to have reached the goals that our ideals have given us and there is nothing more to do but petty squabbling. Take peace for example. In some ways the EU has been brilliantly successful. For in the Western part of Europe, which in a sense was how Europe was seen by the founders at the time, there has been peace. That one fear, Franco/German enmity has more or less evaporated - not many seriously believe in the prospect of Franco/German war. As, Weiler says, the idea of Kohl or Mitterand[180] talking of the necessity for Europe because of the need to keep the peace between Germany and France seems laughable. What has happened is that the EU seems to have achieved its goal - there appears to be peace and security within its borders. This also fits into the ideal of prosperity, where notwithstanding recessions, we might see that we have

[178] The analogy is not strict because not even the most institutionalised thinks of the Church as the Kingdom of God! It must be noted that this is only one way of looking at the eschatological dimension of the apostolic group and the early church - one which has been characterised as 'liberal Protestantism ' by James Alison (1996). Of course as he acknowledges this has also been a catholic view of the degeneration of the Gospel message by the Church (see Boff 1986).

[179] This is similar to my discussion of the duty/aspiration distinction in chapter 4.

[180] And this is as true for Schröder/Chirac.

achieved at least a system which keeps destitution at bay. So we do not worry about the other parts of the ideal - self realisation and dignity and the mobilisation of agencies other than the state to work to promote this and counteract the negative tendencies of the market[181].

The ideal of supranationalism clarifies the above. Weiler's vision of the ideal approximated to something like I have been arguing here; a vision of different systems engaging with each other, each inspired by an ideal of openness to the stranger and inclusion as a way of developing themselves individually and as a group. In the context of Europe then, we do not have to look at it as though an overarching and internationalist system is subordinating a local and particular system - we can also see it as another local system in engagement with others. We do not have to see it in a two dimensional way as either local sovereignties or one overarching sovereignty but rather different local sovereignties competing and engaging with each other - the universalism flowing into them through that creative interaction[182].

But what happened? The desire to cure the worst excesses of nationalism has been that which destroys the universalist parts of the ideal. For the answer is seen by some to be a single European state. This is the result of the 'monocular' vision and has resulted in a turning inward. Because we think that we have achieved the ideals (or are on the way to so doing because we are travelling along the road to the agreed destination) we have stopped moving up the ladder of aspiration. Our notion of progression is how to make better what we have now; that is, the state. But because we are now turning inward (and downward, so to speak), we have no way of developing from the exchange an openness to the outside. Our notion of progress is what we have now but something bigger. This neatly mirrors John Millbank's point (see above) that differences are merely quantitative. Prosperity becomes having a larger market with more of the same products; peace becomes part of the conditions for achieving that; supranationalism becomes, as the Union replicates the ways in which the smaller states act, the European state. The supreme irony at the European level will thus be that one of the solutions to the problem of the excesses of the nation state will be making a larger one. But more; for its undoubted partial success will make people forget the wide open-ended universalistic ideal and focus on inward, chauvinistic, and nationalistic policies. We thus begin to build 'Fortress Europe', keeping the alien out of it, purifying it of alien contamination internally (the refugee and migrant worker 'problem'), so that we inside who are really 'Europeans' can enjoy order and

---

181 See my discussion of Catholic Social Theory in chapter 11.

182 See MacCormick (1993; 1995).

prosperity[183]. This works both externally and internally. The wall is there is to keep the other out and in keeping them out we internally begin to purify ourselves from the other in our midst. Growth in these circumstances means, we saw, the reproduction of the same. So the homogenisation of Europe through the market might proceed not only through the homogenisation of products (the 'euro-brand') but the homogenisation of consumers (they become products also) and the ironing out of difference. But there is also something more terrifying. In the name of this 'fortress Europe' that we are trying to create and the European identity that it entails, we also try and purify from within. We see those who are different in culture, religion and values as a danger. We can see this in the growth of European chauvinisms and racism, and the problem of EU , asylum and migrant labour (those who are already in Europe and those about to come in)[184].

Here again growth and progress are seen as more of the same. For convergence (that prospective EU partners begin to conform to EU norms), can be seen as only opening out to the 'outside' if these partners are already like us. Development in terms of the Millbank practice of universalised giving and asymmetric exchange is controlled. For we refuse to be open to whatever the stranger, to whom we are thinking of giving, offers. We control the return by making sure that the recipient is like us and therefore likely to give something we expect (the equivalent) in return - thus freezing development. In looking to the South, we also look to convergence round a particular form of European identity, a sort of Judaeo-Christian 'tolerant' one as against an 'intolerant' Islam. Now this is not to argue that minimum Human Rights criteria should not be applied , nor that some degree of economic convergence is necessary. But we must be careful that attention to abuse outside does not make us blind to abuse internally and that our terms for assimilation are in fact conformity to the abuse of rights we have internally. If, to a degree, we accept those outside as they are then, then our inclusion works not only to change them but also to change us. For in trying to deal with their disruption to our society, it also focuses on how we disrupt our own society without thinking about it. Having to deal with Islamic practice in respect of women through law and other means, for example, should affect the discrimination against women and others that Christian churches practice. The challenge of accepting the

---

[183] It is important, as we have seen, to see these two as linked. Because peace is not to be just the good order of commodity production, it will have to cope with the genuine problems for order and democracy that a polity, seeing good order as not just something that is to be produced by enforcing the market, raises. Since prosperity will also have to do with self-actualisation and substantive dignity of humans, it will involve intervention in the market. The market will be seen as having boundaries and will not be treated as sacrosanct. This will raise the problems of to deal with the bureaucratic organisations that will inevitably have to arise therefrom and we will deal with that in chapter 11.

[184] See Lyons (1997).

'inhuman' from the outside, means that we have to look to our human rights and universalistic structures which cannot remain complacent in the face of that. In terms of the EU in general what this does is to conceptualise the Union, as we have seen, into a system of interlocking normative spheres whose identities and the larger identity of Europe will not be structured vertically. Rather the identities, including the European, one will interlock horizontally.

All the above means that it is important not to let the EU sink into local patriotism and turn inward. What is necessary is to be open to the stranger and not exclude them - for that is the only way that we can grow and develop. Otherwise what appears to be universal becomes narrow and local for it loses the capacity to enfold the outside because it sees no context outside of itself. So the universal can become local and fall foul of the problems of localism. It can do that if treats its community as fixed and certain and is thus certain to whom its rights and equalities can apply to. Judith Butler (1996) takes the above point further. For her the universal is always historically contingent in that it will be always articulated in a certain context. Thus throughout our history certain groups were not recognised as human and this was a way to deny them rights; for why should one have to have allegiance to non-humans? We can see this in our time in respect of Jews, Blacks and homosexuals. For her the universal becomes articulated through challenges to its conventional formulation and the excluded set its contingent limit. Thus the universal becomes an ideal for it is with that ideal in mind that we can go against the limit (the border where exclusion starts) and include in those who are at the moment excluded - continually repeating the process. This also has a reflexive effect on the ideal for this also will be affected by the process. We may adapt the metaphor of the signpost pointing to the 'North' - they also eventually change otherwise the 'the north' becomes a form of idolatry. The guidance to the 'north' will eventually lead us to a new type of signpost. To produce something like a 'Fortress Europe' (see above) runs the dangers of fixing those borders and making the contingent exclusions necessary[185].

---

[185] Thus arguments for cosmopolitanism which base themselves on something like the 'world community of human beings' (see Nussbaum 1996) can also exclude if they don't look beyond. For what makes humans so special? We do not have to postulate beings from the stars to see this. Our present day sensitivity and respect for animals and nature makes the point very clearly. Why should animals be left out? Or for that matter trees? We have seen the rise of transnational organisations that are precisely motivated by that ethical view. We do not have to confine ourselves to animals, for the community of human beings is not as fixed as it appears. What about what some think of as the 'rights of the unborn child'? Is the human community to be seen diachronically or just in single time slices? These questions are important in talking of inter-generational justice as when, for example, we discuss ecological problems and factor in the effect it might have on future generations.

CONCLUSION

What I have been trying to do in this chapter (and will try in the next) is to operationalise 'living lawfully'. Part of the problem, as we saw, was how one could describe a system which was supposed to be whole, the unity of the articulations of law and love, without using the language of separateness in such a way that they become separate spheres and are connected in some sort of zero-sum game. I tried to use the example of the Europe Union to begin to show this. There I showed that traditional ways of looking at the problem of how to conceptualise the legal order that is the European Union had difficulty in seeing beyond either some sort of union of sovereign states or one legal order which overrode all the state legal orders that were members of it (calls for federalism would merely be articulations in terms of zero-sum games)[186]. My aim was to show the legal order as a set of 'interlocking normative systems' where sovereignty would depend upon perspective and would not be an all or nothing thing located in one normative order . Europe as a whole would be the set of these systems - polycentric and understood as a totality of these interlocking articulations. To think of the European legal order as, in our example, extending from the sovereignty of Brussels with the national legal order a subordinate part of it, or the other way round with the Brussels a subordinate part of the national legal order, would be a deformed way of looking at. To look at the European order in this way would be the same as looking at living lawfully and only seeing legalism or the chaos of love.

In looking at it in this way, systems theory also is some help since that helped to explain the modes of this articulation. Here, ironically, the fact that systems theory in its autopoietic form starts off by positing a radical separateness helps us. For it has to develop a range of metaphors to deal with the connectedness that there assuredly is. But I use these metaphors to develop a unity in a way which autopoiesis denies. It is in these articulations and connections that we find reasoning 'in the middle'.

We further developed this idea of unity. For there we saw how we could have an identity which would not necessarily have to be exclusive - for the 'other' against which it defined itself was brought inside. The distinction between the outside and the inside here was itself an internal distinction. Thus we saw how the system is open to the outside in a way which makes it part of the inside but without losing it. We produced then, a system of 'differentiated unity'. This is not, as in the Luhmann image of marriage parties endlessly oscillating between the routine of marriage and the contingency of passion, a sort of 'differentiated disunity'. Rather it is a 'differentiated unity' - a

186 See Weiler (1991).

situation where both parties are neither one in such a way that you cannot distinguish them (undifferentiated unity) or so separate that you cannot see the unity (differentiated disunity). 'Differentiated unity' is a mature relationship though, one where people are together and at the same time are their own person. In that way, they are able to put together their passion and their need for stability and interlock them in some sort of way (Cohen 1974).

We then saw how we could view all of this as a system of exchanging units, at all levels from the individual to different levels of collectivities. We saw how this was the way individuals and communities developed and grew. It stems from the gift of connection (see chapter 6) which starts from the inside and initiates the exchange since it is willing to go outside and make that part of itself and thus continually change and recreate itself. There is where love plays its part - precludes the circles of certainty that, for example, Creon and Antigone drew around themselves and which tries to create everything around it in its own image. This enables us to have, 'journey' image of Europe.

That image shows us a necessary and a desirable pattern of social and political organisation because (a) it challenges each normative order, and stops the ideals of each from becoming frozen and distorted, (b) it prevents an illegitimate hierarchy, where the lower systems function only to subvert the higher system, and (c) in the interaction and negotiation between orders, and in the mutual accommodation of their ideals, each set of ideals is constantly interrogated and renewed.

CHAPTER 11

LIVING LAWFULLY

INTRODUCTION: THE LAW SCHOOL AT AUCHENSHUGGLE

We finished the last chapter with the idea of many interlocking and exchanging units whose existence and identity was to be seen in their flux. In this chapter I wish to develop these themes by looking again at democratic ordering. Through studying the problems as instantiated in the European Union and beyond, I intend to show what it is to make a legal system work where legality (respect for rules) and particularity are held permanently in tension. I start where we began by looking at democratic ordering and how the lone voice of Stephen can both be part of the community and itself be *truly* heard. This time I do not start with Stephen but with another, nameless, lone voice. Through this also we shall come to see models of democratic ordering which see the seeming oppositions that we have talked about, of market and welfare and the like, as deeply interconnected. I start then by looking by examining these points through a discussion of the organisational turmoils of a (fictional) Law School.

At the University of Auchenshuggle big changes are being planned in the Law Faculty. Alone among Faculties of Law in the country, the Faculty is not a single administrative entity. It is divided into seven departments corresponding to different branches of law and theory. These are administrative entities in their own right, hold their own budgets and are responsible for their own courses - the Faculty of Law is where all these units meet. But it is a bit more complicated than that and there is some integration of the units. Though departments run their own courses, the degree itself is a Faculty degree and students are not allocated to the various units but are treated as Law Faculty students. So the Faculty itself can in certain instances be seen, not as an overseeing entity, but rather as a department or individual administrative unit.

For some, this state of affairs was seen as somewhat inefficient. Not only because there was some duplication of administrative effort but also because they thought that this arrangement made for exclusivity and inwardness, thereby narrowing down law as a field of scientific study. Against this, some argued that it was precisely these 'exclusionary' circles, ring-fencing certain areas that in a greater unit would not get so much help, that enabled the Law Faculty of Auchenshuggle to be so innovative and strong in contrast to other law schools in the country.

A movement for unification arose whose aim was to abolish all the departments and to have one single Law School, one administrative unit, and one department. The leaders of this movement predicted great advantages for this arrangement - there would be administrative efficiency and the elimination of exclusivity would free teaching and open research in the law. A committee was appointed to produce a plan to show how a unified structure would look. This was duly done and the structure was debated at a Faculty meeting. Many arguments were raised. A particular point of concern to both sides was what was taken to be the centralising and anti-democratic nature of the structure. A key committee in the old structure - the 'co-ordination committee' - would now no longer be representative of the old units but would be smaller. Senior members of staff dominated the debate but on occasion junior members of staff voiced their fears. These were somewhat different from the points made by the former who were more concerned with protection of territory, resources and the like. The more junior members voiced the fear that the new structure would lessen chances of their voices being heard. It is important to note that this was not merely a fear that their interests would not be taken into account and that they would be at the mercy of a powerful command structure. They were also afraid that their positive inputs into the scientific and other organisation of the Faculty would have no point of entry.

Some members of the Faculty who wished to use it to drive through a more, as they saw it, democratic structure in the new Faculty picked up this point. For many years they had been concerned that the departmental structure created too many slippages for the Faculty to be an effective democratic instrument. Power had slipped from the Faculty to where it was difficult to tell. For them this was an opportunity of re-asserting the power and the democratic nature of the Faculty. They were against what they saw as the managerialists who were in favour of taking power away from the Faculty and giving it to small select committees who would, the managerialists thought, get the work of the Faculty done through efficient and rational decision taking. So the democrats saw the junior staff view as a chance to democratise the new law school; to make the Faculty a stronger forum and especially to make more representative and thus larger the powerful co-ordinating committee.

Two connected points need to be noted here. Firstly the 'democratic' solution proposed assumed the integration of the Faculty into a single unit and was, in a sense, predicated on that. This missed the point of the junior member of staff. She was claiming that her voice was not being heard, that in the shake-up what was being lost was the easy possibility, in the small units as they existed before, of her making comments and providing input. She was in fact, the Stephen of the Law Faculty.

The solution of the strong and 'democratic' faculty or representative committee thereof would not address the problems of the faculty Stephen or of the Faculty as a whole (though it might still be an useful institution). For the proposed re-organisation would have the effect of making it harder for people to get their voices heard. This would be detrimental not only to his own interests but also to the interests of the Law School as a whole - for one needs innovative ideas and this would be blocking one of their sources. Doing away with the system of departments effectively left no bridge between the individual and the Faculty and in the Faculty it was difficult to speak because of the mass of competing voices. There was no system of co-ordination only the strongest and most powerful got heard. A representative co-ordinating committee would not necessarily solve this problem. For it would not ensure that individual voices got heard. The individual voices would be lost in the representative and, the more one tried to prevent that, the larger that committee would become until it became the Faculty as a whole (see chapter 1).

Previously the problem was ameliorated because of the small departments, which made it possible for voices to be heard and filtered through in many different ways. At the same time it made the control of decisions and the control and organisation of the work of the Faculty easier. There was, one might say, a system of 'micro-control'. What this meant, for example, was that teaching policies and loads would be organised in small groups of similar interests, which would enable teaching to get done. But more than that, it would enable people to have an input into how, when and what one should teach. The particularities of the individual situation would be taken into account. With the new system, it was felt by some that this would go. The flexibility of a system, which was able to take into account the particular needs of the individual teacher and the particular teaching situation, would be lost. In the name of transparency and democracy we would have a centralised system where everyone would be allotted an equal workload. The way this would be done would be by contact hours alone, it would not matter how and whom one taught. Notional contact hours would be allotted supervisions of doctoral students and the like. These rules would be applied and everyone would know that they were doing the same amount of work, on these criteria. No one was against the equality in teaching loads and this is of course very important as a protection for junior members of staff. But a negative effect of this system would be that, especially in a large faculty, the mutual adjustment for the infinite and diverse particularities of each person would be harder. The rule bound system would be transparent and fair, and it would also be easier to apply. But something important, the particularity of the situation and that of the students and teachers would be lost. The teacher for example would disappear to be seen in terms of contact hours.

What faculty Stephen meant was not that the best way for people to have their voice was to be in small units, as they were before, separate and apparently self-contained, or even just have the facility to be able to work on their own. For there, the integrationalists were right when they claimed that this narrowed the scientific work of each member of the Faculty, enclosed as they were in narrow self-contained, and sometimes self-interested, units. What was needed was a porous architecture which enabled units to be open and exchange with the outside - thereby restructuring themselves. In so doing they would drag the outside in. At the same time the whole context of their world would be the Faculty which would exist in this mutual exchanging and re-structuring. So what we would have is a system of mutual exchanging at different ontological levels which would constitute the Faculty. The implication of this would be an arrangement consisting of a rich skein of institutions that mediated between individual and the Faculty. They would cross over departmental boundaries but would not abolish them totally. They would be at different levels within the Faculty network - would be above or below departments. They would have different functional levels, teaching, research or administration, for example. They would be staffed by those appropriate for those particular roles. Without this, as we saw, voices would less easily be heard. But it would also have another effect. Since 'unification' would destroy all associations except central ones the individual would not have mediated relationships to the centre but only a direct individual one. This would foster distrust since faculty member would only relate to another member through the centre. There would be no horizontal relation. Though they would all be members of the Faculty, their duties would be realised, not in their interaction with their fellows but with what was allotted to them by the centre as their part of the collective endeavour (teaching hours and the like). And in that centre, as we saw, their voice would be difficult to hear. It would engender an intense individualism since working in common would be seen as not working in trust with others but as individual units of the plan. We would have a Soviet style system[187].

AUCHENSHUGGLE AND THE EU

What does the fable of Auchenshuggle tell us about EU governance? Firstly, that it should not be taken in by the 'monocular vision' that MacCormick (1993) criticises. We should not then see the solution to the constitutional architecture of the EU as a larger state - indeed it would be an ironic to see the solution to the depredations that the nation state caused in Europe as being a bigger one! But this is the result of the view that sees the solution to the problems of the 'democratic deficit' as merely a European Parliament[188] which would ultimately represent a European people. The European Stephen however, needs not only to be represented but to have a voice. The European Parliament is an important body and will have many functions in respect of control and as a particular forum for debate. We cannot however allow it to coalesce into a parliament of a state for that will have the effect of producing a homogeneous identity - something which will subsume the voices of differing individuals and groups. Not subsuming voices will be effected by the rich skein of cross cutting groups at different levels and functions which in their interaction enable individuals and groups to realise themselves while at the same time feeding into the general identity of the group. Thus, just as the Law School of Auchenshuggle would gain its identity in the mutual give and take between different individuals and differing groups of individuals organised as 'old' departmental units and groups which cut across these units (and this would enable both individuals and groups and the Law School to grow), so too the EU might been seen as a complex interaction of groups at differing levels, functionally and territorially - some cutting across old nation state boundaries and some not. So, this rich skein of cross cutting institutions means that people interact with each other through and in different groups in a series and family of connections which is in the end the general identity.

---

[187] Soviet power and Thatcherism have, ironically, some similarities. Following Fukayama (1996) we can say that the form of market organisation depends upon the institutions of sociability in a society. Capitalism, as we saw in chapter 6, depends paradoxically upon trust. The problem with the introduction of the market in the Soviet Union was that soviet power had more or less destroyed all middle institutions and thus institutions of sociability. The individual only had a direct relation with the state. All potential middle institutions were state sponsored. In situations like this the only way that large scale market organisation can exist is through state intervention. But with the destruction of the Soviet state that appears to have gone only to reappear again in the form of the old apparachiks and criminal elements - a truly fascist criminal state. Thatcherism itself, with its insistence on there being no community but only the individual, also destroyed middle institutions (though obviously not to the same extent and in the same way) and spread a culture of distrust and greed which reached its apogee in the heady days of the City where greed was good. A feature of the Thatcher system was a quangocracy staffed by conservative placemen which ensured that middle institutions were government run and not associations of sociability and mediation.

[188] See Weiler (1999) for a general discussion of this.

The point is not merely looking for representation or clarity. Rather it is to produce a form of governance that can bridge the gap between the local and the centre which in differing ways enables the individual's voice to be heard but without thereby destroying the group. Auchenshuggle and the EU then, show us how an order embodying the risks and articulations that I have set out in the book might look. Part of what I have been advocating has some affinities to what used to be called 'civil society'. But there is more. We can expand and better understand this vision by drawing briefly from theoretical strains to which it owes much, and has much in common with. I turn then briefly to examine three such theoretical strains; Catholic Social theory, deliberative democracy and associative democracy[189].

a) Catholic Social Theory

Firstly, we see here how market and welfare are connected (see chapters 5 and 6). We saw how and Joseph Weiler (1994) singles out three ideals with which the European project began. The second of these was prosperity. We saw how this was more than just material success. To be sure material success is important - the European project was a 'Common Market' which needed to rebuild after the destruction and poverty that the war left. But it also has other connotations; of dignity and worth; of autonomy and the ability to make one's own living; and with this the ability to make life easier for others; to bind ourselves to each other so that we can all become prosperous. Thus, as Weiler claims, though it contained the desire to rebuild economic strength necessary after the destruction of the War and in the shadow of the great competitive blocs of Communism and America, there were also strong elements of transnational economic solidarity contained therein. Again this is not surprising, since much of this resonates with the values of Christian Democracy.

Maurice Glasman (1996) details some of this, especially how it was developed by Bishop Wilhelm Emmanuel von Ketteler of Mainz. Glasman shows how von Ketteler developed a position which while it criticised the capitalist market was also against statist welfare solutions. The principle of subsidiarity meant that the excesses of the market could be alleviated by a plethora of intermediary organisations and diverting funds to them would be justified. A distinction was made between private property and capital. Private property was defended in that it enabled people to have spheres of autonomy. However, private property in the sense of capital, was held not to be an absolute right; rather one held in trust and subject to constraint so that it

[189] See Chaplin (1993); Cohen and Sabel (1998); Hirst (1994)

helped rather than prevented individual's self realisation and autonomy. For upholding private property in that latter sense, as Glasman points out, meant the loss of other rights such as those of subsistence. Insofar as the market prevented people from living autonomous lives it was just to intervene. This became the theme for the whole series of papal encyclicals from *Rerum Novarum* to *Laborem Exercens* in which Pope John Paul II writes

> 'Man is a person, that is to say a subjective being capable of acting in a planned and rational way, capable of deciding about himself and with a tendency to self realisation. As a person man is the subject of work......these acts serve to realise his humanity, to fulfil a calling to be a person that is his by reason of his very humanity.' (quoted by Glasman 1996: 39)[190]

Secondly, we must note that the key point of the organisation of social life is that people are not lost in it and in this subsidiarity plays an important role. Subsidiarity derives from the Latin *subsidium* which means help. In this context it means that humans are creatures that are social in the sense that they need help in order to be able to live and to realise their functions. The 'subsidiarity function' does not mean secondary but rather auxiliary (in the sense of helping). For Chaplin (1993), this is a highly 'personalist' vision with higher communities helping lower communities and people realising themselves in their communities. It embodies the Thomist/Aristotelian view of needing to live in community; of being designed for co-operative and social ends. The metaphysics of this is the idea of a series of hierarchically ordered communities each helping man's end. It is thus pluralist in that there are many different kinds of communities all of which are needed for people to fulfil themselves. The state has a duty to offer lesser communities such help as they need in order to perform their functions and it must always allow lesser communities to be themselves. The subsidiary function will relate to different levels of political authority (transnational and national competences etc.) and to other bodies. The principles of when to engage in subsidiarity, Chaplin argues, are vague but superior economic or administrative efficiency is not a necessary or sufficient criterion. What is important is that communities perform their proper moral ends and a higher level substitutes when the failure to do so has a public consequence. This articulation is always difficult.

The problem with this way of looking at it is that it can be too 'statist' a solution to specify the EU and help the European Stephen – it is, to some extent, still predicated on the state which encloses. For the implications of this are that communities are, as Chaplin says, 'hierarchically arranged'. Thus

---

[190] See also Morton (1998)

Calvez and Perrin (1961) see subsidiarity as having a 'one way function' - from the state down. But why, Chaplin asks, should we think that, though humans functions in a diverse set of communities, these are in a hierarchy? Chaplin argues that this need not be the case and we can see it as a two way process with communities being able to aid each other (each have a 'proper' function and a subsidiary function). But this, he says, does not solve the problem for the state. The state appears to be the final context since we cannot specify the ends of the state without reference to what the state can do for other communities whereas, with other communities, one can.

A Protestant version, Chaplin shows, may help though[191]. Sphere sovereignty is a Dutch Calvinist doctrine. God creates people to live within a variety of different communities and the state is supposed to look after them and never subsume them. Within each sphere there was a distinct sovereignty and absolute sovereignty belonged only to God - the whole of society was a complex interlocking mechanism. The state is one sphere among many. Within each of the different social spheres, it has no authority; in these spheres other authorities rule which derive their power not from the State but from God. The state can only recognise or acknowledge the authority in those spheres. Dooyerweerd also posits the horizontal co-ordination of communities. Subsidiarity is also two-way in respect of the state. Other communities can aid the state to produce good citizens - its unique subsidiary function is that it aids other communities in a uniquely public and legal way (that is its character). For Dooweryeerd this is the harmonious co-ordination of the spheres. Subsidiarity is the way by which we negotiate the articulation between spheres. What is important about it is that it can be seen as both something that can be enforced by the European Court and as something that is not justiciable, but as something that is political and functional. It is in that uneasy articulation between the interests of the particular actors and European Law and not into a collapse into one or the other that decisions should be taken.

b) Associative Democracy

Catholic social theory, as I have expounded it above, has affinities with notions of 'associative democracy' as propounded by Paul Hirst (1994). For him socialism, as practised in the centralised form of the planned economy is an instance of the imperative form of organisation, where there is a top down organisational structure. This has collapsed - co-ordination did not work and the range of services given was not acceptable. However the market model, or what he calls regulation through contract, cannot work without some welfare

[191] see Dooyewerd (1986)

provisions - people expect welfare and you cannot get away without it. Corporatist alternatives in terms of bargaining by employer and worker interests at all levels are difficult because these interests are no longer homogenous - the form of the bargaining does not take notice of local associations and often cuts across groups and interests. The point of associationist democracy is 'to promote governance through democratically legitimated voluntary associations'. This aims at reducing what Hirst thinks of as the greatest democratic deficit - we have organisations running our lives without consent and corporate control is without representation. What is important is not to have a clear public/private divide and the voluntary institutions of civil society - that way of looking at civil society does not work. We need to see them not merely as working between state and society but as in essence crossing the private/public divide. Hirst claims that liberal democracy will not be able to cope with these problems for three reasons. Firstly it concentrates on representative democracy and that is dead for it is no longer a mode of constraint or a mode of co-ordination, but rather a mode of legitimation. Secondly, it is closely tied to the idea of the nation State and that is becoming less and less important. Finally, representative democracy is in some way unable to cope with the idea of democracy. It concentrates on the Rule of Law above everything else and in that sense excludes the voice of the individual, as we have seen. What associationalism will do, says Hirst, is to extend liberalism - it will neither supplant a market based economy nor reduce the level of collective welfare.

> 'Associative economic governance is conceived as extending those forms of social embeddedness of markets that enable market economies to work better, and associative welfare is designed to extend individual choice, which collectivist systems fail to do, whilst offering extensive and primarily publicly - funded services.' (1994: 19)

Democracy should be seen as to do with communication and not necessarily with representation - all representative democracies construct, in some way, 'the represented'. Thus for Hirst the answer is a system of communicating networks, split across the public/private divide, interacting with each other and it is this which will be the foundation of co-ordination. It will enable society to be organised and goods to be delivered by voluntary associations which would be democratic and self-governing. This would be the primary mode of organisation. It would deal with the point that people need others to realise themselves but it would encourage voice since entry and exit would be relatively easy. It would cope with the fact of the decentralisation of political authority and the rejection of the sovereign state. It would mean more mutualism. This model, says Chaplin, is a shift in governance to change its form. The state instead of being the primary provider becomes the guarantor of services. An associational democracy therefore would be a complex network of different groups - the institutions of the state would be 'pluralised and federalised'. We do not however have to see this as a 'state' in the traditional sense but rather as a public power that would set standards. This would involve standards in manufacture to standards in liberties and agencies to policy them. These will be part of the polity in that they themselves will be subject to the cross cutting and interaction - they would not in that sense stand outside the polity itself but be part of that polity's journey. This calls to mind the ongoing process of constitutionalization of the EU. Weiler (1991) details this process and looks at the complex interaction between various bodies that got the thing started. Though this was, in the first instance done with relatively elite groups, there is no reason to think that this 'constitutional conversation' cannot take in more groups and be part of the ordering, definition and normal working of a polity [192] - the system in crisis made normal.

c) Deliberative Democracy

This 'network of cross-cutting agencies' is further specified in the work of Joshua Cohen and Charles Sabel (1998). The point of what they call directly-deliberative democracy is that collective decisions are taken in arenas where local people take part but in so doing must take into account other people in similar situations. This implies both a centralising and local force. For them the conventional interpretations of institutional failure in modern times do not get at the problem. Thus one view is to see, in the Hayekian mode, the problem as a failure to see the limits of regulation and the unconstrained power that rises therefrom. The solution, in that view, is marketisation and a restraint of that power through a rigid Rule of Law (legalism). The other view sees that as precisely the problem and that we need countervailing power to protect us from the vagaries of the market (the collectivist, planned economies of 'socialism')[193].

---

[192] See Weiler (1999)

[193] Cohen and Sabel also reject the view that denies the dichotomy of market and state and sees them both as interlocked together and mutually reinforcing. The preconditions of both, they say, are bonds of trust which can be undermined but not created by incorrect use of state or market. Since these are anterior to the market and the state, it is not clear what policy prescription one can give for creating them. This view makes a distinction between two ontological levels. Their point, more concretely, is that a constitution, for example, will allow many forms of interlocked social arrangements where market and state are mutually intertwined. But the dichotomy will exist, say Cohen and Sabel, between these interlocked arrangements and the constitution which will be anterior and untouchable from within these social arrangements - they are based upon some non-negotiable power, (knowledge, trust etc.). This is Postema's problem in chapter 2. But the whole point of the 'constitutional conversations' of Weiler, and the arguments above, was to show how the outside, in the form of universal standards, can come inside and yet not lose its universality.

Their argument is that the present institutional arrangements do not give us an adequate decision-making procedure for making solutions. Constitutional democracy and the ideal of the equality of the person seems to demand equality in solutions over localities - so constraining the institutions. This sets up the apparatus of the Rule of Law and the separation of powers. But the provision of services and the regulation that go with this need to be tailored to specific particular problems and local conditions. This generates 'ruleless' agencies and pressure grows to constrain their lawlessness. This engenders general rules which generates pressure to abolish in a cyclic movement. We cannot do away with constitutional constraint and merely have democratic control. For then you get what they call a 'pure bargaining democracy' which has no heed for coherence and fairness or even efficiency. For them a form of federalism would not solve the problem since that merely devolves down power to various centres. In this scheme local solutions remain local and are not necessarily shared by other institutions at the same level - the centre merely registers their decisions. There are only vertical connections and no horizontal ones. The lower levels act in isolation from each other.

What is needed, they argue, is a network of institutions so that local solutions can, where appropriate, help other local centres. Cohen and Sabel see deliberative democracy working in units where decisions are taken in a direct deliberative way. This implies reasoning to solutions through what they call policy reasons and constitutional reasons. The job of a court would be to make sure that decisions are made in this way and that constitutional reasons are not neglected. It would not second guess the decision but would send it back if constitutional reasons were not followed. The point of the legislature would be to empower and facilitate problem-solving in arenas close to the problem.

Thus we would have a network of territorial and functional organisations, the members being those concerned and with an interest in the organisation. There might be more agreement on interests than we think and this would show up in direct deliberation. Thus Stephen might not be such a lone voice as he appeared to be. But also, and more importantly, Stephen might be able to act against his interests. This would come about not because he sees himself as having made the decision but because the cross-cutting and deliberative nature of his society might make him more willing to allow other interests and decisions to prevail over his own wishes - he might still see them as not his but the institutional arrangements would make a long term give and take more feasible and plausible for him. As we saw in the nationality example above, you might be excluded today but included tomorrow and this means you are not really excluded because your universe contains both the inclusions and the exclusions. Here then we have an institutional explanation of 'lawfulness', the social arrangements for 'living lawfully'.

We now turn more explicitly to the EU. Oliver Gestenberg (1998) tries to apply Cohen and Sabel to the Union. For Gestenberg, there appears to be a false dichotomy in the legitimation of EC law. One the one hand, we think of its legitimation as being the market with political liberties being kept at the nation state level. This would involve seeing the constitution of the EU as an economic one, since the market is its own justification. Gestenberg goes on to claim that opponents of this view want to see EC law as being legitimated by democratic politics. But they are pessimistic. For, they ask, how could you have that at the EU level? There is no European state within which such politics need to be contained and nor is there likely to be; it would be too large for the types of solidarities needed; it would not be able to have the cultural homogeneity that would be necessary to keep democratic politics and commitment. So, they argue, the inevitable result would be the success of the market and market legitimation. This view then sees the only hope of non-market legitimation in the vision of an (impossible) European super-state. The other view sees the local state as important - the answer being some sort of accommodation between European economic law and the nation state which will be the repository of democratic politics. And these states will not open out in a European identity for that would destroy the homogeneity, which is necessary for democratic politics.

But we need not necessarily think, says Gestenberg, of democratic politics as having to be homogeneous (the outcome of Wolff's argument), nor as aggregative (the mere counting of voices). Drawing on Cohen and Sabel, he thinks of politics (people taking part) as deliberative - a mixture of substantive (policy) and constitutional reasons. To make binding decisions then, one has to appeal to reasons and ways of making them that can appear to be relevant and acceptable to all citizens. This way of making them will not only be instrumental but will have an intrinsic value - a way of exercising one's autonomy in conjunction and with the help of one's fellows. This is ideally suited, says Gestenberg, to a multi-cultural unity such as the EU. It will not be premised upon the state. The decision-making units, being functionally as well as territorially based, will cut across state boundaries and the public/private divide. Part of the function of something like the European Court of Justice will be to facilitate units of transnational problem solving. In this sense it will be something that tries to ensure that at all levels deliberation takes place and that 'constitutional' reasons are adhered to. But it will not necessarily, as we saw, second guess these decisions. Units, including states, will have deliberatively to justify their internal regimes as against others units' regimes - the point will be to facilitate the deliberative comparison of solutions across different local centres. We might see this as another version of the sovereign state and that Weiler (1991) was correct when he saw the court as the central driving figure in this form of the constitutionalization of Europe. But one does not have to see it this way for sovereignty is dispersed. It is the interactions of all the units with each other that produces the whole system which thereby is not a monolithic state one.

CONCLUSION

Looking at the above theoretical strains helps us to appreciate the architecture of 'living lawfully'. Firstly our 'Stephen problem', that of voice is dealt with by distributing the range and possible outlets of voice. Thus, as we saw in looking at Hirst, and Cohen and Sabel, the key was different functional and territorial groups that cut across each other. So part of the way of solving the problem is to make sure there are many and varied opportunities for voice and that there are mechanisms which ensure that each of these can learn, one from the other. Though this implies higher level structures it does not necessarily mean that these would be control the lower ones – rather they would be means by which geographically dispersed units at the low levels could learn from each other.

However, this does not address an important part of the problem, that of the rational legal control that we saw was necessary to legality. How can you get decision making that is both constrained by the rules and can move away from them? I looked at this in chapter 9 and part of the answer to it was the idea of 'paying attention'. This involves, in paying attention to the narrative of the case, knowing when to apply closure with the rule and when to let the story go on and throw him or her out beyond the rule so as to recreate the law anew. This is an important truth about what it is to adjudicate and the experience and personal qualities necessary for that. We saw how much of this stemmed from 'learning virtue', the practice of being steeped in the law and seeing its point.

However, though important, one cannot rely on the skill and attitude of the judges alone. How can one operationalise this within a legal order? We saw, when looking at Cohen and Sabel, that 'constitutional reasons' were one of the criteria for taking deliberatively democratic decisions and that courts would enforce this, not necessarily by second guessing the lower decision but by remitting it back. Here we might say that the court is initiating a dialogue and the decision- making is, in some ways, shared. For the other agency has to re-think that decision under the constrain of 'constitutional reasons, which might be procedural or human rights based. However, if there are still problems then that other court must start thinking its universalism through and engage in what Weiler has termed constitutional conversations. This could spread to include many actors[194]. What is important here is that Postema's paradox is tackled thereby. For we have the universalism of the law reaffirmed but with the potential always to engage in this dialogue (the constitutional conversation) and question itself. So the universalism of the court both constrains and is itself reflexive.

We can develop this idea further along the lines adumbrated in chapter 9. What is necessary is to develop markers by which adjudication can see that it must step outside its system confines. The idea of 'parabolic reasoning' contains some of that but we can specify in the following manner. We can think of the law in its universalism as by and large playing the machine game - it turns over its cycles until something makes it stop the remorseless playing out of its operations[195]. One can think of it as someone putting a spoke in the wheel of the law – it stops turning and we have to find out why. Institutions of lay justice and the jury system might be seen in this way (see chapter 9). The point of these institutions is not necessarily to make a substantive decision about the law but to force the legal system in general to recalculate. Stopping the law's logic is in this sense arbitrary for it will be at random and not necessarily predictable by the system. Judges might become a bit like spokes by the attitude of 'paying attention' but it is also necessary to design systems to achieve this. Part of the way forward would be in juries and lay justice, institutions which can be seen as 'bridging institutions' – they are part of the legal system but also as being the conduit to the outside make the outside part of the system. Also important would be the way discussed by Collins (see chapter 9) where he looks at the way legal reasoning should leave itself open to interested groups and institutions which through this opening become part of the system injecting particularity into it[196]. It is in all of this that we might see a system of 'living lawfully'.

CODA: THE FEAR OF HOPE

A final question remains. Why go beyond? Why not opt for the security of our comfortable world? When we looked at legal reasoning we saw that we can be open if we 'pay attention' to the outside. Why do that? We need ideals and vision, and we need hope. Ideals and vision are closely related. We saw

---

[194] See Weiler (1999) where he has brilliantly showed how this happens in Europe.

[195] This can be the nuanced deductivism of a system of legal reasoning such as MacCormick's.

[196] One way forward here might be an expansion of the *locus standi* rules.

how the vision (the north) inspires the journey and can thus be seen as outside. But is also inside for it transforms the nature of that journey making it a northward one. In the context of Europe we might think of Weiler's founding ideals as both being in the future (something that guides Europe) and in the present, suffusing our idea of Europe now - bringing, as we saw, the future into the present. Vision and hope also go together for the power of the vision gives us the hope to go forward and be open to the outside. What enables this is the openness of a transformative vision. For that gives us the hope to go beyond even if we are frightened of making a mistake. It gives us hope to learn from the mistakes; to accept that it is impossible to live or make a world without them. To go wrong does not mean we are forever condemned - we can go forward.

The loss of hope is not just the hopelessness of despair when there appears nothing that one can do. It is more insidious than that. John Kenneth Galbraith (1992) makes this point. He posits a large group of people in western societies who stay away from the political process because they see there is no point to it. It gives them nothing and they do not see anyway in which they can make a difference to the process. For these there is no hope left. But there is another set, who take part in the process because for them it has, or appears to, deliver. Politics does not change much for it only depends upon marginal changes in that latter group. Why? Because those in that group basically agree and are content with what they have - they have no transformative vision.

How does Galbraith characterise those in this 'culture of contentment'? Firstly, they think that they have their just deserts. What they want and have is achieved by their worth. They are enamoured of 'short termism', they will always prefer short term solutions to long run ones because the future might not arrive and thus they would have lost out to it. Thirdly, they want to keep the state 'off people's backs' especially if this means paying higher taxes. Finally there is the toleration of great disparities in income. In short they are happy in the position that they are in and all their work goes to preserve it. Against this, Galbraith posits the 'underclass' which has always been found necessary in capitalist societies to do the work that the fortunate found disagreeable but was necessary to keep them in affluence. In the past transition (and the possibility of transition) from that class to the favoured prevented eruptions of discontent on a large scale. The class was fluid and always needed to be replenished with new members. But now, he says, things have changed and transition becomes more difficult. The group becomes structurally fixed, structural unemployment comes in. This makes the possibility of containment harder and harder and explosions more likely.

In the culture of contentment 'hope has become redundant', in Duncan Forrester's (1997: 252) telling phrase, and any kind of utopianism is dismissed out of hand. They are happy to believe that this is the best of all possible worlds because for them it is. This is, as Forrester says, 'a comforting notion for the rich and strong'. They have arrived where they were wanting to go, the 'End of History has come'[197] and the 'New World has arrived' and so there is no need for hope and vision.

But there is another way of looking at this as well. It is not that there is no need for hope, rather what we have is a state of hopelessness. For they are not so much contented with what they have as frightened of losing it. Their policies, as shown by Galbraith, are motivated by the fear of loss. They have what they want and want nothing new but perhaps more of the same. They have no transformative vision, their only vision, and their only hope, is of a world that might be like the present one, but bigger. They are like the servant who, in the parable, buried his talent in the earth. That parable should not be seen as a Thatcherite parable but rather one about hope and vision, and fear. The way to lose your life is to protect it and defend it and do nothing more. If you have no hope and no vision then you will act as the servant who, full of fear of the master, buried the talent entrusted to him in the ground so as to protect it. In trying to defend what you have, you will, as did the servant, lose even that. The point is that you need hope and vision in order to be able to see and risk the possibilities in your life. What the parable is saying is that to be content in the way Galbraith has been describing is to be in a kind of fear; to be truly hopeless because you can see no possibility beyond that which you have. And in fact that becomes all you want, the possibility of transformation becomes dangerous and threatening. And one can see this the more as the world becomes increasingly unstable and that instability threatens them. This form of contentment closes the individual off both from themselves and from the world - they do not want the world to be anything other than it is ; they want it to be flat and hopeless . In this sort of world change, and the vision and hope that inspire it, are dangerous - better the devil [sic] that you know.

Thus the vision is transformed insidiously. This brings us back to Millbank's point about exchange (chapter 10). In our urge to control the exchange for the exact and equal opposite of market relations, we do not see beyond our system. We transform everything into something like ourselves and we see the future and its transformation as like the present but bigger and more of it. We close down the possibilities of transformation because we see no difference that could change and transform our journey. Any difference

[197] See Fukayama (1992)

that there is we make into something like ourselves. This cannot produce vision or transformation. And we saw some of this argument when we looked at Europe. What we have is something akin to a culture of contentment in that we do not want to move beyond what we already have, thinking that we have arrived at our destination. In being worried about the transformative possibilities we go back and retreat into our enclaves, the nation states, or we think that transformation will be some more of the same only bigger - the super European State .

This blocks off the contingent opening to the 'beyond' and ensures that, as we saw, the world is flattened and, in the relentless following of its operations reproduces itself in its own image. But this heteronomy of system can also transform what appears to be autonomous and contingent action[198]. Thus Hamish X[199], the charitable bank-teller, could also be someone acting not autonomously, out of love or charity, but heteronomously, in thrall to a particular idea of himself and his clients. So sometimes when we think that we are acting from love or welfare we are only reproducing our image of ourselves. We look to reach outside but all we see is an image which reflects ourselves – 'Mirror mirror on the wall – who is the fairest of them all'[200]. We have become trapped in our discourses. Worse we like it. We do not see anything beyond and we don't care.

This failure to move beyond is to do with the fear of failure and fear of losing what we have. We become so concerned with keeping what we have and lose the hope to move forward. But it is important to note, as I have stressed throughout the book, that we should not think of this as meaning that we must discard certainty and the heteronomy of the universalism of rules - to be in the constant flux of leaping into the unknown. The 'culture of contentment', as described by Galbraith, clearly has negative effects. But the fear of losing what you have is not totally unreasonable, what you have might

---

[198] We can see this in a particular image of autopoiesis - the image of its incommensurable cycles can also be one for the impossibility of looking outside. For in the attempt to do so all that is seen is a reflection of oneself. As Roger Cotterrell (1993: 68) puts it:

'In its efforts to take discourse or abstract communication systems seriously, a sociological perspective should avoid the temptation to reify them. Even autopoietic metaphors may be dangerous to the extent that they portray a world over which individuals have not only lost control but in relation to which they might absolve themselves of responsibility, so it seems, for autonomous action. It is important to recognise the full extent to which, in modern conditions, subject centred reason has been confined, repressed, trivialised and debased in innumerable ways; but it may be possible to do this without actually reducing the sociological status of the individual theoretically to that of a construct or carrier of various social systems, whose human autonomy is retained only as a 'psychic system'.

[199] See chapter 6

[200] The Wicked Queen in *Snow White and the Seven Dwarves*

be good not only for you but for others - what is unreasonable is if the fear of loss prevents one from being responsive.

There are times when the appropriate thing to do will be to stay within an heteronomous system and we must be able to risk that also. Much of the reason for law and legal institutions, for the clarity, predicability that I have talked about comes from the desire to protect ourselves against unrestrained power and the dangers that stem from that. We need this because we are rightly afraid of the destructive force of what can be unleashed without this. This is as, Judith Shklar (1984) puts it, part of the 'liberalism of fear' - and we need it. But as she and Martin Krygier (1999)[201] point out, this is not enough. We also need hope to be able to be responsive, to serve substantive justice to transform our world, to make our institutions and our lives whole. But, Krygier says, to secure these aims does not mean that we must throw away the aims put in place by the 'liberalism of fear'. We must accept that in organising our personal and institutional lives we will live, as he says, between fear and hope, knowing that hard choices will have to be made and that we can never guarantee a solution.

And it is with this inevitable tension that I finish. The way to transform and be open to the other is to pay attention. We learn to do this through vision and hope and one of the ways that this comes about is, as we saw in chapter 7, through the machine-like actions of the system world. There we learn what is the same and thereby know what is different. But doing this has the potential of closing off the outside for us for we can all too easily sink into the black hole of the system and stay comfortably within it. That is a tension that we cannot escape and is the condition of our existence. To move out we have to see the danger of staying in our system world. Rather than hell being other people, we have to see that it is being locked forever into ourselves or other exactly like ourselves. Ironically, we can see this, and be moved by the 'other' who is outside, by the act of creative imagination that sees that we are alike and are one. We are alike in that we are also in need of justice and love; we also need to receive as well as give. Only then will we have the madness, Simone Weil's Divine folly, to hunger and thirst for justice, to create a lawful world.

---

[201] See also Krygier (1997)

BIBLIOGRAPHY

Acton H B (1971): *The Morals of Markets.* London : Longman

Alexy R (1989): *A Theory of Legal Argumentation.* Translated by D N MacCormick, and R Adler. Oxford : Clarendon Press

and Peczenik A (1990): "The Concept of Coherence and its Significance for Discursive Rationality", in 3 *Ratio Juris,* 130-147

Alison J (1996): *Living in the End Times.* (1996 S.P.C.K)

Anscombe G E M (1958): "A Modern Moral Philosophy", in 33 *Philosophy,* 1

Arendt H (1994): *Eichmann in Jerusalem : a report on the banality of evil.* Harmondsworth : Penguin

Atiyah P S (1986): "Form and Substance in Legal Reasoning", in D N MacCormick and P Birks (eds.) *The Legal Mind.* Oxford : Oxford University Press

and Summers R B (1987): *Form and Substance in Anglo-American Law.* Oxford : Clarendon Press

Atria F (1999): *The Powers of Application.* Ph.D. Thesis, University of Edinburgh

Avineri S and De Shalit A, eds. (1992): *Communitarianism and Individualism.* Oxford : Oxford University Press

Austin J (1954): *The Province of Jurisprudence Determined.* London : Weidenfeld and Nicolson

Bańkowski Z and Mungham G (1976): *Images of Law.* London : Routledge and Kegan Paul

Bańkowski Z (1977a): "Anarchy Rule O.K?", in *Archiv für Rechts und Sozialphilosophie.* Bd.4 LXIII/3, 327-337

(1977b): "Subsidiarity, Sovereignty and Self", in K Norr and T Oppermann (eds.) *Subsidaritat: Idee und Wirklichkeit. Zur Reichweite eines Prinzips in Deutschland und Europa.* Tuebingen : J C B Mohr, 1977

and Mungham G (1978): "Law and Lay Participation", in *European Yearbook for Sociology of Law,* 17-31

and MacManus J and Hutton N (1987): *Lay Justice.* Edinburgh : T&T Clark

(1989) "The Rule of Law and Participatory Models of the Legal Process" in H Jung (Hrsg.) Alternativen zur Strafjustiz und die Garantie individueller Rechte der Betroffenen Bonn : Forum Verlag Godesberg

(1994) "How Does it Feel to be on Your Own? : The Person in the Sight of Autopoiesis", in 7 Ratio Juris, 254-266

and White I and Hahn U, eds. (1995): *Informatics and the Foundations of Legal Reasoning.* Dordrecht : Kluwer

and Scott A (1996): "The European Union?", in R Bellamy (ed.) *Constitutionalism, Democracy and Sovereignty.* Avebury Press: Aldershot

and Christodoulidis E (1998): "The European Union as an Essentially Contested Concept", 4 *European Law Journal,* 341-354

(1998): "Parable and Analogy: The Universal and Particular in Common Law", in *Acta Juridica,* 138-163

and Christodoulidis E (1999): "Citizenship Bound and Citizenship Unbound", in K Hutchings and R Dannreuther (eds.) *Cosmopolitan Citizenship.* Basingstoke : MacMillan

and Davis C (2000): "Living In and Out of the Law", in P Oliver; S Douglas-Scott, and V Tadros (eds.) *Faith in Law*. Oxford : Hart Publishing

Beck U (1992): *Risk Society: towards a new modernity*. Translated by M Ritter. London : Sage

Bell J (1986): "The Acceptability of Legal Arguments", in D N MacCormick, and P Birks (eds.) *The Legal Mind*. Oxford : Oxford University Press

Bentham J (1823): *An Introduction to the Principles of Morals and Legislation*. Oxford : Oxford University Press

Biggs H, ed. (2000): "Gendered Readings of Obligations", in 8 (Special Issue) *Feminist Legal Studies*

Boff L (1986): *Church, Charism and Power*. New York: Crossroad)

Bradley A W and Ewing K D (1997): *Constitutional and Administrative Law*. 12th ed. London : Longman

Butler B (1950): *Five Sermons*. Indianapolis : Bobbs-Merrill

Butler J (1996): "Universality in Culture" in M Nussbaum *For Love of Country*. Edited by J Cohen. Boston : Beacon Press, *45-52*

Calvez J Y and Perrin J (1961): *Church and social justice : the social teaching of the Popes from Leo XIII to Pius XII, 1878-1958*. London : Burns & Oates

Campbell T (1983): *The left and Rights*. London : Routledge and Kegan Paul

Campbell T (1996): *The legal theory of ethical positivism*. Aldershot, Hants; Brookfield, Vt : Dartmouth

(2000): "Ethical Positivism and the Liberalism of Fear", in T Campbell and J Goldsworthy (eds.) *Judicial Power, Democracy and Legal Positivism*. Aldershot : Ashgate

Carlyle T (1952): *Past and Present: a journal of scientific history*. Oxford : Oxford University Press.

Chaplin J (1993): "Subsidiarity and Sphere Sovereignty: Catholic and Reformed Conceptions of the Role of the State", in F McHugh and S M Natlale (eds.) *Unfinished Agenda: Catholic Social Teaching Revisited*. New York : Lanham

Chesterton G K (1960): *The Father Brown Stories*. London : Cassel

Christodoulidis E (1994): "The Suspect Intimacy between Law and Political Community", in 80 *Archiv fur Rechts-und Sozialphilosophie* 1-18

(1998a): *Law and reflexive Politics*. Dordrecht : Kluwer

(1998b): (ed.) *Communitarianism and Citizenship*. London: Ashgate

Clarke R, ed. (1992): *Situational Crime Prevention*. New York: Harrow and Heston

Cohen G A (1974): "Marx's Dialectic of Labour", in *Philosophy and Public Affairs*, 235-261.

Cohen J and Sabel C (1998): "Directly-Deliberative Polyarchy", in C Joerges and O Gestenberg (eds.) *Private Governance, Democratic Constitutionalism and Supranationalism*. EUR 18340 EN: Proceedings of COST A7 Seminar 1998, 1-30

Collins Hugh (1986): "Democracy and Adjudication", in D N MacCormick and P Birks (eds.) *The Legal Mind*., 67-82

Collins Harry (1990): *Artificial Experts*. Cambridge, Mass.; London : MIT Press

Cotterell R (1993): "Viewing Legal Discourses Sociologically", in G Skąpska (ed.) *Prawo w Zmieniającym Się Społeczeństwie*, 57-70. Kraków : Wydawnictwo Adam Marszałek.

Graig P and De Bùrca G (1998) *EU Law : Texts, Cases and Materials*. Oxford : Oxford University Press

Davies N (1981): *God's Playground: A History of Poland*. Oxford : Clarendon Press,

Davis C (1997) "Who is my Neighbour", in 48 *The Furrow*, 583.

Deschamps S and Bratingham P (1992): "The British Columbia Transit Fare Evasion Audit", in R Clarke (ed.) *Situational Crime Prevention*. New York: Harrow and Heston

Detmold,M (1984): *The Unity of Law and Morality*. London: Routledge and Kegan Paul

(1989): "Law as Practical Reason", in 48 *Cambridge Law Journal*, 436-471

Dewitz S (1995): "Using Information Technology as a Determiner of Legal Facts", in Z Bańkowski, I White and U Hahn (eds.) *Informatics and the Foundations of Legal Reasoning*. Dordrecht : Kluwer

Dooyewerd H (1986): *A Christian Theory of Social Institutions.* Translated by M Verbrugge, edited by J Witte. California; La Jolla,

Duxbury N (1995): *Patterns of American Jurisprudence.* Oxford: Clarendon Press

Dworkin R (1977): *Taking Rights Seriously.* London: Duckworth

(1985): *A Matter of Principle?.* Cambridge, Mass. : Harvard University Press

(1986): *Law's Empire.* London: Fontana

Eliot T S (1988): *Murder in the Cathedral.* Basingstoke: Macmillan Education

Etzioni A (1995): *The Spirit of Community.* London : Fontana Press

Fine R (1979): *Capitalism and the Rule of Law: from deviancy theory to Marxism.* London: Hutchinson

Fitzpatrick P (2001) *Modernism and the Grounds of Law.* Cambridge : Cambridge University Press

Finnis J (1982): *Natural Law and Natural Rights.* Oxford: Clarendon Press

Forrester D (1997): *Christian Justice and Public Policy.* Cambridge : Cambridge University Press

Frank J N (1942): *If men were Angels: Some Aspects of Government in a Democracy.* New York: Harper

(1973): *Courts on Trial* Princeton: Princeton University Press

Freeman M (1981): "The Jury on Trial" *Current Legal Problems* 34

Fukayama F (1992): *The End of History and the Last Man.* London : Hamish Hamilton

(1996): *Trust.* London : Penguin Books

Fuller L L (1969): *The Morality of Law.* Princeton : Yale University Press

(1978): "Forms and limits of Adjudication", in 92 *Harvard Law Review*, 353-409

Galbraith J K (1992): *The Culture of Contentment.* London : Sinclair-Stevenson

Garfinkel H (1955): "Conditions of Successful Degradation Ceremonies", 61 *American Journal of Sociology*, 420-4

Gestenberg O (1998): "Law's Polyarchy: A comment on Cohen and Sabel", in C Joerges and O Gestenberg (eds.) *Private Governance, democratic constitutionalism and supranationalism.* EUR 18340 EN: Proceedings of COST A7 Seminar 1998, 31-46

Girard R (1987): *Things hidden since the foundation of the world.* Translated by S Bann and M Metteer. London : Athlone

Glasman M (1996): *Unnecessary Suffering.* London : Verso

Golding, M (1984): *Legal Reasoning.* New York : Borzoi Books

Godwin W. (1976): *Enquiry Concerning Political Justice.* London : Penguin

Green L (1988): *The Authority of the State.* Oxford : Clarendon Press

Griffith J A G (1977): *The politics of the judiciary.* London : Fontana

Günther K (1993): *The Sense of Appropriateness: Application Discourses in Morality and Law.* Translated by J Farrell. Albany : State University of New York Press

Habermas J (1986): "Law as Medium and Law as Institution", in G Teubner (ed.) *Dilemmas of Law in the Welfare State.* Berlin, New York : De Gruyter

Hare R M (1961): *The Language of Morals.* Oxford : Clarendon Press

(1963): *Freedom and Reason.* Oxford : Clarendon Press

Harlow C and Rawlins R (1995): *Pressure through Law.* Oxford : Oxford University Press

Hart H L H (1961): *The Concept of Law.* Oxford : Clarendon Press

Hayek F A (1944): *The Road to Serfdom.* London : Routledge and Kegan Paul

(1973): *Rules and Order.* London : Routledge and Kegan Paul

(1976): *The Mirage of Social Justice.* London : Routledge and Kegan Paul

(1982): *Law, legislation and liberty: a new statement of the liberal principles of justice and political economy.* London : Routledge & Kegan Paul

Hegel G W F (1948): *Early Theological Writings.* Translated by T M Knox. Chicago, Ill.

Hillis Miller J (1990): "Parable and Performative in the Gospels and Modern Literature", in J Hillis Miller *Tropes, Parables and Performatives: Essays in Twentieth Century Literature.* Hemel Hempstead: Harvester Wheatsheaf, 1990

Himsworth C M G and Munro C R (1998): *Devolution and the Scotland bill.* Edinburgh : W. Green

Hindess B (1987): *Freedom, equality and the market : arguments on social policy.* London : Tavistock

Hirsch von A, Garland G and Wakefield A (2000): *Ethical and Social Perspectives in Situational Crime Prevention.* Oxford : Hart Publishing.

Hirsch von A (2000): "The Ethics of Public Television Surveillance" in Hirsch von A, Garland G and Wakefield A: *Ethical and Social Perspectives in Situational Crime Prevention.* Oxford : Hart Publishing.

Hirsch von A and Shearing C (2000): "Exclusion from Public Space" in Hirsch von A, Garland G and Wakefield A : *Ethical and Social Perspectives in Situational Crime Prevention.* Oxford : Hart Publishing.

Hirst P (1994): *Associative Democracy.* London : Polity Press

Hirvonen A (1997): "Antigone: The Love of the Goddess of Justice", in Z Bańkowski, K Tuori and J Uusitalo (eds.) *Law and Power: critical and socio-legal essays.* Liverpool : Deborah Charles, 235-258

Hohfeld W (1966) *Fundamental Legal Conceptions.* New Haven: Yale University Press

Honore (1986): "Real Laws" in D N MacCormick and P Birks (eds.) *The Legal Mind.* Oxford : Oxford University Press

Hume D (1962): *A treatise of human nature: being an attempt to introduce the experimental method of reasoning into moral subjects.* London : Fontana

Hunt A (1981): "The Politics of Law and Justice", in *Politics and Power* 4 London.: Routledge and Kegan Paul

Jabbari D (1992): "From Criticism to Construction in Modern Critical Legal Theory", in *Oxford journal of legal studies.* Vol. 12, No. 4, 507

Jackson B J (1988): *Law, Fact and Narrative Coherence.* Liverpool : Deborah Charles

Jackson B S (1991): "Semiotic Scepticism: A Response to Neil MacCormick", in IV *International Journal of Semiotics*, 181-202

Jones J and Sergot M (1992): "Deontic Logic in the Representation of Law: Towards a Methodology", in *Artificial Intelligence and Law* 1992 1:1, 45-64

Jülicher A (1899): *Die Gleichnissreden Jesu.* 2nd ed Freiburg: J C Mohr

Kafka F (1973): *In the penal settlement.* Translated by E Kaiser and E Wilkins. London : Secker&Warburg

Kamenka E and Tay A (1975): "Beyond Bourgeois individualism: the Contemporary Crisis in Law and Legal Ideology ", in *Feudalism, Capitalism and Beyond.* Canberra : ANU Press

Kant I (1979): *Lectures on Ethics.* Infield and MacMurray Methuen

Kelman M (1987): *A guide to critical legal studies.* Cambridge, Mass.; London : Harvard University Press

Koestler A (1976): *Darkness at Noon.* London: Hutchinson

Kinsey R (1979): "Depotism and the Rule of Law" in R Fine et al (eds.) *Capitalism and the Rule of Law.* London : Hutchinson

Krygier M (1997): *Beyond Fear and Hope.* ABC Books

(1999)): "Ethical Positivism and the Liberalism of Fear", in T Campbell and J Goldsworthy (eds.) *Judicial Power, Democracy and Legal Positivism.* Aldershot : Ashgate

Le Grand J and Estrin S (1989): *Market Socialism.* Oxford : Clarendon Press

Leith P (1986): "Fundamental Errors in Legal Logic Programming", in 29 *The Computer Journal*, 545-552

(1990): *Formalism in AI and Computer Science*. New York, London : Horwood

Luhmann N (1985): *A sociological theory of law*. Translated by E King and M Albrow; edited by M Albrow. London : Routledge & Kegan Paul

(1986): *Love as Passion*. Cambridge : Polity

Lyons C (1997): "A Voyage around Article 8: A Historical and Comparative evaluation of European Citizenship", in 1997 *Year book of European Law*

MacCormick D N (1978): *Legal Reasoning and Legal Theory*. Oxford : Oxford University Press

(1981): *Hart*. London : Edward Arnold

(1986) : "The Interest of the State and the Rule of Law", in P Wallington and R Merkin (eds.) *Essays in Memory of Professor F.H.Lawson*. London : Butterworths

and Weinberger O (1986): *An Institutional Theory of Law*. Dordrecht : Reidel

(1989a): "Spontaneous order and the Rule of Law: Some Problems", in 2 *Ration Juris*, 41-54

(1989b): "Legalism", in 2 *Ratio Juris*, 184-193

and Bańkowski Z (1991): "Statutory Interpretation in the U.K", in D N MacCormick and R S Summers (eds.) *Interpreting Statutes*. Aldershot : Dartmouth, 359-406

and Summers R S, eds. (1991): *Interpreting Statutes*. Aldershot : Dartmouth

(1991) "Notes on Narrativity and the Normative Syllogism" in 11 *International Journal for the Semiotics of Law*, 163-174

(1992): "Legal Deduction, Legal Predicates and Expert Systems", in 14 *International Journal for the Semiotics of Law*, 181-202

(1993) "Beyond the Sovereign State" in 56 *Modern Law Review* 1-18

(1994): *Legal Reasoning and Legal Theory*. 2nd ed. Oxford : Clarendon Press

(1994): "*The Concept of Law* and the Concept of Law", in *Oxford Journal of Legal Studies*, 1-23

(1995): "The *Maastricht-Urteil*: Sovereignty Now", in 1 *European Law Journal*, 259-266

(1996): "Defeasability in Law and Logic", in Z Bańkowski; I White and U Hahn (eds.) *Informatics and the Foundations of Legal Reasoning* Dordrecht: Kluwer

(1998): "Norms, Institutions, and Institutional Facts", in 17 *Law and Philosophy*, 301-345

Macintyre A (1990): *Three rival versions of moral enquiry: encyclopaedia, genealogy, and tradition*. London : Duckworth

MacKinnon D (1974): *The Problem of Metaphysics*. Cambridge: Cambridge University Press

Maher I (1998): "Community law in the National legal Order: A Systems Analysis", in 36 *Journal of Common market Studies*, 237-254

Marx K (1970) : *Capital*. London : Lawrence and Wishart

(1974): *Economic and philosophic manuscripts of 1844*. Translated by M. Milligan. Moscow : Progress Publishers

McBarnett D (1981): *Conviction*.. London : MacMillan

Mendus S (1989): "To Have and to Hold: Liberalism and the Marriage Contract", in *Archiv fur Rechts-und Sozialphilosophie*, Beiheft 189, pp 70-79

Menlowe M A and McCall Smith A, eds. (1993): *The duty to rescue: the jurisprudence of aid*. Aldershot : Dartmouth

Millbank J (1996): "Socialism by Gift and Socialism by Grace", in 77 *New Blackfriars*, 632-648

Miller D (1999): "Bounded Citizenship", in K Hutchings and R Dannreuther (eds.) *Cosmopolitan Citizenship*. Basingstoke : MacMillan

Mitchell J and Leicester G (1999): *Scotland, Britain and Europe: diplomacy and devolution*. Edinburgh : Scottish Council Foundation

Moles R and Dayal S (1992): "There is more to life than logic", in 3 *Journal of Law and Information Science*, 182-218

Moral L, MacCormick D N and Bengoextea J (2000). "Interpretation, Integrity and Integration at the European Court of Justice" in J Weiler (ed.) *Collected Courses of the Academy of European Law 1999*. Oxford : Oxford University Press

Morton A, ed. (1998): *Beyond Fear*. Edinburgh : St. Andrew Press

Murphy J (1970): *Kant: The Philosophy of Right*. London : Macmillan

Nicholls D (1995): *God and Government in an 'Age of Reason'*. London : Routledge

Nonet P and Selznick P (1978): *Law and Society in Transition: Towards Responsive Law*. New York : Harper and Row

Nozick R (1975): *Anarchy, state and utopia*. Oxford : Blackwell

Nussbaum M (1986): *The Fragility of Goodness*. Cambridge : Cambridge University Press

(1996): *For Love of Country*. Edited by J Cohen. Boston : Beacon Press

O'Hagan T (1984): *The End of Law?*. Oxford : Basil Blackwell

Orwell G (1997): *Keep the Aspidistra Flying*. London : Secker & Warburg

Pashukanis E.B (1951): "The General Theory of Law and Marxism", in H Babb and J N Hazard (eds.) Soviet Legal Philosophy. Cambridge, Mass.

(1980): *Selected Writings in Law and Marxism*. P Beirne and R Sharlet (eds.) London: Academic Press

Pateman C (1984): "The Shame of the Marriage Contract", in J Stiehm (ed.) *Women's View of the Political World of Men*. Dobbs Ferry, N.Y. : Transnational Publishers

Pease K (1997): "Crime Prevention", in M Maguire, R Morgan and R Reiner (eds.) *Oxford Handbook of Criminology*. Oxford : Clarendon Press, Ch. 14

Perrin C (1996): *Breath from Nowhere: Justice and Community in the Event of Human Rights*. (University of Kent Ph.D. Thesis 82)

Petrazycki L (1955): *Law and Morality*. Translated by H Babb. Cambridge, Mass.

Pierrepoint A (1997): *Executioner* London : Coronet

Plato (1973): *The Phaedrus*. Translated by W Hamilton. Harmondsworth : Penguin

Postema G (1989): "In Defence of French Nonsense", in Z Bańkowski and D N MacCormick (eds.) *Enlightenment Rights and Revolutions*. Aberdeen : Aberdeen University Press

Raban J (1989): *God, man & Mrs Thatcher*. London : Chatto & Windus

Rand A (1966): *Capitalism: The Unknown Ideal*. New York : New American Library

Raz J (1975): *Practical Reason and Norms*. London : Hutchinson University Library

(1986): *The Morality of Freedom*. Oxford : Clarendon Press

Rothbard N (1982): *The Ethics of Liberty*. Atlantic Highlands, N.J. : Humanities Press

Roermund B C van (1996): "The Concept of Representation in Parliamentary Democracy", in *Current Legal Theory*, 31-52

Rose G (1993): *Judaism and Modernity*. Oxford : Blackwell

(1992): *The Broken Middle*. London: Blackwell

(1995): *Love's Work*. London : Chatto & Windus

Rottleutner H (1989b): "The Limits of Law - The Myth of a Regulatory Crisis", in 17 *International Journal of the Sociology of Law*, 273-286

Sanders E P (1991): *Paul* Oxford : Oxford University Press

Sousa Santos B de (1987): "Law: a map of misreading", in 14 *Journal of Law and Society*, 279-299

Schauer R (1991): *Playing by the Rules?*. Oxford : Clarendon Press

Scherdin M (1992): "The Hallo Effect. Psychological Deterrence of Electronic Security Systems", in R Clarke (ed.) *Situational Crime Prevention*. New York: Harrow and Heston

Searle J (1969): *Speech Acts*. Cambridge : Cambridge University Press

Selznick P (1966): "Sociology and Natural Law", in J Cogley *Natural Law and Modern Society*. New York: World Publishing

(1992): *The Moral Commonwealth*. Berkeley and Los Angeles : University of California Press

Sergot M; Sadri F; Kowalski R A; Kriwaczek F; Hammond P and Cory H T (1986): The British Nationality Act as Logic Program", in *Communications of the ACM* 29,5 : 370-386

Shearing C and Stenning P (1992): "From the Panoptican to Disney World: The Development of Discipline", in R Clarke (ed.) *Situational Crime Prevention*. New York: Harrow and Heston

Shklar J (1984): "The liberalism of Fear", in N Rosenblum (ed.) *Liberalism and the Moral Life*. Cambridge, Mass. : Harvard University Press

(1986): *Legalism*. Cambridge, Mass.; London : Harvard University Press

Simmonds N (1993): "Judgement and Mercy", in *Oxford Journal of Legal Studies*, 52-68

Smith S C (1994): "How Law hides Risk" in Teubner, G, Farmer, L and Murphy, T (eds) *Environmental Law and Ecological Responsibility*, 117-144

Strawson P F (1950): "On Referring", in *Mind*, 320-344

Sunstein C R (1996): *Legal Reasoning and Political Conflict*. New York, Oxford : Oxford University Press

Susskind R (1987): *Expert Systems in Law*. Oxford : Clarendon Press

Sypnowich C (1990): *The Concept of Socialist Law*. Oxford : Clarendon Press

Teubner G (1983): "Substantive and Reflexive Elements in Modern law", in *Law and Society*, 239-85

(1986): *Dilemmas of Law in the Welfare State*. Berlin, New York : De Gruyter

(1987): "Juridification: Concepts, Aspects. Limits, Solutions", in G Teubner (ed.) *Juridification of Social Spheres*. Berlin : De Gruyter

Thomas P and Mungham G (1979): "Advocacy and the solicitor-advocate in magistrates courts in England and Wales", in 7 *International Journal of Law and Society*, 164-195

Titmuss R (1980): *The Gift Relation*. London : Allen Unwin

Tönnies F (1955): *Community and Association*. London : RKP

Tolstoy L (1972): The Slavery of Our Times. Translated by A. Maude. London : John Lawrence [see p. 6]

Tolstoy L (1978): War and Peace. Translated by R Edmonds. Harmondsworth : Penguin

Twining W (1984): "Some Scepticism about Some Scepticisms-1", in 11 Journal of Law and Society, 137-172

Twining W (1986): Legal Theory and Common Law. Oxford : Blackwell

Tzonis A and White I (1994): *Automation Based Creative Design*. Dordrecht : Elsevier

Unger R M (1975) *Knowledge and Politics* New York : Free Press

(1976): *Law in modern society : toward a criticism of social theory*. New York : Free Press

(1986): *The critical legal studies movement*. Cambridge, Mass. : Harvard University Press

Veitch S (1997): "Law and 'Other' Problems", in 1 *Law and Critique*, 98-109

(1998): "Doing Justice to Particulars", in E Christodoulidis (ed.) *Communitarianism and Citizenship*. London: Ashgate

Ward I (1997): *Kantianism, Postmodernism and Critical Legal Thought*. Dordrecht: Kluwer

Weber M (1954): *Max Weber on law in economy and society*. Edited with introduction and annotations by M Rheinstein. Cambridge, Mass. : Harvard University Press

(1991) "Science as Vocation", in H Gerth and C Wright Mills (eds.) *From Max Weber: Essays in Sociology.*, London : Routledge, 1991

Weiler J (1991): "The Transformation of Europe", in 100 *Yale Law Journal* , 2403-2483

(1994): "Fin de Siecle Europe", in R Dehousse (ed.) *Europe after Maastricht; An ever closer Union?*. München : Law Books in Europe, 203-216

(1999): *The Constitution of Europe*. Cambridge : Cambridge University Press

Wellmer A (1991): *The Persistence of Modernity*. Translated by D. Midgley. Oxford : Polity

White R (1989): "MacKinnon and the Parables", in K Surin (ed.) *Christ, Ethics and Tragedy*. Cambridge : Cambridge University Press

Wolfe A (1989): *Whose Keeper?* Berkeley : California University Press

Wolff R P (1976): *In Defence of Anarchism*. New York : Harper and Row

Wróblewski J (1992): *The Judicial Application of Law*. Dordrecht: Kluwer

Zeleznikow J and Hunter D (1992): "Legal Expert Systems", 3 *Journal of Artificial Intelligence*, 94-110

INDEX

Law and Philosophy Library

22. E. Lagerspetz: *The Opposite Mirrors*. An Essay on the Conventionalist Theory of Institutions. 1995 ISBN 0-7923-3325-X
23. M. van Hees: *Rights and Decisions*. Formal Models of Law and Liberalism. 1995 ISBN 0-7923-3754-9
24. B. Anderson: *"Discovery" in Legal Decision-Making*. 1996 ISBN 0-7923-3981-9
25. S. Urbina: *Reason, Democracy, Society*. A Study on the Basis of Legal Thinking. 1996 ISBN 0-7923-4262-3
26. E. Attwooll: *The Tapestry of the Law*. Scotland, Legal Culture and Legal Theory. 1997 ISBN 0-7923-4310-7
27. J.C. Hage: *Reasoning with Rules*. An Essay on Legal Reasoning and Its Underlying Logic. 1997 ISBN 0-7923-4325-5
28. R.A. Hillman: *The Richness of Contract Law*. An Analysis and Critique of Contemporary Theories of Contract Law. 1997 ISBN 0-7923-4336-0; 0-7923-5063-4 (Pb)
29. C. Wellman: *An Approach to Rights*. Studies in the Philosophy of Law and Morals. 1997 ISBN 0-7923-4467-7
30. B. van Roermund: *Law, Narrative and Reality*. An Essay in Intercepting Politics. 1997 ISBN 0-7923-4621-1
31. I. Ward: *Kantianism, Postmodernism and Critical Legal Thought*. 1997 ISBN 0-7923-4745-5
32. H. Prakken: *Logical Tools for Modelling Legal Argument*. A Study of Defeasible Reasoning in Law. 1997 ISBN 0-7923-4776-5
33. T. May: *Autonomy, Authority and Moral Responsibility*. 1998 ISBN 0-7923-4851-6
34. M. Atienza and J.R. Manero: *A Theory of Legal Sentences*. 1998 ISBN 0-7923-4856-7
35. E.A. Christodoulidis: *Law and Reflexive Politics*. 1998 ISBN 0-7923-4954-7
36. L.M.M. Royakkers: *Extending Deontic Logic for the Formalisation of Legal Rules*. 1998 ISBN 0-7923-4982-2
37. J.J. Moreso: *Legal Indeterminacy and Constitutional Interpretation*. 1998 ISBN 0-7923-5156-8
38. W. Sadurski: *Freedom of Speech and Its Limits*. 1999 ISBN 0-7923-5523-7
39. J. Wolenski (ed.): *Kazimierz Opalek Selected Papers in Legal Philosophy*. 1999 ISBN 0-7923-5732-9
40. H.P. Visser 't Hooft: *Justice to Future Generations and the Environment*. 1999 ISBN 0-7923-5756-6
41. L.J. Wintgens (ed.): *The Law in Philosophical Perspectives*. My Philosophy of Law. 1999 ISBN 0-7923-5796-5
42. A.R. Lodder: *DiaLaw*. On Legal Justification and Dialogical Models of Argumentation. 1999 ISBN 0-7923-5830-9
43. C. Redondo: *Reasons for Action and the Law*. 1999 ISBN 0-7923-5912-7

Law and Philosophy Library

44. M. Friedman, L. May, K. Parsons and J. Stiff (eds.): *Rights and Reason.* Essays in Honor of Carl Wellman. 2000 ISBN 0-7923-6198-9
45. G.C. Christie: *The Notion of an Ideal Audience in Legal Argument.* 2000 ISBN 0-7923-6283-7
46. R.S. Summers: *Essays in Legal Theory.* 2000 ISBN 0-7923-6367-1
47. M. van Hees: *Legal Reductionism and Freedom.* 2000 ISBN 0-7923-6491-0
48. R. Gargarella: *The Scepter of Reason.* Public Discussion and Political Radicalism in the Origins of Constitutionalism. 2000 ISBN 0-7923-6508-9
49. M. Iglesias Vila: *Facing Judicial Discretion.* Legal Knowledge and Right Answers Revisited. 2001 ISBN 0-7923-6778-2
50. M. Kiikeri: *Comparative Legal Reasoning and European Law.* 2001 ISBN 0-7923-6884-3
51. A.J. Menéndez: *Justifying Taxes.* Some Elements for a General Theory of Democratic Tax Law. 2001 ISBN 0-7923-7052-X
52. W.E. Conklin: *The Invisible Origins of Legal Positivism.* A Re-Reading of a Tradition. 2001 ISBN 0-7923-7101-1
53. Z. Bańkowski: *Living Lawfully.* Love in Law and Law in Love. 2001 ISBN 0-7923-7180-1

KLUWER ACADEMIC PUBLISHERS – DORDRECHT / BOSTON / LONDON